STAR WARS®

AND HISTORY

EDITED BY

NANCY R. REAGIN AND JANICE LIEDL

WILEY

John Wiley & Sons, Inc.

To all our friends in fandom: you share the love.

Cover Image: Pyramids © iStockphoto_000016560757; Night Sky © iStockphoto_000008574407; Princess Amidala and Coruscant cityscape © Lucasfilm Ltd. & TM. All rights reserved.

Cover Design: C. Wallace

Text design and composition by Forty-five Degree Design, LLC

Illustration credits begin on page 324 and constitute an extension of the copyright page.

Published by John Wiley & Sons, Inc., Hoboken, New Jersey
Published simultaneously in Canada

For general information about our other products and services, please contact our Customer Care Department within the United States at (800) 762-2974, outside the United States at (317) 572-3993 or fax (317) 572-4002.

Wiley also publishes its books in a variety of electronic formats. Some content that appears in print may not be available in electronic books. For more information about Wiley products, visit our web site at www.wiley.com.

Library of Congress Cataloging-in-Publication Data:
Star wars and history / edited by Nancy R. Reagin and Janice Leidl.—1st ed.
    p. cm.
  Includes index.
  ISBN 978-0-470-60200-3 (cloth : alk. paper); ISBN 978-1-118-28188-8 (ebk);
  ISBN 978-1-118-28373-8 (ebk); ISBN 978-1-118-28525-1 (ebk)
  1. Star Wars films—History and criticism. 2. Motion pictures and history. I. Reagin, Nancy Ruth, 1960– II. Liedl, Janice.
  PN1995.9.S695S74   2012
  791.43'75—dc23
                                                                    2012028584

Printed in the United States of America
10 9 8 7 6 5 4 3 2 1

CONTENTS

Introduction

The Forces of History and Histories of the Force

Janice Liedl

"The Force surrounds us and penetrates us;
it binds the galaxy together."

—Obi-Wan Kenobi, *A New Hope*

History is like the Force. It surrounds us, sometimes literally, when we walk through old cities and tour ruins or re-creations from decades or centuries past. Historical memories saturate our cultures, sometimes producing shocking and unsettling reinterpretations of the past and its heroes and villains. History also binds us together, if not at the galactic level, still on a broad scale, crisscrossing the globe with stories that bring us closer together in shared wonder and fascination.

1

If you are cut off from knowledge of your own history (and that of your family) you can be misled or even taken badly by surprise, as Luke Skywalker discovers. History even makes for a powerful ally, as Yoda might have observed: because knowing something of the past can help you avoid at least *those* mistakes.

It's good to keep Han Solo's skepticism in mind, however, when comparing history and the Force. No historian would suggest that there's a mystical energy field controlling our destiny or that of the societies we study. Instead, historians emphasize how people are the true key to unlocking the mysteries of the past. Empires don't rise and fall by themselves, slavery isn't inherent in human nature, and even corporations are made up of many different individuals. Some people held more power in history than others by virtue of their birth, profession, or fortune, rather like Padmé Amidala experienced as queen and later senator. But such prominence isn't enough to shield a person from the all-too-human realities of heartbreak and despair, as Padmé found when her husband turned to the dark side. It's the repetition of these familiar themes in history—victory and defeat, joy and sorrow, the urge to possess and control, exploration and loss—that has inspired claims that history repeats itself. In reality, history is made up of millions, even billions, of unique stories waiting to be explored and shared.

Some people will say that laying out these stories is easy, that history is nothing more than establishing "the facts" and handing them to readers. Following the great nineteenth-century scholar Leopold von Ranke, historians have sometimes claimed that their job is simply to "show how it really was," as if history was a single, marvelous painting you could understand in one viewing. The truth is that history is messy, complicated, and always changing with the discovery of new information and new interpretations. That's what Luke realizes after Darth Vader's shocking claim that he is Luke's father. His entire personal history had been up-ended by this revelation that he knows to be true, even as he struggles to accept it.

This wasn't the first time that Luke saw his personal history rewritten around him. In his childhood, his guardians, Owen and Beru Lars, assure Luke that his father had been an ordinary navigator on a spice freighter. Obi-Wan destroys that history in a short order when he hands Luke his father's lightsaber and explains that Anakin Skywalker was a skilled pilot and brave Jedi warrior, who was murdered by Darth Vader. That revelation powers much of Luke's determination to fight the Empire and Vader's evil until he learns to his great distress that Vader isn't Anakin's murderer but Luke's father. In *Return of the Jedi*, when Luke confronts Obi-Wan's ghost in the swamps of Dagobah, Luke isn't only expressing his hurt and confusion; he's also challenging his former mentor's use and abuse of history:

> Luke: Ben! Why didn't you tell me? You told me that Darth Vader betrayed and murdered my father.
>
> Obi-Wan: Your father was seduced by the dark side of the Force. He ceased to be Anakin Skywalker and "became" Darth Vader. When that happened, the good man who was your father was destroyed. So what I told you was true . . . from a certain point of view.
>
> Luke: A certain point of view?
>
> Obi-Wan: Luke, you're going to find that many of the truths we cling to depend greatly on our own point of view.

Changing your point of view about the past isn't easy. Luke eventually comes to terms with the good and bad in his father's past. He writes a new conclusion to Anakin's tragic history with a surprising offer of redemption. In the end, Luke grows enough as a person and as a Jedi to see his father and his own history from a more understanding and forgiving point of view. That ability literally rewrites the history of his galaxy.

The history of the *Star Wars* galaxy goes far beyond the adventures of the Skywalker family, although Anakin's own rise and fall also reveals much about the cultures and traditions active in the galaxy during the time of the Republic's decline. There are grand themes of state-building and destruction set against humble stories of traders, tamers, and farmers. *Star Wars* unfolds personal histories, like the one linking Han Solo to the former owner of the *Millennium Falcon*, Lando Calrissian, or the long-standing friendship between frequent political allies Princess Leia and Obi-Wan Kenobi. We see hints at lost civilizations glimpsed in the ruins of Yavin 4 where Princess Leia and the Rebel Alliance make their last stand against the Death Star. There are venerable institutions such as the Jedi Order, with an intriguing history all its own. Their histories tie into the broader galactic history, sometimes in vital ways, as when tampering with the Jedi Archives led to Yoda chiding Master Kenobi for having lost a planet (a feat earthly historians can never equal). Other groups in the *Star Wars* galaxy have a less savory past, such as the Hutts' criminal enterprises on the fringes of first the Republic and then the Empire. Altogether, these historical elements within *Star Wars* provide depth and color that brings that distant galaxy to vivid life.

The histories we see in *Star Wars* are reflections or expressions of historical dynamics and individuals from Earth's own histories. George Lucas drew upon both myth and his understanding of real history in crafting the stories of the *Star Wars* galaxy, as the essays in this collection illustrate. Each chapter takes one set of individuals or institutions from *Star Wars* and compares it with the real historical counterparts that Lucas had in mind when he created his own heroes, villains, and galactic-spanning organizations and struggles. Lucas provided the scholars who worked on these essays with information about the historical models that were his inspiration for many facets of the *Star Wars* galaxy and characters, reading and commenting on each of these essays as their authors developed them.

This book—the product of our collaboration with *Star Wars'* creator—reveals how historical cultures and people provided the inspiration for the far-away galaxy's characters, societies, and politics in ways ranging from the *soldaderas* of the Mexican Revolution as models for Princess Leia's hairstyle choices and gung-ho attitude, to the more sinister parallels between the fate of the Roman Republic and its far-distant counterpart, which Palpatine undermined in order to create his Empire. Countless reflections of our history and cultures can be seen in the *Star Wars* galaxy, from medieval knightly traditions that can also be found in the Jedi Order to the fear of super-weapons that galvanized the world during the Cold War, which provided the impetus for the terrifying Death Star. Setting our histories against those of *Star Wars* sheds new light on both: many details are freshly illuminated, and some of these revelations are surprising.

Drawing on histories from our own past increases our enjoyment and understanding of the cultures and traditions that gave us Padmé, Leia, Anakin, Luke, Yoda, Obi-Wan, Han, Chewbacca, Darth Vader, Emperor Palpatine, the Sith, and all of the other enthralling figures of the *Star Wars* galaxy. Open your mind to the invisible forces of history and you'll gain a greater appreciation of how that Force is a part of *Star Wars*: a rich and rewarding galaxy that combines history and myth with creative magic.

We will use the following abbreviations in this book:

Star Wars: Episode I *The Phantom Menace* = *The Phantom Menace*

Star Wars: Episode II *Attack of the Clones* = *Attack of the Clones*

Star Wars: Episode III *Revenge of the Sith* = *Revenge of the Sith*

Star Wars: Episode IV *A New Hope* = *A New Hope*

Star Wars: Episode V *The Empire Strikes Back* = *The Empire Strikes Back*

Star Wars: Episode VI *Return of the Jedi* = *Return of the Jedi*

Star Wars: *The Clones Wars* = *The Clone Wars*

PART I

"Only Imperial Stormtroopers Are So Precise"

THE WARS IN *STAR WARS*

"The more you tighten your grip,
Tarkin, the more star systems will slip
through your fingers."

—Princess Leia Organa, *A New Hope*

1

Why Rebels Triumph

How "Insignificant" Rebellions Can Change History

William J. Astore

In the climactic battle scene of *Return of the Jedi*, an openly contemptuous Emperor boasts to Luke Skywalker that he is about to witness the end of his "insignificant rebellion." Such was not the case, as the Rebels end up triumphing against the longest of odds. Interestingly, in 2003, Lieutenant General Ricardo Sanchez, the U.S. commanding general in Iraq after Operation Iraqi Freedom, dismissed the growing insurgency in that country as "strategically and operationally insignificant," an assessment that was proved very much wrong by subsequent events.[1] Rebellions are indeed often very significant and very difficult to defeat, especially when they are driven by powerful ideologies and sustained by committed believers willing to sacrifice all.

Whether in real life or in the *Star Wars* galaxy, history is not always on the side of the bigger battalions. Consider the American Revolutionary War. The British Empire had a larger and more professional army than the American rebels, a far larger and more powerful navy, and a wealth of recent military experience, yet the upstart rebels prevailed. To cite just one year, in 1776 Britain's General William Howe landed thirty-two thousand troops at Staten Island supported by ten ships-of-the-line and twenty frigates manned by ten thousand sailors. Clearly outclassed, George Washington and his Continental Army suffered serious setbacks in New York and New Jersey but still managed to keep a viable presence in the field. Sustain-

> Whether in real life or in the *Star Wars* galaxy, history is not always on the side of the bigger battalions.

B-52 dropping bombs over Vietnam; (inset) Imperial Star Destroyer and TIE fighters pursuing the *Millennium Falcon*. (*The Empire Strikes Back*)

ing them throughout these defeats was a shared belief in the cause of freedom, as made manifest by that year's Declaration of Independence.

Next, consider the Vietnam War. In the 1960s, the American Empire was a global superpower with enormous firepower and space-age technology, yet "pajama-clad" Vietnamese insurgents armed with relatively primitive AK-47s prevailed. Indeed, the Vietnamese had nothing remotely comparable to American military might. A caption stamped on the back of an official U.S. Air Force photo of a B-52 Stratofortress dropping bombs on Vietnam illustrated the "Goliath versus David" theme: "The high-flying, heavy bomber delivers bomb loads of more than 38,000 pounds in strikes against Viet Cong strongholds in the Republic of Vietnam." Yet as awesomely destructive as B-52 bombing raids were, the enemy remained unbowed.[2]

Now, consider the *Star Wars* galaxy. An empire with enormous reach and firepower, with a ruthlessness to match the planet-shattering abilities of its Death Star wonder weapon, meets its demise at the hands of a precocious farm boy from Tatooine wielding a primitive lightsaber and a Rebel Alliance that has little more than a ragtag fleet and a fervent belief in the righteousness of their cause.

Princess Leia briefing the snowspeeder pilots on Hoth. (*The Empire Strikes Back*)

Beneath all of the thrills of lightsabers, Star Destroyers, and Death Stars, the true audience attraction of *Star Wars* is the triumph of hope over oppression at the longest of odds. Indeed, George Lucas titled Episode IV (the original *Star Wars* movie released in 1977) *A New Hope*. That hope was based on the compelling power of belief in *freedom*: freedom from the tyranny of a power-mad Emperor and his murderous henchman, Darth Vader.

This belief is first manifested in the original trilogy by Princess Leia Organa. Throughout the original *Star Wars* trilogy, a determined Leia never wavers in her belief in political freedom, a belief that sustains her quest to restore the Old Republic and its empowerment of individual autonomy. So strong is her belief that it survives torture, administered at the orders of Vader (later revealed as her father), as well as severe personal and organizational setbacks (the capture and freezing of her beloved, Han Solo; the rapid retreat under fire of the Rebels from the Hoth system at the beginning of *The Empire Strikes Back*). It is Leia's backbone that stiffens the resolve of the young Luke Skywalker and that provides a serious counterpoint to the "scoundrel" Han Solo, and it is she who gives the pep talks to pilots before they set off into deadly combat against the Empire. Leia's belief in, and allegiance to, the cause of freedom and restoration of the Old Republic is the force multiplier that proves decisive; such belief is the sine qua non of successful rebellions, whether in the galactic wars of long ago in *Star Wars* or in the real events of the American Revolutionary and Vietnam wars.[3]

Keys to Rebel Success: A Trilogy of Wars

Looking solely at the balance of forces in the American Revolutionary War, in the Vietnam War, or in *Star Wars*, one would be excused from concluding that in each case, the rebels had no chance of prevailing. The material odds overwhelmingly favored the British in the 1770s, the Americans in the 1960s, and the Empire after the collapse of the Jedi and the rise of the Sith Emperor. The results of all three of these wars, factual and fictional, remind us that "might" does not always "make right." As Abraham Lincoln famously noted in his Cooper Union address in 1860, being on the side of the "right" may also make might.[4] Belief in being in the right can sustain a rebellion even at its lowest ebb, whether it be George Washington and the Continental Army at Valley Forge in 1777, the North Vietnamese after the Tet Offensive of 1968, or the Rebel Alliance after Darth Vader's capture of Han Solo and defeat of Luke Skywalker at the end of *The Empire Strikes Back*.[5]

Rebels, in other words, can be vanquished only when their ideas and idealism are extinguished, when their faith in the movement is destroyed. That said, even with a just cause, it is hardly easy for rebels to defeat an enemy in possession of superior material resources and seemingly overwhelming firepower. To borrow an expression from Yoda, rebels must unlearn what they have learned; they must believe they are capable of the impossible, a tall order but one they must sustain through the most harrowing of events and the most trying of times. For although one may not be able to kill an idea, one can kill enough adherents to discourage the rest; such unbounded ruthlessness is not unknown, either in history or in the *Star Wars* galaxy (consider here the annihilation of Leia's home planet of Alderaan by the Empire's Death Star).

Put in concrete terms, rebel movements seek to advance an ideology and to overthrow an existing order by following a strategy known to military theorists as "People's War." Often associated with Mao Zedong, who put its maxims to work in his successful bid to gain control over China during and after World War II, People's War is compelling in its boldness.[6] Its goal: the overthrow of an existing order and its replacement with a rebel-led new order.

Think here of the American Revolutionary War. Its "rebels" spoke of inaugurating a *Novus Ordo Seclorum*, a new order of the ages, an idea

Mao Zedong, successful practitioner of People's War, with Richard Nixon in 1972.

they enshrined in the Great Seal of the United States.[7] As misguided and megalomaniacal as he proved to be, Mao Zedong succeeded in inaugurating a new, communist order in China. Ho Chi Minh in North Vietnam sought independence from colonial domination and the imposition of a communist system in a united Vietnam. And in *Star Wars* Leia and her allies seek nothing less than the overthrow of a totalitarian dictator and a recasting of galactic rule along democratic, rather than autocratic, lines; a rule by republican consensus rather than by imperial fear and fiat.

The rebels' goal in People's War may be easy to state, but the means to achieve a "new order" often prove incredibly complex. These means typically encompass social, economic, psychological, military, and especially political dimensions. As long as the rebels remain convinced of the rightness of their cause, strength of will and endurance usually favor them. Because they are fighting for a belief and an ideal, a quasi-religious calling, they often outlast their opponents, who may be fighting strictly out of duty and for little more than a paycheck.

Consider here the motivation of Hessian mercenaries in the American Revolutionary War, of American draftees in Vietnam, or of the nameless and faceless Imperial stormtroopers of *Star Wars*, and contrast this with the "Give me liberty or give me death!" motivation of the American Sons of Liberty, of revolutionary Viet Cong cadres, or of the Rebel Alliance in *Star Wars*.[8] The latter believe that "the Force is with them," that their cause is just and that they are on the right side of history. This "force" sustains them through the darkest of days and is ultimately the difference between victory and defeat.

> Leia and her allies seek nothing less than the overthrow of a totalitarian dictator and a recasting of galactic rule along democratic, rather than autocratic, lines; a rule by republican consensus rather than by imperial fear and fiat.

People's War: A Trilogy of Phases

Military theorists see "People's War" as passing through three phases.[9] In Phase One, the rebels (or insurgents, hence the term *counterinsurgency*) attempt to build a political infrastructure, while seeking allies among the people, which they do in part by spreading their ideas (or propaganda, depending on one's point of view). Every insurgent— every rebel—should be a "true believer" and thus an ambassador for the cause. At the same time, due to their comparative military weakness vis-à-vis their opponent, they seek to establish safe havens, often on the periphery of the state or the empire (or the galaxy), in inaccessible or impoverished areas where they can draw sustenance from the misery or alienation of the people. The more difficult the terrain for their enemy to negotiate, the better for the rebels, whether it be the narrow streets and forested trails of New England of the 1770s, the central highlands and triple canopy jungles of Vietnam of the 1960s,

U.S. soldiers
confront the punishing
terrain of Vietnam.

or the blast furnace heat of
Tatooine and the freezing
wastes of Hoth in the *Star
Wars* galaxy of long ago.

In this political/cadre-building
phase, intimidation may be necessary,
to include fending off rivals to the rebel
cause. Serious arm-twisting may be needed to
convince fence-straddlers (such as an ambivalent Han
Solo) to join the cause. Once revolutionary cadres are formed, the
rebels take action that is aimed both at undermining the legitimacy of
the established order and at rallying more recruits and converts to the
cause. Naturally, such actions will be labeled by the prevailing powers
as terroristic and treasonous. Thus, in the original *Star Wars*, while
operating under a thin veil of diplomatic immunity, Leia steals secret
plans to the Empire's latest wonder weapon, the Death Star, an act of
treason, as seen from the perspective of the Empire's leaders. Her

The "inhospitable" terrain of Hoth. (*The Empire Strikes Back*)

mission to Tatooine is a classic case of "Phase One" operations, for her goal is to recruit General Obi-Wan Kenobi to join the Rebel Alliance in an attempt to destroy the Empire's latest terror weapon. By the Imperial definition, however, she herself is a weapon of terror, a traitor plotting seditious acts against a legitimate government of which she is a privileged representative.

Leia, of course, sees herself not as a terrorist but as a freedom-fighter. For her, the Empire is a tyrannical monstrosity and is therefore illegitimate. In the view of American revolutionaries, Britain's King George III had similarly made tyrannical demands and had therefore forfeited his "divine" right to their allegiance. In the case of the Vietnam War, the Viet Cong and their North Vietnamese allies saw Americans as foreign invaders and their South Vietnamese allies as American stooges.

Yet it is not enough to organize against illegitimate power: one must act to overthrow it. In all three cases, the rebels recognize that

> Leia, of course, sees herself not as a terrorist but as a freedom-fighter. For her, the Empire is a tyrannical monstrosity and is therefore illegitimate.

risky acts—acts that they know will be denounced as terroristic by the powers-that-be and punished as such—are needed both to weaken the empire and persuade more people to join the rebel cause.

Hence, when enough recruits are enlisted and enough arms are gathered, rebels may then move on to Phase Two of People's War: larger-scale action (to include military operations) to gain control over the political landscape, while further weakening the legitimacy of the establishment. This is when so-called guerrilla tactics come to the fore.[10] Such tactics are typically of the small-unit, hit-and-run variety and place a premium on surprise and political impact. They are designed

Attack of the Rebel Alliance on the Death Star. (*A New Hope*)

not so much to defeat an empire militarily but rather to wear it down, to erode its political will, while perhaps provoking it as well into making further and harsher reprisals that, in breeding resentment and accelerating recruitment among the people, ultimately serve rebel ends.

Thus, the main target of guerrilla operations is not the empire's troops but rather the will and legitimacy of its leaders, although striking at a high-profile military target is often the best way to target that will and legitimacy. Consider the original *Star Wars* movie. The attack against the Death Star is a classic case of guerrilla tactics, of Phase Two of People's War. The rebels obviously have no "death star" of their own

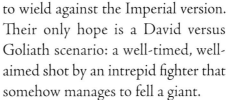

to wield against the Imperial version. Their only hope is a David versus Goliath scenario: a well-timed, well-aimed shot by an intrepid fighter that somehow manages to fell a giant.

At the same time, Leia's very act of stealing the plans to the Death Star touches off a harsh Imperial reprisal that proves vital to the success of the attack and, ultimately, to the Rebellion in general. Although unknown to Leia, Luke Skywalker is key to the Rebellion, but he is at first reluctant to join Obi-Wan Kenobi and leave his home. Yet on discovering the ruthless murder of his aunt and uncle by a vindictive Empire, Luke willingly follows Kenobi into a new life of training to become a Jedi to avenge these murders (and, ultimately, to avenge his real father's seduction to the dark side of the Force, as orchestrated by the Sith Emperor).[11]

American Revolutionary forces accept the British surrender at Saratoga, a surprising Phase Two rebel victory in 1777.

Whenever outnumbered and outgunned rebels stand and fight against a militarily superior enemy, they take a gamble. In *A New Hope*, if the Rebel Alliance had failed to destroy the Death Star, the Rebellion would have been crushed. The Rebels' resolute yet highly risky decision to stand and fight pays off when Luke Skywalker is able to call on the Force to make a kill-shot against the Death Star, seconds before this planet-pulverizing machine is able to deploy its own kill-shot against the Rebel base. This stunning victory, achieved at the longest of odds, demonstrates that the Rebels are a force to be reckoned with.

Like the Battle of Saratoga in the American Revolutionary War or the Tet Offensive in the Vietnam War, the Battle of Yavin that ends with the Death Star's destruction is a key turning point: the "end of the beginning" of an incredibly audacious but ultimately successful rebellion.[12] Winning a major battle, after all, is usually not enough to win a war; powerful empires do not give up their power easily, and they do indeed strike back. When they do, rebel forces, obeying the dictums of People's War, must be prepared to retreat when necessary, to fight delaying actions, to ratchet back military operations, even to go into hiding, licking wounds and marshaling reserves to fight when the timing and conditions are again opportune.

In any rebellion, opportunism is key; so, too, is boldness, with the most dangerous step for rebels to take occurring in Phase Three, the final phase of People's War. In this phase, rebel forces risk it all in a major military assault whose aim is to overthrow the existing order. In *Star Wars*, we witness Phase Three operations in *Return of the Jedi*. In the climactic battle of the trilogy, the Rebels marshal all of their forces in a conventional, all-out assault on the Imperial fleet and its latest iteration of the Death Star. The assault proves to be a trap, one that is sprung by an Empire in full confidence of its colossal power. Yet in Luke the Rebels possess a secret weapon of their own: a leader who gains access to the very core of the colossus but who refuses to betray the Alliance, despite promises of unimaginable power.

In a sense, Luke is a Trojan Horse inserted into the command nexus of the Empire. The Emperor (wrongly) sees him as Vader's natural successor, his new henchman and future enforcer of Sith hegemony. For the Emperor to have turned Luke to the dark side would have been like Britain's King George III turning George Washington back into a Loyalist, or Richard Nixon and Henry Kissinger convincing Ho Chi Minh to give up the fight and accept a divided Vietnam under an American umbrella. Considered in these terms, the Emperor's fervent

Luke as Trojan Horse confronts the Emperor and Darth Vader. (*Return of the Jedi*)

The rebel American horse unseats its imperial master, King George III, in this 1779 satirical drawing.

desire to turn Luke makes perfect sense, for he is the linchpin of the Rebellion. When the Emperor fails in the attempt, however, his true evil blazes forth in a murderous fury that is undeniable even to Vader, who is moved at long last to break free from the Emperor's powerful grip and save his son.

Interestingly, the powerful climax of *Return of the Jedi* represents a return to Phase One of People's War. For in the end, Luke succeeds in turning his father, Anakin Skywalker, back to the Rebel cause. His father ceases to be Darth Vader and returns, if only for a brief moment, to his former place as Anakin Skywalker, the chosen Jedi protector to the Old Republic. This turnabout, a true revolution, marks the symbolic return of republican autonomy and a political process enabled by free debate guided by a philosopher-warrior elite (the Jedi), of which Luke is now the sole surviving member and Master.

This return to the "old ways," this triumph of the Rebellion that ends in the recruitment of Vader to the cause and the death of the Emperor, highlights a vital reality of People's War: its flexible, often nonsequential, nature. For example, while conducting guerrilla operations (Phase Two) against a prevailing power, rebels also continue to build their infrastructure, conduct acts of terror to delegitimize the state, and spread propaganda, all of which are associated with Phase One of People's War. Even during Phase Three—the general offensive—rebels continue efforts associated with the previous two phases. If Phase Three fails, as it did for the North Vietnamese in the Spring Offensive of 1972, the rebels simply return to the previous two phases, biding their time until the next opportunity presents itself for a general offensive, which it did for North Vietnam in 1975.

The complex and nonlinear nature of People's War was expressed by the historian John M. Gates when describing the U.S. military's difficulty in coming to grips with the decisive North Vietnamese invasion of 1975. In his words:

> American conventional war doctrine does not anticipate reliance upon population within the enemy's territory for logistical and combat support. It does not rely upon guerrilla units to fix the enemy, establish clear lines of communication, and maintain security in the rear. And it certainly does not expect enemy morale to be undermined by political cadres within the very heart of the enemy's territory, cadres who will assume positions of political power as the offensive progresses. Yet all of these things happened in South Vietnam in 1975.[13]

Even in cases where the rebels overestimate the weakness of the enemy and lose large-scale battles, they have the option, if managed correctly, to slip back into the earlier two phases of People's War, striving to weaken the established order before the next general offensive aimed at securing victory. What ultimately sustains them through setbacks and dark times is belief: a belief that may become a quasi-religion, a force (or the Force, if you will) that multiplies their efforts, making them far more powerful than the sheer size of their army would indicate on a bloodless balance sheet.

In *Star Wars* and in the two historical analogs (the American Revolutionary and Vietnam wars) considered in this chapter, we witness the triumph of People's War against seemingly long, if not impossible, odds.[14] One can almost hear the voice of Yoda intoning, "Judge me by my size, do you? And well you should not. For my ally is the Force, and a powerful ally it is." A small, seemingly "insignificant," rebellion can grow to remarkable strength when the proper strategy is followed, the right recruits are marshaled, and a compelling belief provides a luminous, force-multiplying vision.

Yoda lifting Luke's X-wing out of the swamp on Dagobah. (*The Empire Strikes Back*)

After Yoda lifts Luke's X-wing fighter out of the swamp in *The Empire Strikes Back*, a chastened Luke gasps and then says, "I don't believe it." "That is why you fail," the wizened Jedi Master replies. Princess Leia believes in the Rebel cause of freedom; Luke Skywalker comes to believe; so, too, in the end does Darth Vader; and that is why they do not fail.

Why Empires Lose: A Trilogy of Reasons

> Well, it is a little exaggerated. We're applying an $18,000,000-solution to a $2-problem. But, still, one of the little mothers was firing at us.
>
> —U.S. pilot in Vietnam[15]

History, whether in a purely fictional-cinematic form as in *Star Wars* or in the very real dramas of the American Revolution and Vietnam, is fascinating precisely because one can imagine alternative events and endings.[16] By imagining how the Empire could have prevailed in *Star Wars*, how the British could have put down the American rebellion, and how the United States could have achieved its objectives in Vietnam, one can draw some suggestive lessons and have some fun. Yet in all of these cases, three critical flaws hampered imperial attempts to maintain their grip. In order of importance, these were overconfidence that led to underestimation of the enemy, indiscriminate reprisals that led to renewed rebel opposition, and an overreliance on technology and firepower that led to civil and nonmaterial factors being undervalued to victory.

People's War, however, is no fail-safe strategy to victory; it is difficult but not impossible for empires to counter. In the first two decades of the twentieth century, the United States defeated a serious insurrection in the Philippines, and after World War II, Great Britain put down a communist insurgency in Malaya.[17] Rebels, in other words, do not always win. Yet key to any lasting imperial triumph is never to underestimate the rebel enemy. As Luke Skywalker says to the Emperor in *Return of the Jedi*, "Your overconfidence is your weakness." The Emperor's riposte "Your faith in your friends is yours" proves untrue, but only with help from a most unexpected quarter (more on the Ewoks in a moment).[18]

Consider the U.S. war in Vietnam. Until 1968, Americans were nothing but confident that they would ultimately prevail in defeating the communist insurgency, thereby preserving a (somewhat) independent South Vietnam. Indeed, despite clear evidence to the contrary, such as the decisive North Vietnamese victory over the French at Dien Bien Phu in 1954, U.S. military officers agreed with President Lyndon Johnson that North Vietnam was basically a "raggedy-ass little fourth-rate country," which had no hope of prevailing against the world's foremost superpower.[19] That events soon proved otherwise was due in large part to American overconfidence. Similarly, the British believed in 1776 that a sufficient show of force would cow the American rabble into dour acceptance of the established order, but ill-managed efforts to split New England from the rest of the colonies succeeded only in driving more colonists from a wider area into the ranks of the rebels.

When it comes to resisting rebel insurgencies, overconfidence often emerges as a cardinal, even fatal, flaw of empires. As overconfident empires stumble, dashed hopes for quick and easy victories often lead to internecine fighting and savage reprisals that only exacerbate previous setbacks at rebel hands. In classic People's War, both sides vie for the hearts and minds of the people, who are much more than passive spectators. In a classic metaphor used by Mao Zedong, the people are the "sea" in which the rebel "fish" swim. If an empire can make the sea do its bidding, the fish cannot thrive and have nowhere to hide. Yet if the rebels can wrest control of the sea from the empire, the latter will wither and eventually die.

In the American Revolutionary War, as well as in Vietnam, enough of the people turned against the empires involved to allow the rebels space in which to swim and thrive. The people did so often because of heavy-handed, even murderously violent, repression and reprisals by these empires that generated resentment, recruitment, and rebel resurgence. Such a dynamic is captured in the *Star Wars* trilogy. As mentioned earlier, Luke joins the Rebellion only after the Empire murders his innocent aunt and uncle. Though left unsaid in the original *Star Wars*, it is logical to assume that the Empire's apocalyptic destruction of the planet Alderaan generated as much sympathy for Leia and the rebellion as it terrified wavering star systems into toeing the Imperial line. And in *The Empire Strikes Back*, Lando Calrissian sells Han Solo to Vader, only to join the Rebel cause when Vader ups the ante, insisting as well on the surrender of Leia and Chewbacca, a demand he backs up with a threat of a permanent military occupation of Lando's profitable but less-than-entirely-legal gas mine.

Because unprincipled empires believe only in themselves and their own prerogatives of power, they have a habit of acting imperiously, even viciously, when they are frustrated in their (overconfident) designs—a flaw that opportunistic rebel troops exploit to their benefit. When not intimidating or torturing or killing them, empires may also be oblivious to the "little people" within them, another weakness that a crafty rebel force can readily exploit. Consider events on the forest moon of Endor in *Return of the Jedi.* Its indigenous civilization of Ewoks is literally beneath the Empire's notice. The Ewoks themselves are not so much persecuted as they are shoved aside or flattened under the feet of Imperial Walkers. In the eyes of the Empire, a subject society such as the Ewoks that relies on spears, rocks, booby traps, and similar "primitive" weapons and techniques is a nonfactor.

It is not so much what the Empire does to the Ewoks as what it fails to do that proves decisive to the Rebellion. On first encounter, the Rebels themselves are not immune to dismissing the Ewoks as feckless "primitives" and therefore of little use. Finding themselves snared in a booby trap, Luke and Han confront a band of Ewok hunters whose small stature and cute furry faces initially amuse more than they impress. Amusement turns to concern as Luke and Han are trussed up and marched off. It quickly becomes apparent they are to become the main course at a feast in honor of C-3PO, the translator-droid whose golden sheen makes him something of a minor deity among the Ewoks.

Ewoks in action against Imperial stormtroopers, using rocks to disrupt their mission. (*Return of the Jedi*)

George Lucas has said that he had the Viet Cong in mind when he created the Ewoks, and one can see why.

Yet it is not the Force that Luke employs to levitate C-3PO that wins the Ewoks over to the Rebel cause. Rather, it is the respect the Rebels come to show for the Ewoks, as they share with them their collective struggle against the Empire. In a light-hearted and seemingly inconsequential moment, Ewok tribal elders proudly proclaim that Luke, Han, Leia, and the rest of the Rebel team are now members of the tribe, an event that has profound implications for the victory to come.

George Lucas has said that he had the Viet Cong (VC) in mind when he created the Ewoks, and one can see why.[20] Like the VC in the Vietnam War, the Ewoks are smaller in stature than their enemy and possess little in the way of advanced weaponry (whereas the VC dug pits and employed bamboo Punji sticks as weapons, the Ewoks have a hankering for logs, swinging, and rolling, as well as nets). Like the VC, what the Ewoks do possess is superior knowledge of the local terrain and an ability to blend into that terrain. Their eventual revolt demonstrates that clever tactics aided by the element of surprise can prove effective even against an enemy that possesses superior technology and devastating firepower.

Despite their stature and low-tech weaponry, there are just enough Ewoks to confuse an elite Imperial force at a crucial moment, a diversion that enables the Rebel Alliance to disable the new Death Star's protective energy field. Without this brave (and costly) diversionary assault by the humble Ewoks, the crucial offensive would have failed, even if Luke had somehow still prevailed in his personal duel with the Emperor.

The torturous terrain of Vietnam was alien to U.S. soldiers, but not to members of the Viet Cong, like this man.

The *Millennium Falcon* and other Rebel ships confront the Imperial fleet at the Battle of Endor. (*Return of the Jedi*)

Indeed, the Battle of Endor sequence in *Return of the Jedi* illustrates the Rebel Alliance's growing sophistication as they combine all three phases of People's War to disrupt the Empire's entire system of command and control simultaneously. Whereas the Empire is strait-jacketed by its dependence on the Emperor's personal attention and control, the Rebels rely on decentralized execution and improvisation within a general strategic framework. At Endor, the Rebels launch a combined arms assault by collected forces (the Rebel fleet and the Ewoks) against the full span of Imperial conventional forces, while selected elites of committed Rebel units (Rogue Squadron and Lando Calrissian against the new Death Star; Han, Leia, and the commandos against the Imperial Legion on Endor; even Luke against the Emperor and Vader) engage, disrupt, and ultimately destroy crucial command nodes. With the Emperor fully engaged in personal combat with Luke, Imperial forces are bereft of timely and authoritative instruction to supplement the orders already in place. Thus, they fail to develop a coherent and appropriate response that would allow them to bring their superior strength to bear.[21]

However transitory it proved, the Ewoks' success on Endor highlights another key weakness of many materially driven empires: an overreliance on technology and firepower as being decisive. Consider the U.S. military in Vietnam. It employed every advanced (and terrifyingly destructive) technology it could think of (short of nuclear weapons) to defeat the VC insurgency. B-52 strategic bombers on "Arc Light" raids (incredibly, the U.S. military dropped 6.7 million tons of bombs on Southeast Asia, the equivalent of more than four hundred Hiroshimas in explosive power), defoliants such as Agent Orange, napalm and cluster munitions, tanks and artillery, helicopter gunships, even electrified fences and sensors.[22] Virtually every high-tech weapon in the U.S. inventory was tested in the Vietnam laboratory, and all came up wanting.

Even worse from an American perspective: the widespread devastation wrought by these weapons convinced many Vietnamese to join the rebellion, even as it persuaded many Americans of the immorality of their own military and senior civilian leaders. An undeniable lesson emerged (that many Americans still seek to deny): The U.S. military did not lose the war because the American people lost patience on the home front or because antiwar protesters stabbed the military in the back. Rather, military excesses and overly optimistic assessments ("We see the light [of victory] at the end of the tunnel," General William Westmoreland, the U.S. commanding general in Vietnam, was saying in 1967), driven by overconfidence, led a "silent majority" of Americans to lose faith in their military and its leaders, so much so that a minority of Americans turned against their own government to sympathize with the plight (and even the goals) of the Vietnamese rebels.[23] Thus, the U.S. military lost the Vietnam War not because it was betrayed by the people but because its leaders betrayed the ideals of the people.[24] One of the key betrayers here was President Richard M. Nixon, Lucas's model for the Emperor (Palpatine/Darth Sidious), as discussed further on.

The same is true of the Empire in *Star Wars*. Its approach to Rebel dissent is to build ever-bigger and more powerful weapons to annihilate the dissenters. Rule by fear, by shock and awe, is the method to its growing madness. As Grand Moff Tarkin says to Leia in *Star Wars*, once the Empire demonstrates the power of its Death Star vengeance weapon, dissent will be quashed forever.[25] Only Vader sees more clearly. In reply to Admiral Motti's boast that "This station is now the ultimate power in the universe," Vader tells him not to be "too proud of this technological terror you've constructed. The ability to destroy a planet is insignificant next to the power of the Force."

Putting a less mystical spin on Vader's dissenting insight, a clear lesson of Vietnam is that destructive space-age technology is not enough to compel assent to imperial demands, especially when rebel resistance is supported and sustained by a powerful ideology. By highlighting the spiritual and nonmaterial factors that sustain successful rebellions, *Star Wars* provides an invaluable reminder to military theorists of all stripes.

Because of this trilogy of critical flaws—the Emperor's overconfidence, his belief in violent reprisals and rule by terror, and the Empire's faith in "Death Star" technology—the Emperor and his minions hardly bother with political suasion and mobilizing popular support, a key tenet of counterinsurgency (COIN) strategy. A less cocky, less power-mad Emperor would recognize that the iron fist of murderous reprisals needs to be balanced by the velvet glove of conciliatory rhetoric. Subject peoples can tolerate considerable oppression if it is softened by reassurances of safety and security. Put differently, victory in COIN is derived not so much from military action per se as it is from military action that creates time and space for civil means (to include police action) that seek both to marginalize the rebels and preserve the people's support.[26] Empires can do this by focusing on the pro-establishment minority, rallying them to the cause of neutralizing the rebels, while at the same time encouraging compliance (often in the name of security and order) among the rest of the people.

Yet the Sith Emperor will have none of it. Instead of seeking inclusion and a broader base of support, his actions are exclusive and narrow his base of support. Indeed, his "base" rests on the jackbooted excesses of stormtroopers, the intimidating power of Star Destroyers, and the sorcerer ways of the Sith. When the former are neutralized and the latter (Darth Vader) is turned to the Rebel cause, the Emperor is lost.

Evil Incarnate?: The Emperor, Vader, and the Rebel Cause

At first glance, the *Star Wars* universe appears incredibly simple, a Manichean realm in which the Rebels are the forces of good, and the Empire and especially its leaders are the forces of evil. Certainly, the Emperor and Vader recall real-life totalitarian analogs such as Adolf Hitler and Heinrich Himmler (the head of the notorious SS, or *Schutzstaffel*) in Nazi Germany or Josef Stalin and Lavrentiy Beria (the head of the NKVD, or secret police) in the Soviet Union. Yet interestingly, in portraying the ascent of Senator Palpatine, who becomes the evil Sith Emperor, Darth Sidious, Lucas says he had Richard Nixon in mind as a parallel, as well as other historical dictators who subverted democracies.

Surely, this is less than fair to Nixon, who, despite all of his faults, had positive qualities to go along with his paranoia, his abuse of power, and his betrayal of the U.S. Constitution.[27] Yet Lucas is making a more subtle point here, one in which we can view Nixon and even Senator Palpatine as fallen figures, talented men who fell prey to their own overweening ambition and all-consuming paranoia.

All of us have tendencies toward the dark side, Lucas suggests in *Star Wars*. As Yoda confesses, the path to the dark side is easier, quicker, more seductive. It grants to its followers the illusion of limitless power. Palpatine, in his quest for absolute power, gives himself up entirely to the dark side. He may cloak his quest in polite, diplomatic language, coyly asking for "emergency" powers, so that he might restore order and calm to an increasingly unruly galaxy. Yet his true megalomania is revealed in *Revenge of the Sith*, when he baldly states, "I am the Senate," echoing the absolutist illusions of King Louis XIV of France, who famously declared "I am the State." Even worse, Palpatine seduces Anakin Skywalker, Luke's father, by twisting Anakin's honest, yet forbidden, love for Padmé into a fevered pursuit of boundless power

Emperor Palpatine, also known as Darth Sidious. (*Return of the Jedi*)

President Richard Nixon flashes a V for victory on the campaign trail in California in 1968.

whose goal it is to cheat death for the sake of his beloved. Her death in childbirth completes Anakin's tragic descent into evil, his bottomless despair being exploited by the pitiless Sith Emperor to complete Anakin's transformation into Darth Vader.

In detailing the psychodrama of the Emperor and Vader, we appear to have traveled far from rebellions and People's War. Yet surely the *Star Wars* universe is a reminder that power corrupts us all, and that absolute power corrupts absolutely. Even Senator Palpatine emerges as something more than a wolf in sheep's clothing. Like Nixon, perhaps, he is a man of considerable gifts who is led down a dark path by an unquenchable thirst for power, a thirst unconstrained by moral qualms due to Palpatine's (and Nixon's) mistrust of nearly everyone around him.

As grim as that reading of human nature may be, *Star Wars* also serves as a reminder that power, however dark or evil, will never fully extinguish hope, and that its relentless exercise will always generate resistance. Hitler and Himmler, after all, met their demise; so, too, did Stalin and Beria. Anger, fear, and aggression may triumph in the short term, but goodness, if fought for with conviction, courage, and faith, will triumph in the end. Or so the ending of *Return of the Jedi* suggests.

Nevertheless, Lucas's revelation that Nixon was an inspiration for Palpatine casts the *Star Wars* passion play in a new light. Lucas, I believe, is affirming here that there is a thin line between good and evil, love and hate. Put differently, good and evil, love and hate, are dualities that are more labile than we care to admit. Negative emotions and unrestrained compulsions for power and control can channel the noblest of causes—even love—into the darkest of avenues.

> The *Star Wars* universe is a reminder that power corrupts us all, and that absolute power corrupts absolutely.

If Lucas ever returns to *Star Wars* and completes the final cinematic trilogy that was to follow the events of *Return of the Jedi*, one hopes he will develop this theme further. For there will be future perils for Luke, Leia, and Han: the perils of victory, as they strive to adjust to their new status as leaders and power-brokers of an inherently disputatious and disordered galaxy. In the unavoidable reality of the messiness of life, the Sith desire for total dominance in the name of "order" and "security" will never be extinguished, whether in a galaxy far, far away or right here and right now on planet Earth.

A Coda: The United States in Iraq and Afghanistan

In the aftermath of the attacks by al Qaeda on September 11, 2001, are subsequent actions by the United States in Iraq and Afghanistan more consistent with an "Old Republic" advised by Jedi or with an Empire motivated by hatred and revenge? Interestingly, U.S. troops have themselves adopted the Jedi label to describe both their military skills and their noble intent. In the 1980s, field-grade officers who graduated from the School of Advanced Military Studies at Fort Leavenworth, Kansas, became known within the U.S. Army as Jedi Knights.[28] These officers designed the invasion plans both for Desert Storm and the liberation of Kuwait in 1991 and for Operation Iraqi Freedom and the toppling of Saddam Hussein's regime in 2003 (the apparently decisive success of the latter leading to celebrations of their military and specifically their "Jedi" prowess).[29] Eight years later, Navy SEAL Team Six's mission in Pakistan in 2011 that resulted in the death of Osama bin Laden led the *New York Times* to gush that the SEALs were "America's Jedi Knights."[30]

Yet the rapid collapse of Iraq into chaos and civil war from 2004 to 2008 and the stalemate (as of 2012) of Afghanistan raise questions whether the American military can accurately describe itself as being guided by an elite corps of Jedi-like masters. Indeed, since 9/11, the American way of war has often seemed more imperial than benevolent. Consider the U.S. military strategy of the moment in Afghanistan. It is designed to put down Taliban rebels or insurgents, hence the descriptive term *counterinsurgency* or COIN. Yet its goal is also to win the hearts and minds of the Afghan people by protecting them from violence, as well as by offering them hope, usually in the form of billions of dollars in aid. It further involves moving heavily armed and armored troops into close contact with the locals (who are not always pleased with what they see as a foreign and potentially menacing presence in their midst) and of partnering with them in ways that are intended to be attuned to local cultural concerns and priorities.

Such an approach seems tailor-made for U.S. Special Operations forces, one of those branches of "Jedi Knights" the U.S. military fancies it possesses. At the same time, however, the United States has adopted a far more aggressive and destructive approach to "winning" in Afghanistan. Call it the imperial or "Death Star" approach. How else to describe the building of a colossal U.S. embassy in Kabul and a sprawling network of steroidal military bases?[31] These are arguably American analogs to the Imperial Death Star and Star Destroyers of *Star Wars.* The United States proceeds to garrison these bases with "warriors" and mercenaries, while at the same time isolating them (in the name of "force protection") from the majority of the Afghan people.

Amazingly, few Americans sense the tension—indeed, the contradiction—inherent in these approaches. In places such as Afghanistan and Iraq, the United States seems to believe it can be both Luke Skywalker and Darth Vader, both cunning and courteous Jedi Knight and kinetic Dark Lord of imperial power projection. Whether the aggressive jackboot of imperial military action is consistent with the "knowledge and defense" actions of skilled Jedi advisers remains to be seen. Yet

Imperial stormtroopers; (inset) American forces in anonymizing body armor. (*A New Hope*)

it is difficult to envision how a country can have it both ways. Over time, the elite skills and good deeds of the U.S. military's "Jedi" will likely prove insufficient to erase the looming and darker presence of its militarized embassy, its sprawling network of bases, and the destructive power of its weapons among the Afghan people.

The United States has adopted a far more aggressive and destructive approach to "winning" in Afghanistan. Call it the imperial or "Death Star" approach.

As the U.S. military engages in what is now euphemistically termed *kinetic* operations (deadly combat, in plain speak) in Afghanistan, the Afghan rebels have demonstrated a surprising ability to weather American firepower, while employing indigenous knowledge and homegrown technology of their own. American warmaking relies heavily on high-tech weaponry and the profligate expenditure of ammunition and munitions, from .50-caliber machine gun rounds to grenades to 30-mm cannon and heavier mortar and artillery rounds to 2,000-pound bombs dropped by B-1 bombers, all in support of platoon- and company-level operations.

Pacification by massive firepower, however, inevitably leads to noncombatant casualties and collateral damage that undermine the counterinsurgency strategy of winning Afghan hearts and minds. In his book *War*, the celebrated journalist Sebastian Junger recounts how, after one such instance of unintended civilian casualties, the Afghan elders of Yaka Chine met to declare jihad against American forces in the valley, despite apologies and appeals made by the U.S. commander at the scene.[32]

In countering this massive use of firepower, Afghan rebels make do mainly with rifles, even World War I–vintage bolt-action Lee-Enfields, the Afghan equivalent to the Rebel lightsaber, together with rocket-propelled grenades (RPGs) and a few machine guns. Like the Ewoks, however, the Afghan "primitives" have "force multipliers" of their own, as Junger, who was embedded with U.S. combat troops, recounts:

> For every technological advantage held by the Americans, the Taliban seemed to have an equivalent or a countermeasure.

Apache helicopters have thermal imaging that reveals body heat on the mountainside, so Taliban fighters disappear by covering themselves in a blanket on a warm rock. The Americans use unmanned drones to pinpoint the enemy, but the Taliban can do the same thing by watching the flocks of crows that circle American soldiers, looking for scraps of food. The Americans have virtually unlimited firepower, so the Taliban send only one guy to take on an entire firebase. Whether or not he gets killed, he will have succeeded in gumming up the machine for yet one more day.[33]

A menacing Tusken Raider. (*A New Hope*)

In the eyes of the Afghan people, one might imagine that U.S. troops, with all of their heavy weaponry, ordnance, and armor, recall the heavy-handed presence and trigger-happy cockiness of Imperial stormtroopers in *Star Wars*. For the self-anointed American Jedi, such an image would naturally be difficult to perceive.

I have also heard, from U.S. officers stationed in Iraq and Afghanistan, of a tendency for U.S. troops to refer to Iraqis and Afghans as "Sand People" (the violent and vicious desert nomads of Tatooine in *Star Wars*) and to comment disparagingly about their dirty homes and disgusting habits.[34] For troops hailing from the material comforts and the antiseptic luxuries of twenty-first-century America, such comments are predictable, if not exactly expedient. More important, such comments (and there are far worse) reveal a certain contempt that is more consistent with a high-handed and hegemonic empire than it is with an enlightened corps of Jedi.

As U.S. troops deploy across the "galaxy" of planet Earth (and estimates suggest that in 2011, U.S. Special Forces were deployed to an astonishing seventy countries, with plans to expand to a further fifty), seeking ostensibly to combat terror and to spread freedom and democracy, will they use their considerable "force" for knowledge or defense, or will they forever be on the attack?[35] In the increasing production and use of robotic aerial drones (with such nicknames as "Predators" and "Reapers") on assassination missions, so eerily reminiscent of the replicated clones of *Star Wars*, will they succumb to the temptation of the dark side in a febrile quest for "full spectrum dominance" of the globe, however it may be couched in benevolent terms?[36] Or will they come to recognize, in the wise words of Yoda, that "wars not make one great"?

Such questions, stimulated by the richness of the *Star Wars* galaxy, are not easily answered, even as they grow ever more vital by the day.

Yoda tells Luke that "wars not make one great." (*The Empire Strikes Back*)

"Someone has to save our skins.
Into the garbage chute, flyboy!"
—Princess Leia, *A New Hope*

2

"Part of the Rebel Alliance and a Traitor"

Women in War and Resistance

Janice Liedl and Nancy R. Reagin

As the shuttle *Tydirium* approaches the forest moon of Endor in *Return of the Jedi*, Princess Leia Organa, a key member of the Rebel strike force, is filled with apprehension. Their mission is dangerous, maybe even suicidal. The Rebels are relying on stolen codes obtained by their own spies to bypass tight Imperial security. That will be only the start of the challenges she knows they face in the vital mission to take down the massive generator protecting the second Death Star. Most of the Rebels, Leia included, are dressed in forest camouflage, a time-honored guerrilla warfare tactic, to increase their chances of moving undetected once they close in on their objective. If captured,

Leia is more than a figurehead; she is an active participant in bringing down the Empire. (*A New Hope*)

Leia and her comrades will be treated as traitors by an implacable enemy that sees them not as worthy soldiers but as "Rebel scum." Leia is right to be worried about what fate they face as resistance fighters: our history and her own galaxy's past show that women were not spared when they took part in the irregular warfare of the resistance fighter. Yet the Empire should be worried, too, because it faces a resistance made all the stronger by the women who lead and support the Rebel forces.

Princess Leia is a spy, a saboteur, and a guerrilla, as well as a leader in the overthrow of Palpatine's tyranny. She wasn't the first woman to fight those battles. In the egalitarian societies of the *Star Wars* galaxy, many women engage in battles against Palpatine's plotting. From the Clone Wars heroics of Ahsoka Tano, Anakin Skywalker's daring and resourceful Padawan, to Mon Mothma's grave and measured guidance as the Alliance's Chief of State, women fight for

Historical women battled overwhelming opponents as resistance fighters.

liberty. Historical women, many of them drawn from French history, such as Joan of Arc, Charlotte Corday, and the women of the French Resistance during World War II, also battled overwhelming opponents as resistance fighters on the battlefield and behind enemy lines.

A Symbol of Hope

Since the French Revolution of the late eighteenth century, a woman has led France, at least when France was symbolized in the arts. An image of the classical goddess of Liberty was used to urge on the commoners against the oppressions of the king and his Ancien Regime. Dressed in Roman-style clothing and wearing a hat known as a Phrygian cap, an ancient symbol of freedom, this Revolutionary icon was known as Marianne as early as 1792. Even after the Revolution

Marianne had come to symbolize the French ideal of liberty by 1830.

During World War I, Americans understood Joan of Arc as a symbol of liberation from tyranny.

came to a sputtering end with Napoleon's seizure of power, Marianne's image remained strongly connected to a French national culture. During the July Revolution of 1830 and many times after that, Marianne was employed in nationalistic art to represent the freedom-loving ideals of France, particularly against oppression by reactionary or foreign occupiers.[1]

Another feminine image of resistance to oppression that became popular in the nineteenth century was that of Joan of Arc, the medieval warrior who had inspired France's leaders to reclaim French territory from English occupiers. She was sometimes presented as leading the people in ways similar to Marianne and was used even by the U.S. government (an ally of France) during World War I as a symbol for French liberation from oppression.

The Maid, the Countess, and the Padawan

Military command is often seen as a male preserve. Great generals in history have almost always been men, but there have been rare occasions where women have not only commanded resistance armies in name, as did Queen Zenobia in antiquity, but actually led these forces on the battlefield. The medieval French warrior Joan of Arc is among the most famous of women war leaders. Being a young woman, she seemed doubly unfit to lead a warrior's life. That was the thought of many at the time, both among the French forces she rallied to win back the kingdom for the French heir to the throne, Charles, and for the English forces, desperately seeking to hold onto the French crown that the English king, Henry V, had claimed in the Hundred Years' War.

By her background and training, Joan was anything but a warrior. A farm girl from the Burgundian village of Domrémy with a deep devotion to her religious faith, teenage Joan believed that she was commanded by heavenly voices to go into France and come to the aid of the dispossessed king Charles. Joan was frightened; she pointed out that

Joan of Arc led the resistance against the English occupation of France in the 1400s.

she was only "a poor girl who did not know how to ride or lead in war." Within a few months, however, she had taken up the voices' challenge and traveled to the court of the French ruler, where she proved herself worthy of respect by the uncrowned king and his courtiers. Joan of Arc learned to handle a horse and maneuver in heavy armor. She was eventually given command of an army to raise the siege of Orléans. With this victory, the French celebrated Joan as the Maid, whose rise to prominence demonstrated God's support of their cause. Wearing custom-made armor and wielding a sword she'd miraculously discovered behind the altar of a monastery church, Joan became, as one contemporary noted, "a captain, going to command in war, to draw her pay and her equipment, and to serve according to the size of her large heart."[2]

> To the end, Joan of Arc posed a daunting figure who inspired fear in her enemies.

Newly called to service as Anakin's Padawan in her early teens, Ahsoka is remarkably young for the position and somewhat unseasoned. Yet the Republic's battle against the Separatist forces requires the Jedi to muster all available members, and the young Togruta is quickly thrust into the heart of the action, joining Anakin and Obi-Wan

Ahsoka bears the Jedi warrior's burden of command. (*The Clone Wars*)

Kenobi at the Battle of Christophsis. Within a short while, "Snips" is commanding troops on her own with sometimes disastrous results, as when her reckless pursuit of the enemy at the Battle of Ryloth leads to the death of half of her squadron of pilots. The young Padawan is desolate at the results of her recklessness but eventually finds a balance between personal bravery and careful leadership.

These were lessons Joan of Arc didn't learn until after she'd achieved her greatest triumph, seeing Charles VII crowned as king of France in July 1429. Her king played at politics, negotiating a truce with the Duke of Burgundy, who had, until then, supported the English. Joan was irritated at King Charles's disinclination to aggressively pursue the retreating English. She pushed for battle, following the English to Paris, where she experienced her first defeat and a costly one, at that. By one account, five hundred were dead after the initial assault, and a thousand more were wounded. Some of Joan's contemporaries believed that the failure to take Paris broke her will. In any case, it helped seal her fate as she became increasingly sidelined in the French king's court and council, while she sought to continue her campaign to drive the English out of France. To the end, she posed a daunting figure who inspired fear in her enemies.

According to accounts of Joan's final battle, even though her force was small, her spirit was undaunted. She rode forward with her standard raised high as she joined the melee: she "held herself in her armor and with gestures just like a captain leading a great army." This would be her last foray. In May 1430, Joan of Arc was captured by the Burgundians at Compiègne and was handed over to her English enemies to be tried as a heretic and eventually burned at the stake. She was not even twenty years old when she died.[3]

Centuries later, another inspirational woman leader rose up to help lead a resistance movement. Countess Constance Markievicz was, despite her name, an Anglo-Irish aristocrat and deeply resented the British rule over Ireland. A women's rights activist, she married a Polish count, and the two settled in Dublin, where she became involved in

After the death of Constance Markievicz in 1927, Ireland memorialized the resistance fighter and politician.

the Irish nationalist movement in 1908. Markievicz founded a paramilitary nationalist group, Fianna Éireann, for Irish teens, male and female. She encountered hostility when she joined Sinn Fein but persisted, despite the heckling her elite status earned her from other Irish nationalists, rather worse than the teasing Princess Leia received from Han Solo.

In 1916, everything changed for Markievicz and for Ireland. That was the year of the Easter Rising, an armed insurgency designed to drive the British out of Ireland. Lieutenant Markievicz held an officer's rank in the Irish Citizen Army and took her position seriously. She went into battle wearing her uniform and wielding her revolver. The Rising failed, however, and Markievicz surrendered to British authorities, along with the rest of her unit. She was the only one of almost a hundred women prisoners kept in solitary confinement, rather like Princess Leia on the Death Star.

Although Markievicz's conviction could have carried the death sentence, the judge changed the penalty to life in prison. Markievicz was actually released as part of a greater amnesty in 1917 but soon was back in prison for antigovernment activism. In 1918, she was the first woman elected to the British House of Commons, an honor she pointedly refused to take up, preferring instead to sit in the new Irish parliament, Dáil Éireann, when it was first convened. Today, Ireland celebrates Constance Markievicz as one of the nation's resistance heroines.[4]

Keep Mum, She's Not So Dumb!

Joan of Arc, Constance Markievicz, and Ahsoka Tano fought their enemies with weapons and sometimes in pitched battles. Many other women were rebels but in much less visible ways. As spies, women were particularly capable of making a contribution to a war effort. Because of prejudices about women as weak or incapable, few historical women were considered to be military threats, even when their nations were occupied by hostile powers. Loreta Velazquez boasted of performing amazing exploits as a spy for the Confederacy during the American Civil War. According to her, "For certain kinds of secret service work women are, out of all comparison, superior to men. One reason for this is that women, when they undertake a secret service job, are quicker witted and more wide awake than men, they more easily deceive other people, and were less easily imposed upon."[5]

Leia was a spy and a courier on behalf of the Rebel Alliance to Restore the Republic. (*A New Hope*)

In the opening of *A New Hope*, Princess Leia relies more on the protections due her as a senator than as a woman when she tries to bluff her way out of Darth Vader's control. Even when captured, she is still a successful spy, sending R2-D2 off to Tatooine with the Death Star's plans entrusted to her by other spies for the Alliance. With her selfless drive and determination, Leia would have felt at home with many of the other women who spied for their cause and their country. Like Leia, countless other women spied in earnest and to great effect. Among them was Rose Greenhow, who ran a spy network of almost fifty Confederate sympathizers in the Civil War. After her father died, Rose's aunt and uncle took her in, and she spent several years at their Washington boarding house, which served the likes of two-term vice president John Calhoun. Widowed in 1854, Greenhow became a mover and a shaker in Washington politics, supporting James Buchanan in his candidacy and during his term as president. His successor, Abraham Lincoln, was as loathsome to Rose as Palpatine became to Padmé by the time of the Clone Wars: Greenhow sought to oppose Lincoln as the Civil War began, since she saw him as a "tyrant."

Rose Greenhow frustrated even President Lincoln with her spy network on behalf the Confederacy.

Guided by the belief that "all's fair in love and war," Greenhow used her connections with Washington's elites, particularly its military men, to uncover secrets she could pass on to Confederate leaders using a secret cipher. Many members of Greenhow's spy network were also women. One sixteen-year-old she recruited, Bettie Duvall, smuggled important intelligence to General Beauregard on papers tucked into her imposing crown of upswept hair, a trick that might have worked for Princess Leia, as well. With that information provided by Greenhow's spy network, the South was able to handily counter the North's maneuvers at the First Battle of Bull Run in 1861.

Greenhow's high profile and Southern sympathies made it impossible for the Washington widow to escape notice for long. President Lincoln set Allan Pinkerton, the head of the new Intelligence Service, to keep a special watch on her, and that vigilance soon paid off. Uncovered as a key Confederate spy, Greenhow was put under house arrest. Even that failed to stem the tide of secrets she harvested and passed on. Exasperated, the Union leaders eventually exiled her to the Confederacy,

Blondes aren't necessarily dumb: a 1942 British poster warning against female spies.

Careless talk costs lives: The Empire's slogan evokes World War II propaganda. (Lucas Licensing artwork)

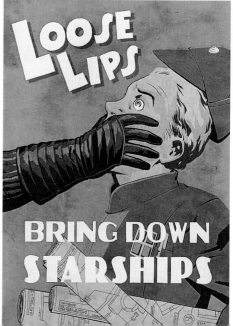

and she continued to do her best to support their cause until her death by drowning in 1864.[6]

The success of female spies such as Loreta Valazquez and Rose Greenhow and the notoriety achieved even by failed spies such as Mata Hari during World War I—who was recruited by the Germans to spy on the French, but whose efforts never amounted to much—caused later wartime governments to blame women for intelligence leaks. British authorities during World War II feared that men in the armed services seemed particularly willing to disclose their rank and where they were stationed to attractive women.

Yet the image of a lone seductive spy surrounded by gullible men is misleading. One more truth that Greenhow's story highlights is that spying was rarely a solitary occupation. Greenhow had many acquaintances and accomplices in and around Washington who helped her uncover and deliver news of the Union plans. All of these women who were successful spies built on their relationships to gather and transmit

Mon Mothma notes that many suffered and died to help the Rebel Alliance in its struggle against the Empire. (*Return of the Jedi*)

intelligence. Some paid with their lives, just as Mon Mothma notes that many Bothans did in bringing the Alliance news of the second Death Star's secret construction installation at Endor. Whether in their galaxy or ours, spy networks such as these were crucial in helping underdog powers such as the Rebel Alliance hold their own against their opponents.

The Princess and the *Partisanes*

Princess Leia embodies all of the traits we associate with a resistance fighter when she takes up a blaster to strike back against the Imperial forces on Endor. Many historical women fought against oppressors, although not all went so far as to take up weapons. The Spanish Civil War began in 1936 after the military leadership (supported by Spanish fascists) rose up against the democratic government of the Spanish Republic, leading to three years of bloody civil war. Women supported both sides in more traditional roles, but the militias defending the Republic also welcomed women as combat volunteers in the initial stages of the struggle. More than a thousand women served as *milicianas* defending the Republican zones during 1936.

> "Fancy me, a weak woman, and now I can manage a gun with the ease that I used to wield a needle."
> —*Carmen, a* miliciana

One journalist interviewed a *miliciana* named Carmen, who had been a seamstress in Madrid before the war. She volunteered for the militia, initially planning to do laundry and sewing for the male soldiers, but took a combat role after seeing several comrades killed. A few months later, the same journalist ran into her again and noted that Carmen herself was surprised at how much she had changed, since she had become proficient with a rifle: "Fancy me, a weak woman, and now I can manage a gun with the ease that I used to wield a needle."[7]

After the German invasion of France in 1940, thousands of loyal French citizens joined various Resistance groups dedicated to defeating their Nazi occupiers and those who collaborated with them—among the Resistance groups were more than ten thousand women. Some contributed in very low-key ways: providing food and shelter in "safe houses," hosting meetings and passing on vital intelligence, and using passwords and code names in order to protect the network, even if they were caught and tortured. The very appearance of normality—doing laundry, minding children—helped disguise many women's Resistance efforts. In the workplace, female secretaries or low-level civil servants could conceal their contributions to the Resistance, forging identity cards or other paperwork. One secretary made carbon copies of anything "interesting" that she typed, allowing her to tip off the local Resistance if the police were planning a raid.[8] Women, in fact, often made up the backbone of resistance movements in France, Italy, and elsewhere in occupied Europe, providing much of the infrastructure for the resistance against the Germans.[9]

Because French men were subject to a labor draft and were carefully watched by the government, French women had relative freedom of movement that many used to their advantage. As Brigitte Friang, a Resistance member, later commented, "In the 1940s, we still had the weakness of paying less attention to a woman and a man meeting, in the road, in a restaurant, in trains, than two men meeting." Young single women were particularly valued in Resistance recruiting as having both the free time and the unassuming status to work for their cause in a variety of roles: serving as couriers, even smuggling goods and people under the authorities' watch.[10] Women's presence in markets, for example, was seen as normal by the Germans. This meant that women could take on quite risky roles, as one member of the Italian Resistance noted, "Naturally the Germans didn't think that a woman could have carried a bomb, so this became the woman's task."[11]

As we saw earlier in the United States during the Civil War, women could play key roles in espionage networks, as well. Marie-Madeleine Fourcade, an executive secretary whose boss was arrested by the Gestapo, used the information her employer had gathered before the

A group of *maquis* men and one woman in 1944. Women were a vital minority in the French resistance to the Nazis in World War II.

war to build up one of the most important intelligence networks in occupied France. Her sex protected her from suspicion for a long time; later, even the British authorities were surprised to find out that their main French intelligence chief had been a woman.[12]

At the same time, French women were not expected or welcome in a direct military role, although they were active in the armed forces of several of the other Allies and filled combat roles in the Soviet Union's military. Charles de Gaulle accepted women into the French military only in order to free up men for combat roles. It was commonly accepted that war was man's work, and this meant that few women were accepted in the *maquis* as *partisanes*, full-time, gun-carrying female fighters.

Some women persisted against the attitudes and obstacles, among them Georgette Gérard, an athletic engineer who joined the Resistance in 1940 and was one of only two women known to have led a *maquis* group. Under her direction, they ambushed and sabotaged the Germans so effectively that the Gestapo targeted her directly in the winter of 1943–1944. When she was captured, she was imprisoned by the

Germans in Limoges under horrible conditions. The *maquis* leader survived, thanks to the timely appearance of French liberation forces. Rather like Luke Skywalker and Han Solo breaking into the detention area of the Death Star, French forces freed the prisoners, narrowly averting a massacre of Gérard and her fellow captives.[13]

It's clear that many women performed vital roles in the resistance to oppression, even if they never fired a weapon. Some avoided violence in principle, just as Duchess Satine of the New Mandalorians did during the Clone Wars. At least a few were deliberately sidelined when it came to anything the male leadership felt was unsuitable for women. Others were fully employed in supporting roles. These jobs, often in communication, supply, and transport, were not only key to the success

Even command wasn't always safe: Leia and other support staff faced danger evacuating Hoth. (*The Empire Strikes Back*)

of their resistance movements or rebellions, but, despite being out of direct combat, were still very dangerous undertakings. The Alliance is a perfect example of this: the countless ordinary mechanics, technicians, medics, dispatchers, and other support staff who scramble to evacuate Hoth in the face of an Imperial attack certainly don't get off easy.

Consider the women of the SOE, Britain's World War II–era Special Operations Executive. Although many were employed on British soil in war-support jobs as typists, drivers, and clerks, some fifty or so were recruited by Vera Atkins to infiltrate on the continent ahead of the soldiers on D-Day. To recruit and place women in such roles was unprecedented in the British military tradition. There were protests, lawyers for the executive noting women's particular vulnerability in such situations: "Though all SOE's agents would be without uniforms and therefore liable to be shot as spies, women agents would have even less legal protection in the field than men." Nevertheless, dozens of women drawn from various nationalities took up Atkins's call to form a core of women radio operators and intelligence officers capable of coordinating the Allied invasion with *maquis* groups on the ground in France.[14]

The risks were enormous, and many of the agents were compromised, some immediately on landing in poorly managed parachute jumps. Others were betrayed by double agents within the organizations or captured in Gestapo raids. As the Allied Forces moved across France, making contact with their supporters on the ground, few of these women were still in place with their Resistance groups. Not knowing what happened to these women was too much for Atkins, back in London. In early 1945, she crossed the channel to find out what had happened to her many missing agents, particularly the women who had little to no protection of rank. She worked on the war crimes tribunal and pursued these matters in interrogations, investigations in the concentration camps, and through sheer, dogged determination uncovered the truth. For many of her agents, the trails led only to reports of their deaths.

Nancy Wake was a spy, a courier, and a saboteur: one of the Gestapo's most wanted, due to her work in the French Resistance.

Some SOE operatives made it through the war. One such was the Australian Nancy Wake, who had moved to Paris in the 1930s, working as a journalist before she married a Frenchman and joined him in Marseilles. Wake lived through the fall of France to the Nazis in 1940 and soon became involved in the resistance to the German occupation and the collaborationist Vichy government. At first, her contributions seemed minor, at least according to her own memory. She began by providing supplies to the local Resistance group and shelter for Allied soldiers caught behind enemy lines and finally worked as a regular escape courier, assisting people to cross the border into Spain. The Germans dubbed her "the White Mouse" and began to close in on the young married woman. Wake was forced to leave her husband and make the dangerous trek across the Pyrenees into Spain in 1943. Her husband was captured, tortured, and killed by the Germans in retribution.[15]

Within a year, Wake was back in France, parachuted in to assist in running a *maquis* group. She soon showed herself more than up to the challenge. Hearing a report that thousands of German soldiers were targeting their group, the White Mouse set out with twenty Resistance fighters to relieve their comrades. When some of the teenage *maquis* fled after coming under fire, Wake turned into a veritable fury, standing up in the middle of the woods and throwing every foul insult she could muster at the cowards who fled. Shamefaced, most of her soldiers returned, and they were able to save the day.[16]

Just as they had in Marseilles, the authorities pursued Wake and the other members of the Resistance. They were always on the run, often evacuating a temporary headquarters location while closely pursued by their enemies. Just as Princess Leia escaped in the withdrawal from Hoth by the skin of her teeth (and the skillful piloting of Han Solo), so, too, did Wake experience the terror of close pursuit. At one point, she was chased out of a *maquis* headquarters under such a close attack that from her speeding car pursued by a German Henschel, she could clearly see the pilot's goggles and helmet as he tried to shoot her. A few days later, she carried out an act of everyday heroism none the less remarkable, biking more than three hundred miles in three days to get a new radio and codes for her group after a disastrous withdrawal.

Wake's drive and persistence were stunning. Just as the Alliance leaders did with Yavin 4, Wake soon appropriated an old residence (the Château de Fragnes, near Montluçon) as new headquarters for her Resistance group. Where the Rebel Alliance used that vantage point to take down the Death Star, the *maquis* attack was almost as spectacular. They destroyed the nearby Gestapo headquarters in a tightly organized operation where every member, including Wake herself, raced in at midday to leave a hand grenade in each room, surprising the unaware staff with their sudden arrival and shocking mission. The resulting explosions utterly demolished the headquarters.[17]

Armed and Dangerous

Resistance fighting could get dirty—and not just literally, as when Princess Leia takes a slide into a garbage masher in the Death Star. Sometimes, desperate times called for desperate measures, up to and including assassination. In the Bible, you can read of the daring Jewish widow Judith, who figuratively cut off the head of the Assyrian army threatening her town when she killed the general, Holofernes. Sometimes the assassinations were much more calculated and crass. In *Attack of the Clones*, the Separatist leader, Count Dooku, puts a bounty on Padmé that is taken up by the bounty hunter Jango Fett, who in turn employs Zam Wesell. In the guise of a human woman, Zam has established herself as a formidable assassin. Her final target eludes her, however: Zam fails to kill the senator. Instead, she is captured by Obi-Wan and Anakin. Before the bounty hunter can reveal her secrets, she is silenced by Fett.

Not every assassin was in it for the money. Charlotte Corday was a principled assassin during the French Revolution of the late eighteenth century. Originally a true believer in revolution, Corday became disenchanted as the revolutionary regime became increasingly radicalized and devoted to terror and oppression. She determined to strike a blow against these policies by assassinating Jean-Paul Marat, a journalist and a revolutionary leader. On July 13, 1793, Corday succeeded in her plan, stabbing Marat while he was in his bath. Some considered Corday a heroine, but few would publicly support her during the worst excesses of the Revolution's radical phase. Corday expressed no remorse for her assassination but faced her judges with a calm satisfaction that she had rescued France from a force for evil.[18] A speedy trial by the government resulted in her execution: more legal than but just as lethal as Zam Wesell's end outside a seamy Coruscant dive.

Charlotte Corday believed Marat's death would free France from revolutionary terror in 1793.

Obi-Wan Kenobi frequently tangles with women who are as dangerous as Corday, even if they sometimes fight on his side. The Zabrak bounty hunter Sugi leads a band of mercenaries during the Clone Wars and reluctantly teams up with the Jedi when they face a common enemy. Sugi is violent, especially fond of her powerful rifle and vibroblade to settle conflicts, but also intensely honorable. When offered more money to switch sides in a conflict, she instantly refuses, considering the proposed deal an insult to her code of conduct.

THE PEOPLE'S WAR

Rebel movements seek to advance an ideology and to overthrow an existing order by following a strategy known as "People's War."

In *Star Wars*, Leia and the Rebel Alliance want to overthrow a dictator who rules by fear and fiat and recast galactic rule along democratic lines. Similarly, America's founding fathers hoped to inaugurate a Novus Ordo Seclorum, a new order of the ages, an idea enshrined in the Great Seal of the United States.

Small wonder the Rebel's symbol is a stylized version of the seal, with two wings framing two branches like ribbons, topped by a star point. Almost two hundred years later, however, the United States found itself fighting to preserve its own empire in a People's War against a different set of rebels, in Vietnam.

THE PEOPLE'S WAR, PHASE 1

Military theorists see "People's War" as passing through three phases. In phase one, the rebels try to build a political infrastructure while seeking allies among the people, in part by spreading their ideas.

Princess Leia's mission to Tatooine is a classic example of the latter. She wants to ask former Jedi general Obi-Wan Kenobi to join the Rebel Alliance in an attempt to destroy the Empire's weapon of mass destruction; because her ship is captured, she invites him via hologram. In the same way, Samuel Adams formed a Committee of Correspondence in 1772, which sent out letters from Massachusetts to potential allies in other colonies, protesting the tightening grasp of the British crown and asserting "the rights of the colonists . . . to communicate and publish the same to the world as the sense of this town." Their letters must have been persuasive: Committees of Correspondence were rapidly created, and they became the revolutionary cells throughout the colonies that led to the First Continental Congress.

Leia, of course, had something more tangible to offer than letters: the plans to the Death Star.

THE PEOPLE'S WAR, PHASE 2

This phase calls for larger-scale actions, including guerilla tactics. These involve small units and hit-and-run attacks, and they prioritize surprise and political impact. The goal isn't to win a war but to wear down an enemy's resolve.

The attack against the first Death Star exemplifies a phase two operation, calling for a single sling bullet to bull's-eye a giant as if it were a womp rat, as did Washington's raid against Britain's Hessian forces in Trenton, New Jersey, on December 26, 1776. To achieve surprise, he ferried soldiers and artillery across the Delaware at night through floating ice and a snowstorm. Unsupported, but undaunted, he attacked with great success, suffering only 9 dead and wounded to the Hessians' 120. He captured a thousand prisoners plus arms, powder, and artillery.

Crossing back proved even more difficult, whereas Luke and Han just had to race back to their Yavin 4 base.

THE PEOPLE'S WAR, PHASE 3

In any rebellion, the final phase is the most dangerous, when everything is risked in a major assault to finally overthrow the existing order.

The Rebels' Battle of Endor is America's Battle of Yorktown. On September 28, 1781, Washington's Franco-American force of nearly nineteen thousand men besieged a series of British redoubts and batteries on Virginia's York River, as the French navy blocked the mouth of the Chesapeake Bay. Washington then dug trenches and placed artillery, and on October 9 opened fire. After this softening, he took two of the redoubts on October 14, turning them against the British. He foiled a British counterattack the next day and placed more guns on the sixteenth. After a British retreat failed, their General Charles Cornwallis sent out the white handkerchief on October 17. Upon receiving word in London, Prime Minister Lord North reportedly said, "Oh God, it's all over."

Although John Trumball famously depicted Cornwallis surrendering, he was absent from the ceremony by choice, unlike the Emperor after Endor, who was disintegrated along with the second Death Star.

SUSTAINING THE PEOPLE'S WAR

Given the asymmetry of the People's War, a rebel force will have many setbacks. Washington, for instance, suffered far more Battles of Hoth than he enjoyed Yavins, and the North Vietnamese failed in their 1972 Spring Offensive, although they won in 1975.

What ultimately gets the rebels through these setbacks is a belief, a will, a spirit that that multiplies their efforts. As Yoda said, "Judge me by my size, do you? And well you should not. For my ally is the Force, and a powerful ally it is." Or as Patrick Henry declared on March 23, 1775, to the Virginia House of Burgesses, "Is life so dear, or peace so sweet, as to be purchased at the price of chains and slavery? Forbid it, Almighty God! I know not what course others may take; but as for me, give me liberty, or give me death!"

What does an empire have? Cloned stormtroopers. German mercenaries. Napalm. Blackwater private contractors. But ideals can sustain a rebel force even if the other side has deeper pockets.

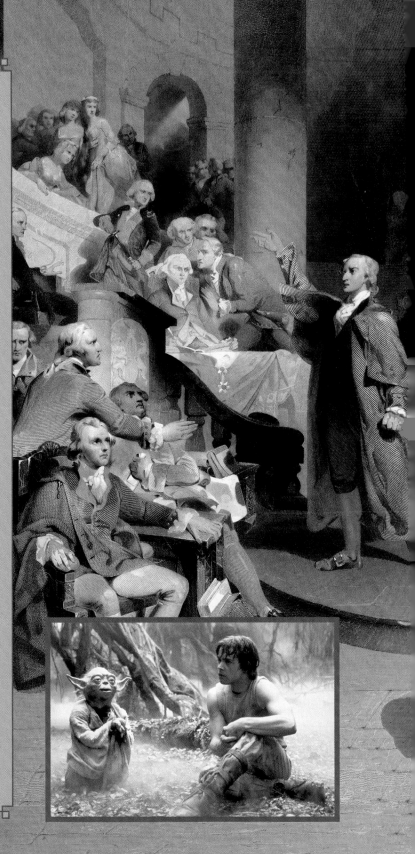

Asajj Ventress versus Luminara Unduli and Ahsoka Tano: women warriors fight for and against the Republic. (*The Clone Wars*)

Zam Wesell isn't the only Separatist female assassin. In *The Clone Wars*, we meet Asajj Ventress, who is apprenticed to Darth Tyranus, Count Dooku's secret Sith identity, during the Clone Wars and who frequently battles the Jedi in her missions. Early in the wars, Dooku dispatches her to either free or permanently silence the Trade Federation viceroy Nute Gunray after the Jedi captures the Neimoidian. In the resulting battle, featured in "Cloak of Darkness," she faces down one of the most formidable Jedi fighters, Luminara Unduli, and only Ahsoka Tano's timely intervention saves the day. Ventress is renowned as an assassin but, unlike Corday, fails in her chief target: she repeatedly seeks to slay Obi-Wan Kenobi, but the Jedi Master survives her attacks and schemes.

Disguise was another important tactic in a resistance fighter's arsenal. Many women resorted to the obvious disguise of dressing as a man. In fact, that was one of the chief charges against Joan of Arc in her heresy trial. Dressing as a man was illegal in many jurisdictions, right up to the twentieth century. When Princess Leia infiltrates Jabba's palace on Tatooine disguised as Boushh, she is unrecognizable. The unisex outfit and the muffling helmet make it impossible to distinguish her real identity as she works to free Han Solo from his carbonite bondage. Something must have given her away, of course, because when she releases Han, Jabba and his court are waiting to confront them both. Relying on disguise was risky business but a risk that was worth taking, just as much for those seeking to free their comrades from Gestapo jailers as for Leia, Chewbacca, Luke, and Lando working to rescue Han from Jabba.

Not every disguise was so inspiring. Many women working for a resistance cause disguised themselves in humble ways: as servants, laborers, schoolgirls, and occasionally prostitutes or mistresses. These disguises couldn't have always been easy to bear, just as when Ahsoka Tano wears a slave collar in an undercover operation during which Anakin and Obi-Wan pose as slavers.

Women of the French Resistance employed disguises to aid in their Resistance work. Sometimes they needed to improvise even further when the disguise fell through or didn't bring the desired results. That was the case for Lucie Aubrac, one of the earliest organizers of the

Leia employs a key resistance tactic when she infiltrates Jabba's palace in disguise. (*Return of the Jedi*)

resistance against the Vichy regime. She raised a family while editing a journal for the Resistance and founding a hit squad devoted to rescuing captured comrades. In 1943, the mission became personal. Her husband and coleader, Raymond, had been captured by the authorities. Raymond was destined for cruel torture at the hands of the infamous Klaus Barbie. Knowing that certain death awaited her husband, Aubrac sprang into action. She scouted a nearby hospital, where she pretended to be a doctor. In a smock and wearing a stethoscope, Aubrac was able to rescue several of their agents and acquire a sample of live typhus bacteria. She planned to infect Raymond with candies containing the typhus in order to prevent his torture and execution, but that plan fell through, and Raymond's transfer to Germany loomed. Forced to improvise, Aubrac and the rest of her hit squad intercepted the prison van transporting her husband. Three German guards died, and thirteen prisoners, including Raymond, were freed, due to their rescuers' daring act of disguise and cooperation.[19]

Resistance: Something Old and Something New

Women have contributed to resistance movements from ancient times to the modern day and in increasing numbers. In the Mexican Revolution of 1910–1920, women supported the revolution with supplies, safe houses, and reporting, and some, such as Dolores Jiménez y Muro, worked their way up to be at the heart of the resistance fight.[20] The numbers and the importance of women in rebellion continue to grow. By some estimates, as many as two-thirds of the Sandinistas fighting in Nicaragua in the 1970s were women, and this wasn't only at the lowest level. Four of the seven military commanders at the fight for León in 1979 were female. Prominent in the Sandinista leadership was

Commander Two, Dora María Téllez, only twenty-three years of age when she became a spokesperson of the revolution.[21]

When resisting an invading force or an oppressive regime, women often practice subversive acts that are concealed within the performance of traditional roles: providing food and safe houses for the *maquis*, typing up useful forgeries and carbon copies of secret documents, or smuggling bombs in a marketing basket. Yet war, revolution, and political upheaval also offer women an oppor-

A female supporter in the Mexican Revolution. Her hairstyle, sometimes worn by women during Mexico's Revolution, helped inspire Princess Leia's. (*A New Hope*)

tunity to escape the constraints of tradition in support of their cause. Just as Leia sheds the garb of a princess and disguises herself as a male bounty hunter, so Joan of Arc was able to don armor and lead troops against the English. During the Clone Wars, Sugi is a mercenary leader who ruthlessly executes a pirate who threatens her crew. Ahsoka is assigned to Anakin as his Padawan, in hopes that responsibility for her will temper Anakin's impulsive and rash ways. Instead, while fighting for the Jedi Order against the Separatists, Ahsoka is even more reckless than her Master. Lucie Aubrac rescued her husband from the Gestapo, and Charlotte Corday carried out a carefully planned assassination in order to save innocent lives—all "unfeminine" feats that could never have occurred in peacetime. Sometimes women started in a more traditional expression of resistance support and ended up in combat, such as Carmen the Spanish seamstress who became a *militiana*. In both supporting and leading roles, women are now integral to every modern revolution, something that Princess Leia and other women of the *Star Wars* galaxy would have appreciated.

"For over a thousand generations, the Jedi Knights were the guardians of peace and justice in the Old Republic."
—Obi-Wan Kenobi, *A New Hope*

3

Elegant Weapons for Civilized Ages

The Jedi and Warrior-Monks throughout History

Terrance MacMullan

The *Star Wars* galaxy brims with fascinating people, places, and things. Yet even in a galaxy with suave Corellian smugglers, breathtaking Tatooine binary sunsets, and awesome Death Stars, nothing rivals the allure of the Jedi. Millions found their imaginations fired by the simple description of the Jedi given by an old wandering knight who explains that "for over a thousand generations, the Jedi Knights were the guardians of peace and justice in the Old Republic."[1] While the Jedi—with their sorcerers' ways and elegant weapons—stand as a unique vision from long ago in a galaxy far, far away, they also represent a response to an eternal struggle to reconcile the ideal with the real, the spiritual with the physical, the easy way with the right way. They are the realization of the universal hope that power be placed in the hands of people wise enough to use it justly. Once we recognize this, we can see the Jedi as another glorious chapter in what Joseph Campbell called "the one, shapeshifting yet marvelously constant story that we find."[2]

A careful student of *Star Wars* and history discerns a recurring pattern, similar to a musical theme that emerges and recedes throughout a symphony, which harmonizes the tales of the Jedi and other spiritual warriors. These extraordinary people combine the discipline necessary to manifest incredible physical power with the wisdom to know that such strength must be used only in the service of a higher purpose. They show that before there can be a cunning warrior in whom the Force is strong, there must first be a monk wise enough to feel the Force. This chapter examines the parallels between the Jedi Knights and three renowned societies of warrior-monks from history: the Shaolin monks of China, the samurai of feudal Japan, and the Knights Templar of the Crusades. Each of these comparisons reveals different facets of the Jedi as warrior-monks. The example of the Shaolin monks helps us understand their vision of the one energy that unifies the entire universe. The samurai cast light on the Jedi's unique mind-set, especially their detachment even in the face of death. Finally, tracing parallels with the Knights Templar illuminates the Jedi's moral dualism— the belief that the universe is a battleground in a cosmic struggle between good and evil—as well as the risks of virtue in a corrupt world.

This chapter demonstrates that the virtues that we so admire in the Jedi have been manifested by flesh-and-blood people from a variety of past cultures and organizations. Although it appears unlikely that any of us will ever be able to use the Force to move objects telekinetically or trick guards, we *can* tap into a real spiritual force that might help us forge lives of greater nobility and virtue.[3]

"Ancient Weapons and Hokey Religions": The Origin of the Jedi Order

The Jedi origin stories highlight the unavoidable tension between the deadly warrior and the serene monk that lies at the core of the Jedi's being. According to the world beyond the films—the Expanded Universe of *Star Wars*—thousands of years before the Battle of Yavin in *A New Hope*, there lived on Tython a group of seers who felt both

A school for keepers of the peace: Jedi progress through ranks from Youngling to Master, similar to many historical martial orders. (*Attack of the Clones*)

the serene and benevolent side of the Force, which they called Ashla, and its destructive and malevolent aspect, called Bogan.[4] These people were not warriors but mystics and philosophers who were drawn to this ever-present energy as a source of wisdom.

The members of the Jedi Order are bound by a number of proscriptions shared by many other monastic communities throughout human history. Jedi adhere to a very precise dress code that marks them not merely as Jedi but as Jedi of a particular rank. Jedi normally enter the Order as Younglings and then strive to progress through the ranks of Padawan, Knight, and Master. Every Jedi obeys some appropriate authority within the Order, whether it is the Master who guides each Padawan's training or the members of the Jedi Council who hold ultimate authority over all Jedi. Jedi fill many different roles of service to their Order and the Republic, including generals, investigators, diplomats, and archivists. Whether battle-hardened commander or quiet librarian, all Jedi are trained to wield their signal weapon—the lightsaber—only as a measure of last resort. The light side of the Force teaches the Jedi to be compassionate to all life, but their knowledge of the dark side prohibits them from developing intimate relationships. Celibacy prevents them from suffering divided loyalties or unfit attachments that might cause them to be seduced by the dark side of the Force.[5] Just as in earthly monastic societies, many Jedi struggle with this rule, and some even violate it, with devastating consequences. Indeed, one of the most cataclysmic chains of events in the *Star Wars* saga is triggered when Anakin Skywalker's tender passion for his forbidden love, Padmé Amidala, turns obsessive and destructive.

The Jedi are a potent moral force when they successfully balance the humility and obedience of the monk with the warrior's pride and valor. They become spiritual beings *in* the mundane world of matter, technology, politics, and desires, who are not *of* this world. They feel the deeper truths of peace, calm, and harmony but choose to engage with discord, scum, and villainy, in the hopes their mastery of physical force and the spiritual Force might make things right.

"It Binds the Galaxy Together": *Qi*, the Force, and the Shaolin Monks

The earliest community of warrior-monks whose story parallels that of the Jedi still prays and trains today in a monastery near the mountains of Henan Province in China. Although their origins are shrouded by a veil of legend, we know that from the Shaolin Monastery there arose a cadre of *Seng Bing* ("monk soldiers") who submitted to a rigid monastic code; shunned fame, wealth, power, and other worldly desires; and studied a universal energy force that imbued them with great vitality and physical power. During their long history, they cleared the surrounding countryside of dangerous animals, protected their neighbors from bandits and pirates, and served the government of their people. They suffered persecution by a vengeful emperor and witnessed the destruction of their temple. They even rescued a princess or two!

A more civilized age: pagodas decorate the site of the famed Shaolin Temple, founded in 495.

The story of the Shaolin monks begins with the founding of their temple in 495 by a Buddhist monk from India named Batuo.[6] By decree of the emperor Xiaowen, this temple was erected at a central location near the imperial capital of Louyang, much as the Jedi Order built its longest-standing Temple on the capital world of Coruscant in close proximity to the Senate chamber.[7] The Shaolin monks were originally tasked with the spiritual mission of studying and promulgating Buddhism. In both cases, these spiritual beings became warriors only when forced by fate, as in the seventh century when the monks of Shaolin confronted bandits attacking the monastery and its neighbors.

Other Shaolin stories provide more evidence that the spiritual preceded the martial. Perhaps the most significant is the tale of Bodhidharma, a legendary early abbot who lamented that the monks were too feeble for the rigors of Chan (or Zen) meditation. Having been raised in a warrior family in India, Bodhidharma was trained in the *vajramushti* fighting system, which he taught the monks for the sake of improving their vitality. Soon the monks became known as the most formidable fighters in all of China. Supposedly, the system of physical exercise developed by him was the basis of the well-known Shaolin ch'uan-fa (Kung-fu) system.[8]

Although it is impossible to verify Bodhidharma's exact contributions, we know that soon after his tenure, the "Shaolin Temple became a center of excellence for the fighting arts with martial artists from across China making a pilgrimage to the temple to practice with the monk-soldiers."[9] The monks practiced martial arts primarily as a means of cultivating vitality; as Buddhists, they fought only defensively and for the purpose of protecting innocents. This is reminiscent of Yoda's admonition to Luke that "[a] Jedi uses the Force for knowledge and defense, never for attack."[10] Their earliest warrior training focused on the staff: a sacred and defensive weapon that had long been the symbol of the Buddhist monk.[11] They studied a multitude of staff forms, just as the Jedi learn the seven lightsaber forms.[12] Later they developed unarmed martial arts forms, such as the *Nizong quan* or

For knowledge and defense: Shaolin monks were renowned for their daring fighting styles and fearless military service.

"Wild-Beast Fists," which were based on the movements of animals.[13] Similarly, Jedi lightsaber forms were patterned on the behavior of animals and bore their names, such as Form IV *Ataru:* The Way of the Hawk-Bat.[14]

Many of the daring exploits of the warrior-monks of Shaolin closely mirror those of the Jedi. Just as Obi-Wan Kenobi and Anakin Skywalker shield Senator Padmé Amidala against an assassination attempt in *Attack of the Clones*, in the seventh century a Shaolin monk named "Jue Wen died leading a detachment of thirty Shaolin monk soldiers on a mission to save Princess Yong Tai from a planned assassination."[15] The Shaolin monks earned their reputation as fearsome fighters while serving the imperial government of China during military campaigns, just as the Jedi Guardians protect the Republic against its enemies. Both groups performed two distinct military functions: they were leaders of regular combatants, as well as elite front-line fighters capable of deciding entire battles with their incredible abilities.[16]

The legendary figure Bodhidharma offers a wealth of comparisons with the venerable Jedi Master Yoda. Both were skilled martial artists, as well as wise spiritual teachers. They shared a mastery of cosmic energy that granted them abilities that defied belief. Legends say that Bodhidharma meditated in a cave for nine years so intently that he drilled holes through solid rock with his gaze.[17] Other tales have him floating across the Yellow River on a single reed.[18] These wonders compare to how Luke Skywalker learns the power of the Force when Yoda tells him to lift his X-wing fighter out of Dagobah's swamps. Skywalker, shackled by doubt, tries but fails. The diminutive Master then uses the Force to gracefully lift the fighter out of the swamp and onto firm ground. Most remarkably, both Masters even achieved a kind of resurrection: Yoda's spirit appears to Luke after the Battle of Endor, and Bodhidharma was said to have appeared to his student Song Yung three years after his death.[19]

True Masters: Bodhidharma and Yoda had both served their orders as teachers and leaders. (*Attack of the Clones*)

These stories of two great masters from two very different worlds underline the most important similarity between the Shaolin monks and the Jedi Knights. These spiritual warriors shared a common belief that the universe is not really the mundane world of separate objects governed by luck and probability. Instead, the universe is a single whole unified by an invisible, ever-present, and living energy that the Jedi call the Force and the Shaolin monks called *qi*.

Obi-Wan describes the Force as "an energy field created by all living things. It surrounds us and penetrates us. It binds the galaxy together."[20] Jedi study a living Force that grants them not only incredible physical and sensory abilities, but also telekinesis, healing abilities, and mind control over the weak-willed. Yet they also feel a deeper—possibly sentient—side called the Unifying Force, which is the energy felt at the cosmic level of galaxies, space, time, and even fate.

> The universe is a single whole unified by an invisible, ever-present, and living energy that the Jedi call the Force and the Shaolin monks called *qi*.

少林寺

Temples as targets: Like the Jedi Temple, the Shaolin Temple was destroyed by fearful government forces but eventually was rebuilt. (*Revenge of the Sith*)

The monks of Shaolin were one of many communities in China who studied the phenomenon they called *qi* (sometimes written *ch'i*).[21] *Qi* is also a ubiquitous, invisible energy that underlies all things. Master Waysun Liao explains that "[a]ccording to the legendary theory of Yin and Yang, *ch'i* exercises its powers ceaselessly, moving in a balanced manner between the positive (constructive) and the negative (destructive) powers."[22] Dedicated study and cultivation of *qi* affords vitality, sensitivity, and even enhanced physical abilities. Early *qi* masters used internal energy circulation and acupuncture techniques to heal,

just as the Jedi use the art of *Curato Salva*.[23] The Shaolin monks first cultivated *qi* for its own sake and only later learned to move this energy into their limbs and weapons to become terrifying warriors.

The power wielded by warrior-monks across these worlds led to persecution by political figures who sought scapegoats to deflect public attention away from their own thirst for domination. The second Jedi Temple on Coruscant is invaded during the bloody Jedi Purge in 19 BBY and is eventually reduced to rubble (as seen in *Revenge of the Sith*).[24] Similarly, the Shaolin Temple was twice destroyed—first in 574 and again in 845—as part of an imperial purge of Buddhism as a supposedly traitorous cult.[25] Both temples were rebuilt by their resilient monks: Master Luke Skywalker returns his renewed Jedi Order to a new Temple on Coruscant, and the rebuilt Shaolin Temple still houses a brotherhood of monks who keep alive their ancient traditions of Chan Buddhism and martial arts.

The pen and the sword in equal measures: seventeenth-century samurai Miyamoto Musashi excelled at both fighting and philosophy.

Bunbu itchi means "the pen and the sword in equal measure." It summarized the samurai's obligation to balance their mastery of warfare with civilized endeavors, such as classical literature, calligraphy, and Confucian philosophy.[31] We see this philosophy in the life of Miyamoto Musashi: a *ronin* or masterless samurai whose unparalleled swordsmanship helped him survive countless battles and duels. After his only defeat, which came at the hands of a wandering monk armed only with a pair of short staves, he retired to a mountaintop cave. There he penned one of the classics of Zen philosophy and sword fighting, *The Book of Five Rings*, and produced masterpieces of painting, calligraphy, and even woodcarving.[32] Although proficiency with the pen distinguished the samurai from mercenaries and enabled them to perform their civic and administrative duties, their mastery of the sword was even more crucial. The long sword did not only *protect* the samurai's life: it *was* the life, the symbol, and the soul of the samurai. A graceful weapon steeped in spiritual significance, it was "an instrument of life and death, purity and honor, authority and even of divinity."[33] We can compare this to the Jedi's reverence for the lightsaber.

The Jedi's "elegant weapon for a more civilized day" also resonates with spiritual and symbolic significance.[34] Materially, it consists of a hilt that ignites a blade of pure energy that can slice through almost any substance and, in the hands of a trained user, can reflect blaster fire. Practically, a lightsaber is often the only thing protecting a Jedi from death. When Master Kenobi returns Anakin's lost lightsaber, he scolds his Padawan, saying, "Anakin, this weapon is your life" (*Attack of the Clones*). Spiritually, the lightsaber is the Jedi's soul. One of the final tests facing a Padawan is to assemble his or her own lightsaber. Thus, the lightsaber is not only a sign of the Padawan's maturity, but is also a unique and deeply personal mode of self-expression.

From their earliest days, the Jedi were mindful of the dangers of the dark side of the Force. To help future adepts along the narrow path to the light side, the Jedi live by the strictures of the Jedi Code. The classical expression of the Code based on the writings of Jedi Master Odan-Urr reads,

> There is no emotion; there is peace. There is no ignorance; there is knowledge. There is no passion; there is serenity. There is no chaos; there is harmony. There is no death; there is the Force. A Jedi does not act for personal power or wealth but seeks knowledge and enlightenment. A true Jedi never acts from hatred, anger, fear or aggression but acts when calm and at peace with the Force.[35]

Just as the Jedi live by and meditate on the Jedi Code, so the samurai lived according to their own arduous code of *Bushido*, "the way of the warrior."[36] *Bushido* was not so much a systematic system of ethics as it was a set of guidelines pertaining to dress, deportment, and behavior on the battlefield. Samurai retainers owed absolute obedience to their master, just as Jedi Padawans implicitly obey their Masters and all Jedi are to obey the decrees of the Jedi Council.[37] Finally, although *Bushido* was not a monastic code, it mandated a frugal, sober life marked by the cardinal virtues of loyalty and obedience.[38]

A later version of the same Zen philosophy taught by Bodhi-dharma at the Shaolin Monastery guided a samurai's spiritual life and

"Some Damned-Fool Idealistic Crusade": The Jedi and the Knights Templar

Just as the chroniclers of the Clone Wars record the valiant deeds of Jedi leading their outnumbered clone troopers against the vast droid armies of the Separatists in a galactic war that stretches from the Core worlds to the Outer Rim, our own historians preserve tales of remarkable warrior-monks who survived not only battle, while perennially outnumbered, but also starvation, solitude, and ultimately betrayal in a faraway realm they called Outremer. These were "men whose bodies were protected by iron and whose souls were clothed in the breastplate of faith."[47] They are still renowned in history, legend, and myth as the Knights Templar.

These European Christian crusaders were powerful warrior-monks whose aggression was restrained by social codes and spiritual doctrines. They were esteemed above other knights for their austerity, devotion, and moral purity. Like the Jedi, they practiced individual poverty within a military-monastic order that com-

Mighty fortresses: headquarters for the Jedi and Templar orders were sites of training, diplomacy, learning, and defense. (*Attack of the Clones*)

manded great material resources. Both knightly orders demanded celibacy and obedience from their members, who in turn were revered as paragons of honesty, wisdom, and bravery.

Although there had been Christian monastic and military orders before the Templars, it was only "[i]n the warrior-brothers of the Temple [that] the meekness and humility of the true monk were united with the courage and noble intent of the virtuous knight."[48] Just as the Jedi evolve out of a spiritual community that originally has no martial aspirations, the French knights who formed the Knights Templar had no interest in starting a military order. After more than ten years of combat in the Holy Land, these war-weary knights wanted to atone for their sins by forming a lay religious community or joining an established monastery. Yet the Christian king of Jerusalem, Baldwin II, "persuaded Hugh of Payns and his companions to save their souls by protecting pilgrims on the roads."[49] On Christmas Day 1119, these warriors took vows of poverty, chastity, and obedience—just the same

as any Christian cleric—and created one of the earliest orders of Christian warrior-monks.[50] Their formal name was the Poor Fellow-Soldiers of Christ, but they became known as the Knights Templar because their original headquarters, the al-Aqsa mosque of Jerusalem, was believed to occupy the spot where Solomon's Temple had been built. The Temple served as headquarters, arsenal, fortress, and home for these knights, just as the Jedi Temple does for the Jedi. In time, the

Wise knights: both the Jedi and the Templars were governed by a council of high-ranking members. (*The Phantom Menace*)

Templars created an intercontinental network of fortresses and temples, just as the Jedi archives, academies, and temples span the galaxy.

The Templars "quickly became the fighting arm of the Church, having allegiance only to the pope and the grand master."[51] Similarly, Jedi are the peacekeepers of the Republic who obey the chancellor and the Jedi Council. The Jedi are governed by a Jedi Council of twelve senior members, headed by a Grand Master, just as all of the major decisions of the Templars were made by the twelve members of the Grand Chapter headed by the grand master. As membership in the Jedi Order requires strict adherence to their code, so the Rule that governed the Templars "stipulated attendance at services together with the canons, communal meals, plain clothing, simple appearance and no contact with women."[52] Templars "were to dress in white, symbolizing that they had put the dark life behind them and had entered a state of perpetual chastity."[53] Although their white robes were emblazoned with a red cross after 1143, their hooded mantles bore a great resemblance to Jedi attire.

Due to their exceptional training and zealous devotion, the Templars were both commanders and elite combatants. This matches the Jedi's dual capacity as either front-line fighter or commander of a military unit. The most famous instance of Templars serving as unit commanders was during the Second Crusade in 1148, when the Christian army of King Louis was in danger of disintegration after a harrowing passage through the Cadmus Mountains. Louis couldn't lead his heavily armored knights through unfamiliar terrain, so he turned over his command to the Templar master Everard des Barres. The army survived the ordeal only because des Barres "divided the force into units, each under the command of a Templar knight whom they swore to obey absolutely."[54]

More important than their dual roles in war was that the Jedi and the Templars fought simultaneous battles on two very different planes: the physical and the spiritual. Both groups saw themselves as crusaders in an ancient war between the forces of light and the armies of evil.[55] The Templars believed that they were sanctified warriors protecting God's land and faithful flock against heretics in league with Lucifer. Of course, the Muslim Seljuks and Mameluks with whom they clashed *also* saw themselves as the faithful servants of God and his one true faith: Islam. Consequently, the Muslim warriors waged battle with every bit as much moral conviction and certitude as the Crusaders.

History teaches that "there were heroes and villains on both sides" (to quote the opening crawl from *Revenge of the Sith*), and each army committed horrifying atrocities. Christians, for their part, saw their armed crusade in Outremer as an echo of a deeper spiritual struggle against the forces of evil, because they were called to a "dual vocation of battling physical enemies as well as spiritual ones."[56] Their patron Bernard of Clairvaux emphasized this dual struggle when he described the Templars as "a new kind of knight . . . who devotes all of his energies to the struggle on both fronts, against flesh

> Both [the Jedi and the Knights Templar] saw themselves as crusaders in an ancient war between the forces of light and the armies of evil.

and blood and against the evil spirits in the air."[57] More deadly than the armed warriors beyond the walls of their fortresses were the inner spiritual demons that threatened to damn their souls through temptations of selfishness and sinful errors, greed born out of fear.

Where the Templars saw themselves as fighting evil on two fronts, the Jedi undeniably fight evil in body and spirit. From the time of the Force Wars of Tython, the Jedi are for millennia the final bulwark protecting the galaxy from Sith domination. Their struggle against the Sith is such a defining feature of the Jedi Order that the Jedi nearly slip into oblivion when they delude themselves into thinking that the Sith have been extinguished at the Battle of Ruusan. Without their evil opposites, the Jedi lapse into complacency and are caught unawares by the Sith's brilliant revenge under Darth Sidious in *Revenge of the Sith*. Every Jedi's soul is also a battlefield in the contest between passion and compassion, anger and peace. As warriors, as well as monks, Jedi have to walk a razor's edge by being fierce enough to vanquish their foes without being pulled to the dark side by anger.[58] Many of the most gifted Jedi—including Count Dooku and Anakin Skywalker—lose their balance and succumb to the allure of the quick but corrosive path to the power of the dark side.

The power of the dark side: Luke's struggle with his fears mirrors medieval admonitions to fight spiritual evils. (*The Empire Strikes Back*)

Compassion and killing: twelfth-century Bernard of Clairvaux excused the Templars' warlike ways, despite conflicts with Church ideals.

As warriors, as well as monks, Jedi have to walk a razor's edge by being fierce enough to vanquish their foes without being pulled to the dark side by anger.

These dualisms—warrior and monk, good and evil, physical and spiritual—lead to a number of tensions and contradictions in the lives of these virtuous warriors. The Knights Templars' existence posed a theological paradox for the Church. As Christians, they were required to obey the imperative to turn the other cheek and love their neighbor and practice nonviolence. Yet as warriors, their primary function was to kill any of their Muslim neighbors who opposed Christian conquest of the Holy Land. This theological conundrum was resolved by the venerable Bernard of Clairvaux, who "announced the Templars as the champions of a higher struggle in which homicide, which was evil in Christian eyes, was really malecide, that is the killing of evil itself, which was good."[59] Bernard thus offered the rationalization that the Templars were not violating Jesus's clear edicts against violence because they were not actually killing *people*. They were killing evil that just happened to be *inside* people.[60]

The Jedi also struggle to reconcile the ideals of the Jedi Code, which requires that Jedi show compassion and use their powers only to defend, and the realistic demands of their war against the Sith, which sometimes require that the Jedi show no mercy. When Mace Windu confronts Supreme Chancellor Palpatine after he learns that he is the Sith Lord Darth Sidious, Windu disarms his opponent and has Sidious apparently at his mercy. Anakin urges Windu to follow the Code by showing mercy and allowing Sidious to stand trial. Windu protests that Sidious is too evil to let live, even though killing an unarmed combatant violates the Jedi Code. Like Bernard, he sees his opponent less

as a man who has done evil than as evil itself residing within a man. Unfortunately, Windu has no idea how right he is: Sidious has orchestrated the entire encounter so that his apparently pathetic position beneath Windu's lightsaber, combined with Anakin's fear of losing Padmé, will overwhelm the young Jedi, causing him to strike Mace Windu and turn against the Jedi.

Jedi and Templars alike struggled to balance monastic virtues with martial ones. As monks, they needed to humbly resign themselves to fate and renounce the mundane world. Yet as warriors, they were called to change the world by force of arms and proudly turn the tides of fate. Templars feared the sin of pride, not only as Original Sin of Christian theology but as "[t]he biggest stumbling block on the path to this new religious knighthood [and] an attitude long encouraged and reinforced within the military aristocracy."[61] As warriors, the Templars were required to develop exceptional physical abilities, which sometimes led to knightly arrogance. The Templars eventually resolved this problem through a kind of compromise: "a Templar had to maintain the utmost humility as an individual while feeling intense pride in belonging to the Temple."[62] They seemed to have learned this lesson too well, because it was the Templars' uncritical obedience to authority—and not their pride—that proved to be their undoing.

The Jedi also struggle to balance the selflessness required of them as members of a monastic Order with the fear, pride, and other passions that come naturally to normal creatures. It is easy to recall a number of Jedi who show excessive greed, arrogance, and fear: Anakin laughing as he plummets his airspeeder through the skylanes of Coruscant, Obi-Wan confronting General Grievous and a huge force of droids on Utapau *by himself*, Luke setting off to rescue his friends from Vader's grasp before completing his training. Yet it is in the life of the Jedi Master Qui-Gon Jinn—the tall, aloof, and curt paragon of compassion—that we best see how the warrior's virtue of fearlessness becomes his

"Reckless he is": Jedi such as Obi-Wan find fearlessness one of their greatest assets. (*Revenge of the Sith*)

greatest weapon: from his bravado in his rescue of Queen Amidala from Naboo, even though the planet has been occupied by the massive Droid Army of the Trade Federation, to the moment when he and his Padawan casually saunter into a hangar guarded by dozens of droids and promptly reduce them to scrap. Moreover, his faith in the Force and its prophecy is demonstrated in his response to the Jedi Council's decision that Anakin is too old and fearful to be trained as a Jedi. He is tenacious in his commitment to train the boy, with or without their assent. By placing incredible power in the hands of a person whom he believes to be the one who will bring balance to the Force, Qui-Gon Jinn sets in motion a chain of events that ends with the destruction of the Sith Order and the return of balance between good and evil in the galaxy under Luke Skywalker and the New Republic.

Sacrificial knight: Jacques de Molay was arrested and executed on King Philip IV's orders.

The final pattern shared by the Templars and the Jedi concerns their remarkably similar betrayal by trusted rulers. The Templars' betrayal began in 1307 with King Philip IV of France's plan to consolidate the Templars and the Hospitallers (a smaller order of warrior-monks) into a single crusading force under his command. His stated intention was to use this combined order to recover Outremer territories lost to Muslim forces in 1291. After the grand masters of both orders rejected the king's plan, Philip plotted to seize the Templars' considerable assets. The Templars had accumulated enormous wealth since their foundation and represented an irresistible target to an impoverished monarch such as Philip, who

Knights to pawns: even the greatest warriors of the Templar and Jedi Order, such as Ki-Adi-Mundi, were vulnerable to betrayal. (*Revenge of the Sith*)

was already deeply in debt to the Order. The Templars also made a monarch such as Philip uneasy, because they were an independent military force—exempt from taxation—that could move freely within his borders.

On Friday the 13th of October, 1307, Philip's men executed a secret warrant to arrest as heretics all of the Templars in France, including their grand master Jacques de Molay, who had served the day before as a pall bearer at the funeral of the king's sister Catherine.[63] This treachery is reminiscent of Supreme Chancellor Palpatine's plan to destroy the Jedi Order through the issuance of Order 66: one of the contingency plans that the clones have been trained to obey during their conditioning on Kamino. This order commands the clone troopers to destroy every member of the Jedi Order, even the Jedi who have served as their comrades and commanders for the last four years.[64]

Both orders were also dishonored by slanderous propaganda campaigns. The Templars were charged with crimes that were deemed deeply offensive to medieval Christians: denying and spitting on the cross, homosexual acts, and worshiping profane idols.[65] For their part, "the Jedi were painted as the real traitors of the Clone Wars: imperial

propaganda implicated the Jedi in the creation of the clone troopers and the manipulation of the Senate."[66] Very few knights survived either massacre.

We glean two important lessons from these stories of betrayal. The first is that those who strive for virtue are especially imperiled in a world filled with deceit and villainy. As powerful as these knights were, they were outwitted by adversaries who relied on cunning, instead of courage. The second lesson is that an excess of either greed or fear can prove fatal. The Templars perished in part because of their power and wealth. They also naively trusted Pope Clement V—who initially absolved the Templars of their guilt in 1308 but then gave in to Philip's pressure and suppressed the Order in 1312—when there was clear evidence that the king had designs on their property and was circulating scandalous rumors about them.[67]

Darth Sidious counts on the Jedi's misplaced pride in their collective ability to feel the Force when he unfurls his plan for galactic domination without their notice. Only Yoda senses that the Jedi have become dangerously proud. He warns Kenobi and Windu that the arrogance they lament in Anakin Skywalker is "a flaw all too common among Jedi." Even members of the Jedi Council as venerable as Ki-Adi-Mundi and Mace Windu are blinded by their excessive pride in the inherent moral purity of all Jedi. They refuse to accept evidence that Count Dooku is behind the plot to assassinate Senator Amidala, saying that Dooku is incapable of such treachery by virtue of having once been a Jedi.

A final meaningful parallel is that the epilogue of the Templars' sad story reads much like the prologue of the Sith's rise to power: both tell of an evil and secret brotherhood hell-bent on revenge. According to legend, a handful of Templars survived the purge, thanks to their vast land holdings, secret dens, and global web of contacts. As centuries passed, this cabal clung to the shadows and grew into a powerful occult brotherhood driven by their lust for revenge against the French Crown and the pope. An eighteenth-century account claims that the Freemasons inherited and perverted the Templars' mission, adding a "vow of vengeance against the kings and priests who destroyed their Order, and against all religion."[68]

"No Such Thing as Luck"

Histories of the exceptional men who lived and died as Shaolin monks, samurai, and Knights Templar remind us that the Jedi are not alone in seeing that we are not *really* crude, material creatures who beg for good fortune and die for good when our flesh goes cold. People from our histories formed similar societies dedicated to preserving peace and fighting on behalf of innocents too weak to defend themselves. All people, on whatever world they might live, *need* these stories. These tales kindle the hope and courage we need to reject the corrupting allure of greed, resist the seductive power of anger, and, above all, live in the face of death and change. The Jedi are the first but not the last to look beyond the desires bound to this world to live in the light of the brighter truth that we are "luminous beings," as Yoda instructs Luke, who partake of a common, unifying, cosmic energy, whether we name it Ashla, *qi*, *spiritus*, or the Force.[69]

"I will not let this Republic that has stood for a thousand years be split in two."
—Chancellor Palpatine, *Attack of the Clones*

4

"A House Divided"
The Causes and Costs of Civil War

Paul Horvath and Mark Higbee

The *Star Wars* saga may appear to be just entertainment—great storytelling, stunning visual effects, and terrific adventure on an epic scale. Yet the galaxy we see there also reflects humanity's real history of conflict and economic exploitation more than many fans may realize. The films center on two galactic civil wars, just as American history pivots on the Civil War. Both plot lines turn on the course of civil wars and their causes and consequences. Furthermore, brutal economic exploitation and political division are imbedded in the *Star Wars* galaxy, just as they exist in much of our history. Different civil wars have had quite different causes: some were fought over political rivalry, religious disputes, and economic conflict. Some resulted in the overthrow of oppressive leaders. Others demonstrated deep divides on policy and politics. All were devastating to the people who lived through them.

Separatists, Revolutionaries, and Those Loyal to the Empire

Take the wars that led to the creation of Imperial Rome. In the last decades of the Roman Republic, powerful nobles vied to control the government and the wealth that implied, going head-to-head in a series of costly civil wars. Julius Caesar vied with Pompey the Great before emerging as the ruler of Rome. His nephew Octavian tangled with Mark Antony and Cleopatra in another civil war that spanned the Mediterranean and cost thousands of lives. When he emerged victorious, Rome celebrated a "Pax Romana" with his assumption of absolute rule that was just as hollow as the "peace, freedom, justice, and security" that Anakin believes Palpatine will provide by eliminating the Republic.

In the seventeenth century, a different type of civil war broke out in Britain between forces loyal to England's Parliament and supporters of King Charles I. This British Civil War had economic and political causes complicated by religious disputes between Puritans and the

This 1643 woodcut made light of the real divide separating families and neighbors during the British Civil War.

king's traditional church. From 1642 to 1649, the war raged and the people suffered horribly, often at the hands of their nearest and dearest, as neighbor turned against neighbor. When the king was defeated, his execution didn't bring the democratic republic that some parliamentary supporters had envisioned. Ironically, the victorious parliamentary leader, Oliver Cromwell, wielded more absolute power than King Charles had ever enjoyed: a feat that Palpatine would have applauded.

Political revolutions sometimes share the attributes of a civil war. The American Revolution deeply divided communities in some of the thirteen colonies, as pro-revolutionary Patriots struggled for local control with the so-called Loyalists, who wanted to stay under the rule of the "mother country." Before the war's outbreak, Patriots tarred and feathered dozens of Loyalists, pouring pitch-black liquid pine tar over their victims, then coating the tar with feathers and parading them around the town in humiliation

The Tory's Day of Judgment: Patriots prepare to tar and feather a Loyalist during the American Revolution.

and disgrace. A Virginia shoemaker was tarred and feathered just before the Revolution for "King-worship," while a Connecticut mother was threatened with tarring and feathering in 1776 because she named her newborn son for a British general.[1] Patriots forced Loyalists to sign "loyalty oaths" to the Revolution; if they refused, the Loyalists were jailed and their property was confiscated. Loyalists formed pro-British militias in areas where the British army was operating, often engaging in pitched battles with pro-revolutionary forces, especially in the South. When the Patriots won and the British were forced to withdraw, tens of thousands of Loyalists left the new United States and emigrated to Canada so that they could remain under the rule of the British Crown.

The Russian Revolution of 1917 began a multiparty civil war that lasted almost six years. The ruling tsar was deposed by the leadership of the Russian parliament, supported by a population that was weary of the losses inflicted by Russia's involvement in World War I. The provisional democratic government that replaced the tsar was itself overthrown by the Bolsheviks—led by Vladimir Lenin—eight months later. This kicked off a bloody, multiparty civil war, as the Bolshevik Red Army fought not only the anti-Bolshevik White Army, but also

In both the *Star Wars* galaxy and America's history, civil war sparked atrocities and featured charismatic freedom fighters, even as it divided and destroyed families and communities.

regional and nationalist insurgent groups seeking to break away from what became the Soviet Union, along with foreign armed forces that tried to intervene. As in other civil wars, civilians paid the heaviest costs: both the Whites and the Reds carried out massacres and summary executions of groups they suspected of supporting the other side, and constant warfare combined with drought to produce mass famines and epidemics. After the Whites lost, hundreds of thousands of their supporters fled Russia, just as the American colonial Loyalists had fled to Canada after *their* side lost the Revolution.[2]

The American Civil War is possibly the best parallel for the civil wars that afflict the *Star Wars* galaxy. There is no mastermind to rival Palpatine, of course, and his particular brand of political skullduggery was absent. Instead, the American Civil War is understood by serious

A street barricade in Moscow during the Russian Revolution— fighting filled the streets of many Russian cities.

scholars and students of history to have resulted, in complex ways, from slavery—and this was universally understood by Americans during the Civil War but forgotten by later generations. Nevertheless, the two plot lines of *Star Wars* and the U.S. Civil War contain some striking parallels in the events leading up to the outbreak of war. In both the *Star Wars* galaxy and America's history, civil war sparked atrocities and featured charismatic freedom fighters, even as it divided and destroyed families and communities.

"Have You Come to Free Us?": The Roots of Civil Wars

The *Star Wars* saga includes two different civil wars. The first of these involves the Trade Federation, later included in the Confederacy of Independent Systems, fighting to separate from the Galactic Republic. This struggle is shown in *The Phantom Menace*, *Attack of the Clones*, and *Revenge of the Sith*. In the remaining three films, *A New Hope*, *The Empire Strikes Back*, and *Return of the Jedi*, a different but equally relevant civil war takes place, as individuals and star systems that are subjects of the Empire rebel. The Empire has ruled its subjects with absolutist and arbitrary force. Both of these civil wars echo events that have taken place in our own history, although in vastly different ways: "It is a period of civil war. Rebel spaceships, striking from a hidden base, have won their first victory against the evil Galactic Empire . . . Pursued by the Empire's sinister agents, Princess Leia races home aboard her starship, custodian of the stolen plans that can save her people and restore freedom to the galaxy."[3]

As the opening text to *A New Hope* declares, the war between the Alliance to Restore the Republic and the Empire is a civil war. From Princess Leia Organa's viewpoint, the Alliance represents the true political traditions of the galaxy that were abandoned with Palpatine's illegitimate seizure of power. Subverting and corrupting the Republic from within, his Empire has become a force for evil and oppression. For Darth Vader and his master, Leia is the illegitimate force: a spy, a Rebel, and a traitor. This dispute seems purely about politics and ideology. The Alliance to Restore the Republic, as its name suggests, seeks a return to the old form of galactic government and the freedoms it protected. The Empire fights to maintain its control over the galaxy and all within it. In many ways, this deep divide over the ideals of legitimate government and how far centralized governments should control regional rulers resembles the split seen between the North and the South in the later stages of the American Civil War.

Compare this divide with the coming of an earlier civil war in the galaxy: "Turmoil has engulfed the Galactic Republic. The taxation of trade routes to outlaying star systems is in dispute. Hoping to resolve the matter with a blockade of deadly battleships, the greedy Trade Federation has stopped all shipping to the small planet of Naboo."[4]

The opening words of the *Phantom Menace* set the tone for the Clone Wars to come. The conflict in the films begins with an economic motivation: in order to overcome the Republic's confiscatory taxation, force is necessary.[5] This has parallels in the complaints made by some colonists before the outbreak of the American Revolution: "No taxation without representation." Similarly, the American Civil War resulted from attempts of the slaveholding class of the South to avoid any risk that the democratically elected government of the United States would confiscate the slaveholders' property or endanger their political power. When Abraham Lincoln won the presidency in 1860, the losers in a national political election refused to accept the result of the election for the first time in American history. The winners, the Republican Party, promised to both halt slavery's expansion into new territories and to protect it in the states that had slavery—but this was nonetheless a threat to the means by which slave states maintained their wealth.

The American Civil War was thus caused by slavery and its course greatly shaped by the wartime actions of the slaves themselves—but it

As a Jedi, Qui-Gon Jinn has the Republic, not the abolition of slavery, as his first priority. (*The Phantom Menace*)

Lincoln was reluctant to take up the antislavery cause, even when the Civil War began.

was not a war sparked by moral concerns with ending slavery. As the war began, nobody in the Lincoln administration professed a desire for a war that attacked slavery; instead, Lincoln proclaimed that he would not touch the rights of slaveholders in the existing slave states. Similarly, the Jedi and the Republic were willing to turn a blind eye to the moral issue of slavery, at least in Anakin's day, as demonstrated in this exchange between Anakin and Qui-Gon Jin:

> Anakin Skywalker: I had a dream I was a Jedi. I came back here and freed all the slaves . . . have you come to free us?
>
> Qui-Gon Jin: No, I'm afraid not.

Of course, there were plenty of moral arguments against the continuation of slavery before the Civil War voiced by a small Northern minority, the Abolitionists. The Abolitionists were for the immediate emancipation of all slaves in the United States and didn't want to reimburse slave owners for even a penny of their lost "property." In contrast, Southern leaders were devoted to protecting slavery above all else: after the election of Abraham Lincoln as president in November 1860, they declared their states independent of the United States, in order, they said, to protect and perpetuate the slavery that was the foundation of their wealth and property. The rest of the United States refused to accept any act of secession, and civil war resulted. For the seceding states, it was a war to protect and expand slavery, and for the North, it began as a war to preserve the Union. Yet over time, the North's war objectives changed, and it became a war of liberation, a war to save the Union by destroying slavery. Thus secession, meant to preserve slavery, produced a war that the North concluded could not be won without destroying slavery.[6]

Slavery was deeply rooted in both the American political system and in the economy of the *Star Wars* galaxy, however, and it was not easy to uproot.

> Padmé Amidala: I can't believe there is still slavery in the galaxy. The Republic's anti-slavery laws . . .
>
> Shmi Skywalker: The Republic doesn't exist out here.

Leading up to the nineteenth century, the most extensive system of slavery in history—now called "Atlantic slavery"—developed in the Western Hemisphere under European colonialism. In Africa, countless wars were fought for the purpose of enslaving people and selling them into the transatlantic commerce in human beings. The trade in human beings was the most profitable and strategically influential commerce in the world—much as petroleum is today. People from Africa and goods produced by slave labor on New World plantations, including sugar, indigo, rice, tobacco, and coffee, were the dominant world commodities. Profits from slavery yielded about a third of the capital formation of Britain in the 1770s, and slave-grown products contributed immeasurably to the rising standard of living in the centers of the empire.[7] In large part, the capital that financed industrialization was produced from slave labor and slave trading. Any proposal for the universal and immediate emancipation of all slaves seemed foolish and irrational to many: abolitionists seemed to be calling for a reduction in society's wealth, just as foolish as Padmé's expectation that antislavery laws will be enforced across the Republic.

> Slavery was deeply rooted in both the American political system and in the economy of the *Star Wars* galaxy, however, and it was not easy to uproot.

After the invention of the cotton gin (a simple machine that extracted the fiber of the cotton plant from the burr mixed with seeds and thereby made the fiber usable) in 1793, cotton plantations spread quickly across the South. The cotton plantations were entirely dependent on slave labor, just as the vast Hutt empire

Working a cotton gin.

relies on cheap slave labor, and slavery grew fast in the United States: in terms of territory, in its political and economic importance, and in the number of slaves. Cotton quickly became the key product for the new industrial factories of England and New England alike. Consequently, cotton rapidly became the principal crop of the slave South and by far the most valuable product of the entire U.S. economy.

By the 1830s, cotton cultivation had spread, with slaveholders and slaves, westward from the original states into the new Gulf states of Alabama, Louisiana, and Mississippi, as well as into east Texas, Arkansas, and Missouri. Cotton so dominated the economy and politics of the country that it was called "King Cotton." Senator James Hammond proclaimed the power of the South and its master crop in 1858: "The slaveholding South is now the controlling power of the world" and "No power on earth dares . . . to make war on cotton. Cotton is king."[8] The Trade Federation and the Empire display similar levels of arrogance in their own time.

"Begun the Clone War Has": How Wars Divide Republics and Empires

Civil wars don't always begin with major confrontations or pitched battles. The Clone Wars might have opened at Geonosis, but the origins of the conflict date back at least to the Blockade of Naboo and the taxation of trade routes before that. The "Shot Heard Round the World" in Lexington, Massachusetts, where American militia held their own against British troops, happened more than a year before the Declaration of Independence was signed in 1776. Similarly, the American Civil War started small, in one specific state. South Carolina was the first of the slaveholding states to withdraw from the United States after Lincoln's election, passing its "Ordinance of Secession" on December 20, 1860. A few days later, the state's secession convention adopted the "South Carolina Declaration of the Causes of Secession," which depicted Lincoln's election as an "abolitionist" threat to slave owners' continued right to possess slaves, the form of property deemed indispensable to South Carolina's prosperity. With Lincoln's oath of office, proclaimed the Declaration, "The guarantees of the Constitution will then no longer exist; the equal rights of the States will be lost. The Slaveholding States will no longer have the power of self-government, or self-protection, and the Federal Government will have become their enemy." Consequently, South Carolina declared it had dissolved its ties to the United States and "resumed her position among the nations of the world, as a separate and independent state."

John Calhoun, the South Carolina senator who staunchly defended slavery and who championed South Carolina's right to defy federal laws.

Other slave states followed South Carolina's lead, but the Northern states and their elected officials did not willingly allow the United States of America to be dissolved. Despite this, it wasn't until April 1861 that the war started with the attack on Fort Sumter in Charleston Harbor. The first pitched battle took place at the First Battle of Bull Run, two months later. From this perspective, the long gap between the isolated actions of the Trade Federation on Naboo and

Count Dooku, leader of the Separatist Confederacy of Independent Systems. (*Attack of the Clones*)

the Battle of Geonosis makes perfect sense: it often takes a long time to turn from civil dispute to civil war.

In the *Star Wars* universe, the formation of the Separatist Confederacy and its slow road to civil war happen in a very similar fashion to the rise of the Confederate States of America. After the crisis on Naboo detailed in *The Phantom Menace*, the Trade Federation becomes cynical about the Republic and concludes that the corruption and bureaucracy in the Galactic Senate have become too much to bear. When Count Dooku rallies to their cry of unjust taxation, other systems begin to sympathize with their anti-Republic stance. As a result, other groups—the Corporate Alliance, the Commerce Guild, the InterGalactic Banking Clan, and the Techno Union—join the movement. These individual groups bring more than political support to the Confederacy: they are also in the business of battle droid manufacture. The battle droid army of the Confederacy is amassed to overwhelm the peacetime army of the Republic, as well as the few Jedi who are entrusted with keeping the peace.

The Confederacy relies on a massive battle droid force to fight the Republic. (*The Phantom Menace*)

Both the U.S. federal government and the *Star Wars* Republic, on the other hand, were vehemently opposed to secession. "I will not let this Republic that has stood for a thousand years be split in two," says Palpatine in *Attack of the Clones*. Due to the growth of the Separatist Confederacy, in terms of both its membership and its military force, the Galactic Senate confers emergency power on the Supreme Chancellor, Palpatine. "And as my first act with this new authority, I will create a grand army of the Republic to counter the increasing threats of the separatists," Palpatine declares in a later scene of *Attack of the Clones*. It is at this point that the Clone Wars are inevitable.

Lincoln and the Republicans were elected in 1860 on a dual promise: first, to leave slavery undisturbed in those states that permitted slavery; and second, to stop slavery from expanding into any additional territories or states. Most voters in the North supported this "free soil" position, but the slaveholders felt it was a dire threat to slavery's perpetuation in the United States. It would ensure that over time the slave states' dominance of the U.S. Senate would decline. Since the founding of the Republic, slavery's perpetuation had relied much on the slaveholding class's disproportionate power in the federal government, as well as on the slave system's ability to replicate itself in new territories. Southern elites feared that halting the expansion of slavery into new states would ultimately undermine slavery throughout the nation and thus destroy the source of their wealth.

Lincoln won the 1860 election by securing an unprecedented majority of the electoral college vote, without even being on the ballot in the Southern states. That the North's electoral votes alone could elect a president frightened the slaveholding class: Lincoln won a fair and constitutional election, despite his total lack of Southern support. This seemed to indicate that the Northern majority could enact its will against the slave states, and they would have no recourse.

We do not wish to suggest a parallel between Lincoln and Palpatine. We do suggest that in both instances, a political change at the top of the respective governments led to war. The granting of emergency powers to Palpatine is also the motivation for the second war, pitting Rebels against the Empire. By not ceding emergency power back to the Galactic Senate after the resolution of the Clone War and then dissolving the Galactic Senate later, in *A New Hope*, Emperor Palpatine dominates the galaxy with fear. "Fear will keep the local systems in line. Fear of this battle station," proclaims Tarkin in *A New Hope* (with an arrogance comparable to Senator Hammond's boast about "King Cotton"). This second war has parallels to the American Civil War in its later stages.

Plans and People

Across the South, as U.S. forces invaded Confederate territory, oppression weakened greatly. Wherever Union forces drew near, slaves challenged the order of the plantations, and many slaves escaped to Union lines, obtaining freedom and bringing military intelligence. The actions of heroic slaves who aided the Union, such as Robert Smalls in the first two years of the Civil War, together with Frederick Douglass's propaganda linking the Union cause with the defeat of the slaveholding class, eventually convinced Lincoln's administration and the Northern public that emancipation was the strategic key to defeating the Confederacy. Black communities across the North had organized militias and sought to fight for the United States since the firing on Fort Sumter. Their willingness to enlist, though rejected for the war's first eighteen months, became compelling during the course of the war.

All of this laid the groundwork for Lincoln's decision in the summer of 1862 that the war had to become a war of emancipation, as well as a war to save the Union. Lincoln did not announce his Preliminary Emancipation Proclamation until after the battle of Antietam in September 1862, but he had concluded that summer that emancipation was a military necessity. He waited to proclaim emancipation as a war goal for the United States until after the United States had a victory in battle, so that the move would not seem born of desperation.

In *A New Hope*, the Rebels' destruction of the Death Star is a key military victory, pivotal to the galaxy's future. In the American Civil War, the shift of the North's war aims into a war to destroy slavery, as well as a war to save the Union, was the epic turning point of the war. As Lincoln said when his emancipation policy was criticized in the North, "no human power can subdue this rebellion without the use of the emancipation policy, and every other policy calculated to weaken the moral and physical forces of the rebellion."[9] In *A New Hope*, the Rebels destroy the enemy's most powerful weapon, the Death Star; in the Civil War, emancipation destroyed the Confederates' reason for war, as well as the foundation of their economic system.

Lincoln recognized, along with many in the North by midway through the war, that the black soldiers were indispensable to the hopes of victory by the United States over the Confederates. By the war's end, blacks made up 10 percent of the enlisted men in the U.S. Army and Navy. They proved to be an essential strategic element in the cause of the Union.

One of the most infamous events of the Civil War was the massacre of hundreds of black soldiers of the U.S. Army after their capture at Fort Pillow, Tennessee, by Confederate troops, on April 12, 1864. This massacre occurred after Fort Pillow was seized from U.S. forces by Confederate troops commanded by Nathan Bedford Forrest (a plantation owner who in later years was a leader in the creation of the Ku Klux Klan). These African American soldiers' surrender was not accepted, because the Confederate position was that blacks were not eligible to serve in any army: the Confederates held that they were legally slaves and inferior beings, who could not be granted the status of either a soldier or a prisoner of war (much

> The Rebels destroy the enemy's most powerful weapon, the Death Star; in the Civil War, emancipation destroyed the Confederates' reason for war, as well as the foundation of their economic system.

as the clones are in the *Star Wars* galaxy). W.E.B. Du Bois, the great historian and civil rights activist, described the massacre, noting that some black troops "were burned alive, having been fastened inside the buildings, while still others were nailed against the houses, tortured, and then burned to a crisp."[10]

Although the pretext is different, the proclamation of Order 66 by Darth Sidious in *Revenge of the Sith* and the great Jedi massacre that follows echo the massacre of defenseless soldiers at Fort Pillow. After the Emperor issues the order, clone troopers turn on their Jedi generals and attack them mercilessly. Just as the surrendering soldiers at Fort Pillow were betrayed by their captors, given that the soldiers expected that their surrender would stop the fighting but would not lead to their own deaths, so, too, are the Jedi betrayed by their clone troopers. In leading their troops against the Droid Army, the Jedi are essentially defenseless against the forces that have been under their command just minutes earlier. Shortly thereafter, Anakin Skywalker, now under the sway of the dark side, enters the Jedi temple and slaughters all individuals inside: the Padawans, staff, and Younglings all meet their end by his lightsaber. In both massacres, defenseless lives were lost; people who had no expectation of being massacred were killed in cold blood.

After turning to the dark side, Darth Vader massacres Jedi Younglings and turns on his former friends. (*Revenge of the Sith*)

Their murders were a violation of the laws of war. Lincoln, in 1863, had codified wartime law and then distributed it not only to the U.S. troops but to the Confederacy. Some of these provisions included maintaining communication between enemy forces, truce, prohibiting torture, prohibiting assassination, and protection of prisoners. Certainly, Forrest, as well as the Sith Sidious, but especially Vader, forsook these codes of conduct and perpetrated what are thought of as the most callous of acts thus far in either war. Both the Jedi code and the code of war understood by nineteenth-century Americans were thus violated by leaders who had professed to support these codes.

Nathan Bedford Forrest led the massacre of hundreds of African American soldiers at Fort Pillow. After the war, he led the creation of the Ku Klux Klan.

"You Were My Brother": Border States and Uncivil Divisions

The Civil War is often referred to today as a time that pitted "brother against brother." Sometimes this division was literal, as in the case of brothers Alexander and James Campbell, who fought for the North and the South, respectively, at the Battle of Secessionville in 1862.[11] Divided households were not as common as often supposed today, but families in the border states—such as Kentucky, Missouri, and especially the "Bleeding Kansas" territory—were often divided in their loyalties and military service, even as Anakin and Padmé ultimately choose different sides in the Clone Wars and the newly turned Sith apprentice, Darth Vader, turns his lightsaber on his onetime Master and mentor, Obi-Wan Kenobi, who mourns his Padawan as a brother.

Kansas was so bitterly torn between pro- and antislavery supporters that the Civil War in effect started several years early there: after the

"You were my brother": On volcanic Mustafar, Anakin and Obi-Wan are torn apart by their divided loyalties. (*Revenge of the Sith*)

Kansas-Nebraska Act of 1854 had opened the state to white settlement, supporters of both sides had poured in, seeking to dominate and control the territorial government. Territorial elections were marked by widespread fraud, and the pro-slavery local government that resulted soon faced competition from a second, "shadow" antislavery government based in Lawrence, Kansas. After several violent skirmishes, supporters of both sides took to arming themselves and mounted guerrilla attacks on communities on the other side. By 1856, the territory was in a state of constant low-level warfare, which led it to be called "Bleeding Kansas." The war there essentially persisted through 1865, with communities regularly mounting attacks on neighboring settlements. The border state of Missouri was similarly divided, and by 1861, Missouri had two competing (pro- and anti-slavery) governors and state legislatures, as federal troops battled against a pro-Confederate state militia. The Mandalorians of the *Star Wars* galaxy exhibit a similar division, with Jango Fett's cloned troopers forming the corps of the Grand Republican Army in the Clone Wars, even while his homeworld of Mandalore defects to the Confederacy's cause.

Kentucky senator John Crittenden tried to stay neutral at the start of the Civil War, but ultimately his sons served in different armies.

Kentucky, which occupied a central location between the Union North and the Deep South, is another example of how communities could be torn apart through civil warfare. The state contained both pro-Union and pro-Confederate supporters, and the state legislature, its governor, and Kentucky senator John Crittenden initially attempted to maintain a neutral position between the U.S. federal government and the Confederacy when the war began. The state legislature passed a formal declaration of neutrality in May 1861, but the state's location was too strategically crucial for either side to ignore it. President Lincoln famously commented that "I hope to have God on my side, but I have to have Kentucky." Union forces took up positions just north of the state, in Illinois; Confederate troops constructed forts just across from Kentucky's southern border in Tennessee; and Ketucky's citizens formed two competing state militias, one pro-Union and the other pro-Confederate.[12]

General Ulysses Grant, commander of the Union Army, married into a family that was strongly pro-Confederate.

The stalemate ended in the summer of 1861, when Confederate forces invaded the western corner of Kentucky, and then General Ulysses S. Grant led an invasion of Union forces from the north. Pro-Confederate supporters fled to the southern part of the state to establish a second, "shadow" state legislature in late 1861, and the state became a battlefield for the next two years. Senator Crittenden's own family was torn apart, as his oldest son, George, became a Confederate Army general, while his younger son, Thomas, served as a general on the Union side.

Another prominent Kentucky family—that of First Lady Mary Todd Lincoln—was similarly divided. While Mrs. Lincoln lived in the White House, five of her brothers or brothers-in-law fought for the Confederacy. Three of them died.[13] Like Abraham Lincoln's, General Grant's in-laws were also pro-Confederacy. Ulysses Grant's wife, Julia, came from a Missouri slaveholding family; they were married at her father's plantation, and Grant's parents did not attend the wedding because they disapproved of his marrying into a slave-owning family. Unsurprisingly, when the Civil War began, Julia's childhood friends and her family supported the Confederates.[14]

Although not a blood family, even the Jedi are divided by the Clone Wars: Dooku's defection is matched by many of his peers' during the course of the conflict, including the assassin Asajj Ventress and eventually his replacement, Darth Vader.

"No Time for Sorrows": Costs and Consequences of Civil Wars

The American Civil War took a huge toll in life, blood, and treasure. Out of a total population of 31 million people, North and South, 620,000 died. Of these, 360,000 served in the U.S. military, and 260,000 served the Confederacy. Furthermore, "The number of southern civilians who died as a direct or indirect result of the war," as historian James McPherson has noted, "cannot be known; what *can* be said is that the Civil War's cost in American lives was as great in all of the nation's other wars combined through Vietnam."[15] The Civil War battle of Antietam, September 17, 1862, was the single bloodiest day in American history: 6,000 Americans were killed.[16] Other battles caused even greater loss of life, but over multiple days. Overall, roughly one in four Southern white men of military age was killed, for a ghastly toll of 5 percent of all Southern whites.[17] An even bloodier toll is suffered in the civil wars of the *Star Wars* galaxy, in which the entire planet of Alderaan is destroyed, and vast populations obliterated. Those wars are depicted as involving more destructive weapons than even the new repeating rifles of the Civil War era. The point here is not to compare actual historical casualties to those in the *Star Wars* civil wars, but rather to stress that the high cost in life and suffering of the American Civil War was analogous to

> The high cost in life and suffering of the American Civil War was analogous to the costs of the epic struggles of the Clone Wars and later the Rebels versus the Empire.

the costs of the epic struggles of the Clone Wars and later the Rebels versus the Empire, which is why both have so much dramatic appeal today.

The American Civil War resulted not only in the destruction of slavery in the United States, but in a process of Reconstruction that included the granting of citizenship to the former slaves. This promise of equality, embedded in the 14th and 15th Amendments to the Constitution, was more violated than practiced in the century after the Civil War, but the existence of this promise became a powerful weapon for the Civil Rights movement of the mid-twentieth century. Similarly, the Empire regularly discriminated against nonhumans, while their enemies in the Alliance built their coalition on interspecies cooperation and respect that fully incorporated all sorts of life forms, including Wookiees, Bothans, Mon Calamari, Ewoks, and others.

The economic consequences of the American Civil War varied by region: "If economic devastation stalked the South, for the North the Civil War was a time of unprecedented prosperity."[18] The outcome was probably the same in the *Star Wars* galaxy: certainly, the droid foundries of Geonosis are profitable, as must be the production of every Star Destroyer or measly TIE fighter. In war, the people lose and the corporations win, regardless of one's galaxy.

The second *Star Wars* civil war resembles an Abolitionist view of the American Civil War: both in the United States and in the *Star Wars* galaxy they are wars of liberation.

In *Star Wars*, one civil division, the Clone Wars, is directly followed by another conflict in which the Galactic Empire has become an oppressive force. The second *Star Wars* civil war resembles an Abolitionist view of the American Civil War: both in the United States and in the *Star Wars* galaxy they are wars of liberation. In these films, the Empire has oppressed every free society into submission, with the exception of the Rebel Alliance. The Rebels' call for freedom strongly echoes the moral arguments put forth by Abolitionists. Some Abolitionists appealed to slave owners to repent of the sin of owning slaves by immediately free-

Darth Vader redeems himself and reunites the galaxy when he kills his Sith Master, Darth Sidious. (*Return of the Jedi*)

ing their slaves. This resembles the rallying cry of the Alliance, which calls for personal freedoms that were unjustly kept from them under the yoke of the Empire.

In the final battle scene of *Return of the Jedi*, the murderous Darth Vader, loyal servant to the dark side, is transformed and redeemed by the long-suppressed love for his son: Darth Vader ultimately cannot stand to see Luke Skywalker defeated and killed by the Sith Emperor. Deep inside, he retains the capacity to love, and that love inspires him to rebel at the last moment. Darth Vader turns against the Emperor and kills him, thus ending the second civil war. In doing so, he saves his son, reclaims his humanity, and becomes a free man, just before dying. He is, in the end, redeemed and the galaxy is reunited, ending the divide that split families and cost billions of lives.

During the Civil War, Frederick Douglass held that the horrible loss of life was the price the country had to pay for the sin of slavery—and that the sacrifice was redemptive. In Lincoln's Second Inaugural Address, he expressed much the same idea that Douglass had proclaimed since the war started:

Frederick Douglass,
former slave and
Abolitionist leader.

If God wills that [the war] continue, until all the wealth piled by the bond-man's two hundred and fifty years of unrequited toil shall be sunk, and until every drop of blood drawn with the lash, shall be paid by another drawn with the sword, as was said three thousand years ago, so still it must be said "the judgments of the Lord, are true and righteous altogether."[19]

The experience of the American Civil War made the United States into a nation that could evolve into the country we know today. The people of the *Star Wars* galaxy also pay a terrible price to end oppression and restore freedom. The joyous celebrations that span the galaxy from Endor to Coruscant at the end of *Return of the Jedi*, however, show that the terrible cost is justified to restore freedom to all.

PART II

"Join Me, and Together We Can Rule the Galaxy as Father and Son"

POLITICAL HISTORIES IN *STAR WARS*

"Sounds an awful lot
like a dictatorship to me."
—Senator Amidala, *Attack of the Clones*

THE TOOLS OF DICTATORSHIP

In *Mein Kampf*, Adolf Hitler wrote, "All great movements are popular movements . . . stirred into activity by the ruthless Goddess of Distress or by the torch of the spoken word cast into the midst of the people." Authoritarian leaders can exploit poverty and human misery caused by events such as the Great Depression. They can rely on preexisting nationalist rivalries and resentments or mobilize support by manufacturing the distress, whether through the Battle of Geonosis or the mysterious and sudden fire that destroyed the German Reichstag in 1933.

These movements are often bound together by hostility toward a scapegoat or other imagined enemies. Just as Geonosis led to Supreme Chancellor Palpatine's Jedi Purge, Hitler blamed the Reichstag fire on Communists. On the Night of the Long Knives in 1934, he had some of his own followers murdered to ensure the support of the German military. Throughout the Third Reich, the Nazis created a public culture and educational system that taught Germans that theirs was a "racial community" that excluded German Jews and others who were deemed "undesirable."

CALLED TO WAR

Women have always contributed to resistance movements. Concealed within traditional roles, they carry out subversive acts that are masked as "women's work." They act as spies, couriers, and smugglers. And they have led.

The most unlikely leader was a French farm girl born in 1412. Heavenly voices told a teenage Joan to aid the dispossessed French king. Although frightened, she learned to ride and wear heavy armor. She proved herself worthy at Charles's court, and she was eventually given an army to raise the English siege of Orléans. This victory earned her fame and honor among the French and death at the hands of the English, who burned her at the stake as a cross-dressing heretic.

Joan's struggles inform the trials of Ahsoka Tano. This teenager was young for a Padawan, but the Clone Wars saw her thrust into the Battle of Christophsis. Soon "Snips" was commanding her own troops, sometimes with disastrous results. These setbacks left her desolate but enabled her to find the balance between personal bravery and careful leadership.

ROYAL WOMEN

A long time ago, a charming and intelligent young woman asserted her right to rule a prosperous and sophisticated culture. She was supported by powerful military men from outside her kingdom who helped her overcome stiff opposition. But the men she allied herself with overreached: first one and then the other sought, unsuccessfully, to rule the entire Roman Empire. She fell along with them and died while still young. The twins she bore in her marriage with the second general—a boy and a girl— grew up without her.

This story could be Queen Amidala's, but it's actually Cleopatra's. The Egyptian queen's life demonstrates, as do the lives of many other queens, how much power and peril crowns brought to the women who dared seize them.

THE WARRIOR IS HIS WEAPON

When Obi-Wan Kenobi returns Anakin's lost lightsaber, he says, "This weapon is your life." Indeed, a Padawan must assemble his own lightsaber as one of the last tests before becoming a Jedi. Thus, the weapon becomes a sign of his maturity as well as a unique, deeply personal mode of self-expression.

The samurai had a similar attitude. While they were obligated to balance their mastery of warfare with civilized endeavors such as classical literature, calligraphy, and Confucian philosophy, their mastery of the sword was more crucial. The katana did not just protect the samurai's life; it was the life, symbol, and soul of the samurai. A graceful weapon steeped in spiritual significance, it was, according to Takuan Sōhō, a sixteenth-century master in the school of Zen Buddhism, "an instrument of life and death, purity and honor, authority and even of divinity."

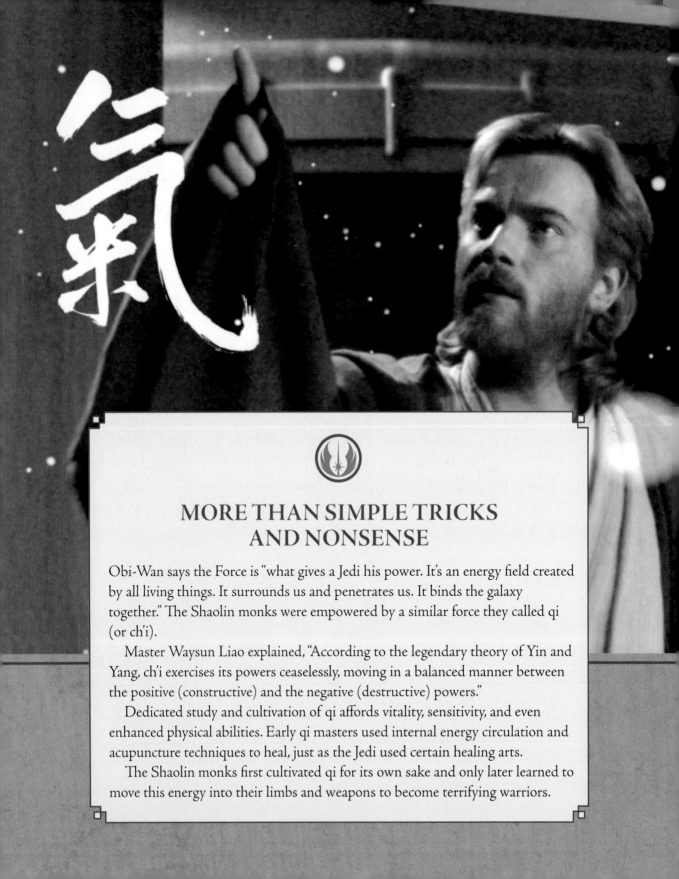

MORE THAN SIMPLE TRICKS
AND NONSENSE

Obi-Wan says the Force is "what gives a Jedi his power. It's an energy field created by all living things. It surrounds us and penetrates us. It binds the galaxy together." The Shaolin monks were empowered by a similar force they called qi (or ch'i).

Master Waysun Liao explained, "According to the legendary theory of Yin and Yang, ch'i exercises its powers ceaselessly, moving in a balanced manner between the positive (constructive) and the negative (destructive) powers."

Dedicated study and cultivation of qi affords vitality, sensitivity, and even enhanced physical abilities. Early qi masters used internal energy circulation and acupuncture techniques to heal, just as the Jedi used certain healing arts.

The Shaolin monks first cultivated qi for its own sake and only later learned to move this energy into their limbs and weapons to become terrifying warriors.

5

I, Sidious

Historical Dictators and Senator Palpatine's Rise to Power

Tony Keen

This idea of a democracy being given up—and in many cases being given up in a time of crisis—you see it throughout history, whether it's Julius Caesar or Napoleon or Adolf Hitler. You see these democracies under a lot of pressure, in a crisis situation, who end up giving away a lot of the freedoms they have and a lot of the checks and balances to some-body with a strong authority to help get them through the crisis.

—George Lucas, audio commentary, *Attack of the Clones* DVD

George Lucas's *Star Wars* saga is, at heart, an adventure story. The political narrative within the movies serves the purposes of that story: the tale of the overthrow of the benign but weak Galactic

Republic, replaced by the oppressive Empire, before the Empire is itself destroyed by the heroes. The story represents the triumph of good over evil.

Nevertheless, as is demonstrated elsewhere in this volume, Lucas clearly used elements taken from actual human history to inform the course of events "a long time ago in a galaxy far, far away." This chapter looks at three instances in the past when a democratic state was overthrown by a dictator, how they parallel Lucas's future (or past) history, and specifically the coup d'état that is carried out by Senator Palpatine from Episodes I to III.

The three historical examples that best parallel Palpatine's rise are found in the lives of Gaius Julius Caesar Octavianus Augustus, Napoleon Bonaparte, and Adolf Hitler. As in *Star Wars*, in each of these cases a republican form of government was replaced by a dictator who received crucial support from many of the republic's own representatives: republican forms of government—in Rome, in Paris, in Berlin, and on Coruscant—thus subverted themselves.

The Roman Republic, Augustus, and the Sith Lord Emperor

The man who has become recognized as the first Roman emperor, Caesar Augustus, was born Gaius Octavius in 63 BC.[1] His great-uncle was the Roman politician Gaius Julius Caesar, who was on his way to the ascendancy within the Roman state. Julius Caesar's impressive military victories and political skills culminated in his appointment in 48 BC to the post of *dictator* and his assassination four years later.

What is now described as the Roman Republic had emerged in the late sixth century BC, after the city of Rome threw out the kings who had ruled it before. By the first century BC, it was in name a democracy, in which every adult male citizen had the vote, and power derived ultimately from the people; hence the use of the phrase *Senatus Populusque Romanus*, known by its abbreviation *SPQR*, meaning that decisions were made in the Roman state by the People, with the Senate, the body composed of ex-magistrates, acting as the people's leaders. In practice, however, the political mechanisms were biased toward the wealthy.

The system was also becoming badly strained. The Roman state had acquired an overseas empire that stretched from one end of the Mediterranean to the other. The political structures that developed to rule a small city-state were not properly equipped for ruling a large empire. The empire had, moreover, brought in a great deal of wealth, which was being monopolized by the elite; this was causing serious social tensions and creating a dissatisfied urban poor, who could be exploited by ambitious politicians.

Furthermore, Roman culture associated political and military leadership, which meant that politicians generally needed to demonstrate their military prowess to achieve high office. This problem was compounded by reforms of the army that had been introduced in the early first century BC to address a problem that the Roman Republic had faced. Originally, men would be recruited into the Roman army only if they owned a certain amount of property. By the second

Marble statue of Augustus in military garb (the *Prima Porta* Augustus), a copy of a lost bronze original, first century BC.

century BC, this pool of citizen farmers from which the infantry had been drawn was diminishing. Rural families were increasingly driven off their farms (and into the cities) by the already rich, who replaced them with slave labor; as a result, there were not enough men from farming households to fill the army's ranks. Abolishing the property requirement for service in the army and recruiting men who had no property addressed the military manpower shortage but left the rewards to be given to Roman troops (who at this point were not yet receiving regular payment) to the generals in command—effectively, this gave Roman generals their own private armies.

Octavius's great-uncle Julius Caesar exploited this to become the most important man in Rome. In 49 BC, he invaded Italy with an army and was made *dictator* for a year.[2] Caesar was able to get this motion through the Roman Senate because most of the members who opposed him had fled with Caesar's main rival, Pompey. In late 48 BC, the Senate renewed Caesar's dictatorship for a year, and in 46 BC, he was appointed dictator for the next decade. Caesar made himself perpetual *dictator* in 44 BC. Caesar had enough support in the Roman Senate to ensure that it supported these moves and enacted appropriate legislation; those

Jean-Léon Gérôme, *La Mort de César* (The Death of Caesar, 1867). This depicts the moment in 44 BC just after the assassination of Julius Caesar in the Portico of Pompey. Caesar's corpse lies in the foreground, as his assassins go forth to proclaim their deed.

who opposed Caesar had either fled or were too frightened to oppose him in any numbers. Assuming the powers of the Roman censorship, Caesar appointed new members to the Senate and increased their numbers to nine hundred men (from the three hundred the Senate had been before). All of these men would be Caesar's partisans. Moreover, Caesar had acquired for himself the power to veto the Senate.

Caesar's dictatorship was seen by some (with some reason) as being tantamount to reestablishing a monarchy in Rome. And so a group of conspirators brought about the assassination of Caesar on the Ides (15th) of March in 44 BC.

The eighteen-year-old Octavius, to the surprise of many, was named in Caesar's will as his heir and became by adoption Gaius Julius Caesar Octavianus. Modern scholars call him Octavian from this point on, and so shall I, though in fact he hardly ever used that part of his name, preferring to stick with Gaius Julius Caesar, for the associations it gave him with his great-uncle.

Octavian moved quickly to secure his recognition as Caesar's heir and establish himself as a major political force in the Roman state. He had to contend with Caesar's right-hand man, Mark Antony, with whom he at first cooperated and then fought. By 31 BC, Octavian had eliminated Antony.

Octavian then set about reforming the Roman state in such a way as to leave himself in control but give the appearance of a restoration of the constitutional norms. In 27 BC, the Senate granted him the title "Augustus" ("the revered one"). It is by this title that we know him from this point on, and we call the Roman state after this point the Roman Empire, as opposed to the Roman Republic—though this distinct division was not recognized at the time.

Portrait bust of Julius Caesar's right-hand man and later Octavian's rival, Mark Antony, first century BC.

"Sounds an Awful Lot Like a Dictatorship to Me": Palpatine's Subversion of the Galactic

Galactic empires in science fiction have been modeled on the Roman Empire since the "Foundation" stories of Isaac Asimov, first published in the 1940s. George Lucas follows in that tradition, and much of the political terminology of the *Star Wars* galaxy (e.g., "Republic," "Empire," and "Senate") are also found in the Roman Empire and could be said to derive from that source.[3] It is plain that the basic structure of Lucas's history derives from the fall of the Roman Republic and the subsequent establishment of a monarchy.

The Senate of the Galactic Republic on Coruscant. Though it is much larger, it shares with the Roman Senate a central location from which the Senate is addressed, and the circular arrangement of the Senators reflects the semicircular arrangement in Maccari's painting. (*The Phantom Menace*)

The Galactic Republic, as we see in *The Phantom Menace*, is democratic and governed by a Senate, just as Rome's was. Senator Palpatine has a pseudo-Latin name that is reminiscent of those of later Roman emperors, such as Constantine, who ruled from 306 to 337. There are also echoes in his name of "Palatine," the name of a hill that stands at the center of the Seven Hills of Rome and is the location of several ancient imperial Roman palaces. This is one of a number of pseudo-Latin names in the *Star Wars* universe; Valorum, the name of Palpatine's predecessor as chancellor, is another. Beyond Coruscant, the architecture of Naboo resembles that of imperial Rome, and the victory parade at the end of *The Phantom Menace* is very like a Roman Triumph.

Senator Palpatine manipulates the Senate in the way at which Octavian proved most adept. He recognizes the problems faced by the Republic—in this case, corruption within the Senate and an excessively influential bureaucracy that hampers his making effective decisions in

> The basic structure of Lucas's history derives from the fall of the Roman Republic and the subsequent establishment of a monarchy.

The triumphal procession on Naboo. (*The Phantom Menace*)

government—and Palpatine exploits them, as Octavian and his predecessors did. He gets himself made chancellor, as Octavian demanded that the Roman Senate make him consul, and before him, Caesar had himself made dictator. Palpatine then (in *Attack of the Clones*) further manipulates the Senate into granting him exceptional powers in order to face the emergency of the impending war with the Trade Federation. This may be compared to the appointment of Octavian, Mark Antony, and another of Caesar's allies, Marcus Aemilius Lepidus, as *triumviri rei publicae constituendae* ("triumvirs for the restoration of the Republic"), and the subsequent granting of special powers to Octavian. Palpatine promises (falsely) that he will give up those powers once the emergency has passed; similarly, Augustus claimed in his propaganda that he had given up his special powers (though, in practical terms, he retained real control).

As with the fall of the Roman Republic, it is important to remember that control of the Galactic Empire is highly dependent on the control of military force. Octavian became the dominant figure in Rome because he commanded the personal loyalty of Roman legions that had once been Julius Caesar's. He subsequently maintained control by ensuring that the provinces where legions were to be stationed were (for the most part) under his command (as the ostensible representative of the Senate). Palpatine's plot succeeds because he creates a private army of clones over which he has direct control; this army enables him to murder the Jedi Knights, the only force capable of opposing him.

A religious element also provides a further connection between Palpatine and Augustus. Religion was extremely important to the Romans, if conceived of somewhat differently from how we understand it now.[4] One of the ways in which Octavian secured his power was to acquire the post of chief priest, *pontifex maximus* (the title survives as "pontiff," one of the official titles of the pope in Rome). In *Star Wars*, Palpatine is assisted in carrying out his coup by his position as Darth Sidious, Dark Lord of the Sith, and the powers he gains from his knowledge of the dark side of the Force. Of course, Palpatine's powers are of a different and more immediate nature, compared with the propaganda benefits that being *pontifex maximus* conferred on Augustus. Yet we should remember that several characters in *A New Hope* (including Admiral Motti, Han Solo, and Grand Moff Tarkin) describe the knowledge of the Force held by the Jedi and the Sith Lords as a "religion."

There are, of course, a number of differences—*Star Wars* is far from being a slavish presentation of the history of Rome as a space fantasy story. Most clearly, *Star Wars* differs in the overt nature of Palpatine's Imperial project, once it is brought out in the open. In *Revenge of the Sith*, Palpatine stands in front of the Senate and proclaims the Galactic Empire: "In order to ensure the security and continuing stability the Republic will be reorganized into the first Galactic Empire! For a safe and secure society."

The enthusiasm of the Galactic Senate for Palpatine's proclamation of the Galactic Empire, which is greeted with loud applause, is paralleled by the Roman Senate's enthusiasm for Julius Caesar. Lucas may well have had this in mind. Padmé Amidala and Bail Organa watch on, powerless, as the orator Marcus Tullius Cicero did in Rome.

Chancellor Palpatine pro-
claims the First Galactic
Empire. (*Revenge of the Sith*)

By *A New Hope*, Palpatine has even gone as far as dissolving the Senate, leaving fear of the Imperial forces (especially of the Death Star) to keep the provinces in line. In a similar way, it can be argued that the presence of Roman legions throughout the provinces of the empire was as much about keeping the conquered territories under control as it was about defending the empire from foreign powers.

The enthusiasm of the Galactic Senate for Palpatine's proclamation of the Galactic Empire, which is greeted with loud applause, is paralleled by the Roman Senate's enthusiasm for Julius Caesar.

Augustus never went as far as dissolving the Roman Senate. Augustus kept the Senate going as a body, and in theory, it retained executive power, with Augustus merely its representative. Augustus is referred to by modern historians as an emperor, but the title he took for himself was *princeps*, "first man."[5] Subsequent Roman emperors maintained the pretense, though it rapidly became obvious that the actual scope for independent action by the Roman Senate was minimal.

Rather than proclaim a new form of state, Augustus went out of his way to give the impression that he had "restored" the old form, and that things had returned to how they were. That sort of rhetoric only occasionally appears in *Star Wars*. One instance is the moment in *Revenge of the Sith* where Palpatine congratulates his new acolyte Darth Vader on restoring peace and justice to the Galaxy, after Vader has murdered the Separatist leaders.

The Senate of the Galactic Republic is in many ways different from the Roman Senate. To start with, it is larger—there are 1,024 delegates to the Galactic Senate, whereas the Roman Senate had (for most of its existence in the Republic) only 300 members. Nor was the Republican Roman Senate geographically representative—it consisted of magistrates and ex-magistrates who belonged to the leading Roman families, drawn from the city of Rome itself and gradually from those areas and families in Italy that had been granted Roman citizenship. Only well after the empire was established were senators admitted who came from outside Italy. In the Galactic Senate, in contrast, each Senator represents a planet, a group of systems, or, in some cases, economic organizations (e.g., the Trade Federation). In this, it more closely resembles the U.S. Senate.

The causes of the wars that wrack Lucas's Republic in the last years of its existence are also dissimilar to those that affected the Roman Republic. In Rome, the civil wars of the last century BC were primarily struggles between individuals vying for supreme power within the Roman state. There were some ideological elements to the struggle, as people fought to preserve the authority of the Senate or for the rich or for the poor, but much of this was cover for personal ambition.[6] The internecine dimension to the fall of the Galactic Republic emerges into the open only in *Revenge of the Sith*, when the last of the Jedi fight for the Republic against the new Empire (though Palpatine has them painted as traitors to the Republic).

The wars that are seen in *The Phantom Menace*, *Attack of the Clones*, and most of *Revenge of the Sith* are different. We first see fighting between bodies that are represented within the Republic but have their own armed forces (Naboo and the Trade Federation). In possessing their own militaries, these planets are unlike the actual provinces over which Rome ruled directly and more like Rome's so-called client kingdoms: states that maintained an appearance of independence, though they had to follow Rome's lead (and were considered by the Romans to be as much a part of the empire they ruled as the provinces were). In *Attack of the Clones*, this has developed into Separatist insurrections within the Republic. These do have similarities to the Social War of 91–88 BC, in which many of Rome's Italian allies seceded because Rome was unwilling to share more widely the privileges of Roman citizenship. Yet the Social War was over long before Octavian made his bid for power, and the Social War was not secretly being manipulated by any of the Roman leaders whose careers profited from their actions in it. There is in Lucas's history a Galactic Civil War, but that term is applied to the later conflict between the Empire and the Rebel Alliance and is a reaction to Palpatine's coup, not a precursor to it.

Palpatine is unlike Augustus in a number of respects. For one thing, he is a lot older. Octavian was eighteen when he began his political career, and although he lived to be seventy-six, he was already sole master of the Roman world by the time he was thirty-two. Palpatine is in his fifties when he first becomes chancellor and in his sixties when he assumes Imperial control (actor Ian McDiarmid was fifty-four on the release of *The Phantom Menace* and sixty when *Revenge of the Sith* was released).[7]

Palpatine is also much less favorably treated in the stories Lucas tells of him than Augustus is often treated in historical accounts. Palpatine is obviously the main villain of the *Star Wars* series, appearing in all but one of the movies and mentioned in the one (*A New Hope*) in which he is not seen. Palpatine is evil, and his actions cannot be seen as having any justification beyond his personal lust for power. He is also ruthless, quite willing to sacrifice his ally Count Dooku in order to draw Anakin Skywalker further toward the dark side.

Augustus was also ruthless when he needed to be. He ordered the execution of seventeen-year-old Caesarion, the child of the Egyptian

Anakin Skywalker, having just executed Count Dooku at the encouragement of Chancellor Palpatine. (*Revenge of the Sith*)

queen Cleopatra. Cleopatra had been Mark Antony's ally and lover, but her younger children were allowed to live. Caesarion died because he was allegedly Julius Caesar's biological son and so a threat to Augustus's claim to be Caesar's rightful heir.

The orator Cicero had been Octavian's supporter in the latter's early career, promoting him against Mark Antony, whom Cicero hated, but when Octavian needed to make an alliance with Mark Antony, he was quite happy to allow Cicero's name to be added to the list of those to be proscribed, in other words, listed as public enemies who could be killed with impunity. Palpatine takes similar actions against his opponents: he declares the Jedi enemies of the Republic.

Sir Lawrence Alma-Tadema, *The Meeting of Antony and Cleopatra*, 41 BC (1885). This depicts the first encounter of Antony (the seated man in a helmet) and the Egyptian queen.

Cicero's head was hacked off by a centurion who caught up with him a short time after the proscription. Supposedly, Augustus regretted that in later life, but he still did it and continued to show little mercy to those who crossed him. He also undoubtedly suspended the normal organs of the democratic state and presided over a military dictatorship. Yet he is often seen as a great man, who did what needed to be done in order to save what could be saved of the Roman state. He is the classic benevolent dictator, a strong leader of the type that Anakin Skywalker advocates to Senator Padmé Amidala in *Attack of the Clones*. As Cicero did with Julius Caesar, she rejects the idea as antithetical to the ideals of a republic.

The final way in which Palpatine differs from Augustus is, of course, that the Roman was successful. He established a system of rule for the Roman

[Augustus] is the classic benevolent dictator, a strong leader of the type that Anakin Skywalker advocates to Senator Padmé Amidala in *Attack of the Clones*.

Empire that, despite many crises, lasted for centuries. It even survived the loss of its western territories and the original capital city; the line of Augustus's successors can be said, with some justification, to stretch to Constantine XI Palaeologus, of Byzantium, who died defending his people against the Turkish storming of Constantinople in 1453. Palpatine's Empire, in contrast, lasts for only twenty-three years before the forces of the Rebel Alliance destroy it.

A Tale of Two Emperors: Palpatine and Napoleon

The English literature scholar Anne Lancashire has observed that the references to the Senate and the Republic in *The Phantom Menace* conjure up Roman history and emphasize the idea of the cyclical nature of history.[8] The notion of repeating cycles of history, in which the *Star Wars* narrative is grounded, perhaps reflects the influence of Joseph Campbell and Campbell's ideas of the cyclical nature of myth. Yet references to the Senate, the Republic, and the Empire do not exclusively conjure up Rome.

For our second historical parallel, we must go forward almost two thousand years in time. Yet many of the terms that are found in the Roman Empire, such as *Senate*, or *consul*, recur in this example. This is because, like many European states of the Early Modern Period, Revolutionary France viewed itself as the heir to Roman culture.

France had been a monarchy until the Revolution of 1789, which led to the establishment of the First Republic in 1792 (as in Rome, replacing a monarchy). As did the new American nation across the Atlantic, the French legislature proceeded to create a constitution for a French Republic in 1791. Like its Roman predecessor, however, the French legislature was hampered by ideological divisions and power struggles from the very outset. Into this situation came a young military officer. Napoleon Bonaparte was in his twenties at the time of the Revolution. From 1792 onward, he was involved in the wars of France, and in 1799, as one of France's few militarily successful generals, he managed to become one of three consuls who were to rule France jointly for ten years, a similar arrangement to the Triumvirate of Octavian, Mark Antony, and Lepidus. Like Octavian in that Triumvirate, Napoleon exploited his position within the Consulate, getting himself made First Consul and then emperor in 1804. Like the other dictatorships discussed in this chapter, there are clearly elements from the history of Napoleon and Napoleonic France that can be compared with the rise of Palpatine.[9]

The French had declared themselves a Republic in 1792, but this First Republic lasted for only twelve years. The Galactic Republic is a much more venerable organization and therefore carries more resonances of the Roman Republic, which lasted for nearly five hundred years before Octavian took sole control. Yet even this period is dwarfed by the twenty-five thousand years of the Galactic Republic's existence.

A Senate was established by Napoleon's 1799 reform of the constitution (the *Sénat conservateur*), and the Senate "vested" the republic in an emperor, thus turning over power to Napoleon; his elevation to the position of emperor was also approved by a large majority of French citizens in a referendum vote. As Padmé Amidala says in *Revenge of the Sith*, "So this is how liberty dies . . . with thunderous applause."

Unlike Rome, where the transition from Republic to Empire was not at the time formally acknowledged, in Napoleonic France the birth of an empire was clearly signaled by Napoleon's coronation in 1804. In his coronation oath, Napoleon claimed that he was taking power as emperor to "maintain the integrity of the territory of the Republic," an assertion that reminds us of Palpatine's pronouncement in *Revenge of the Sith* that the Republic must be reorganized into an Empire "in order to insure the security and continued stability."

Jacques-Louis David, *The Coronation of Napoleon* (1805–1808). Napoleon (standing in the center of the painting) is wearing a garland meant to remind the viewer of a Roman victor's garland, and he is about to crown himself emperor. Empress Joséphine is kneeling in front of him.

As with Augustus, Napoleon came to power on the back of military might. Yet Napoleon was himself an extremely successful military commander, whereas Augustus relied on others, such as his friend Marcus Vipsanius Agrippa, to carry out direct military command. In this respect, Palpatine, who tends to operate through subordinates such as General Grievous or Darth Vader or, when directing the forces of the Republic, Jedi Knights such as Obi-Wan Kenobi, is closer to Augustus than to Napoleon. Napoleon also created an Imperial Guard (*Garde Impériale*). A parallel can be seen in *Star Wars*, where Palpatine also has a body of troops that is sometimes described as the Imperial Guard, who appear in *Return of the Jedi*, though the troops' official name is the Emperor's Royal Guard.

In his coronation oath, Napoleon claimed that he was taking power as emperor to "maintain the integrity of the territory of the Republic," an assertion that reminds us of Palpatine's pronouncement in *Revenge of the Sith* that the Republic must be reorganized into an Empire "in order to insure the security and continued stability."

The wars that made Napoleon's name were largely fought against foreign powers. There were internal rebellions in the First Republic, but Napoleon himself refused to take part in the War in the Vendée, a Royalist rebellion against the French Republic in western France that lasted from 1793 to 1796. He did, however, defend the National Convention

The Emperor's Royal Guard accompanying Emperor Palpatine and Darth Vader. (*Return of the Jedi*)

Jean-Auguste-Dominique Ingres, *Portrait de Napoléon Bonaparte en premier consul* (Bonaparte, First Consul, 1803–1804).

(the Republican legislature) against Royalist rebels in 1795, in the incident that gave rise to Thomas Carlyle's comment about Napoleon's use of "a whiff of grapeshot." This could be compared to the Galactic Republic's wars against the Separatists, though, again, Napoleon was not secretly in charge of the enemies he was fighting.

The fact that Napoleon spent some years as First Consul before declaring himself emperor could be seen as similar to Palpatine's thirteen years as chancellor, before he declared the Empire. Most notably, unlike Augustus, but like Palpatine, Napoleon was eventually defeated. Yet that defeat came about through the actions of external enemies, rather than internal ones—the armies and the population of France remained substantially loyal, and Napoleon remains a respected figure in France today. Unlike Palpatine, Napoleon was not killed at the point of his deposition but was forced to abdicate.

Today Coruscant, Tomorrow the Galaxy!: Nazi Germany and Palpatine

Adolf Hitler, on the other hand, manipulated a democratic republic to gain control over the government, using extra-constitutional means. As with Rome and France, the democratic republic followed the dissolution of a monarchy—in this case, the Weimar Republic was established following the abdication of the German emperor Wilhelm II in 1918, after the defeat of World War I. It should be noted, however, that "Weimar Republic" is, like "Roman Republic" and "Roman Empire," a modern historian's term; the official name for the state remained the *Deutsches Reich*, or the "German Empire."

As in the Roman Senate and the republican French government, the Weimar Republic's legislature, the Reichstag, was deeply divided between ideological extremes from the very beginning, and a large faction within the republic never did accept democratic forms of government. During periods when the economic outlook was good, this system functioned, but the coming of the Depression in 1929 threw the political system into gridlock, which offered Hitler's National Socialist German Workers' Party (the NSDAP) its opportunity.

During the Depression, the Nazi Party gained more seats in every election. By the early 1930s, no party or coalition of parties in the Weimar legis-

Adolf Hitler at a Nazi party rally in Nuremberg, c. 1928.

lature was able to gain an overall majority in elections. Through the influence of conservative politicians, Hitler was appointed chancellor of Germany on January 30, 1933. He then used political intimidation to give his Nazi Party sole power in the German state. A mysterious fire burned down the Reichstag building on the evening of February 27, and the Nazis claimed that the German Communists were responsible, and that the national government was in danger. The parallel to the final meeting of the Galactic Senate in *Revenge of the Sith*—where

Palpatine demands absolute control in order to respond to a "plot of the Jedi to overthrow the Senate"—is a striking one.

After a final set of elections marked by violence and the suspension of constitutionally guaranteed civil rights in March 1933, Nazi storm troopers surrounded the German parliamentary building and refused to allow left-wing representatives to enter. In a chamber thus dominated by Nazi legislators and their allies (much like Caesar's Senate), the Nazis proposed and passed an Enabling Act, which essentially ended democratic rule and proclaimed Hitler the dictator of Germany. In 1934, Hitler proclaimed himself Führer ("leader"). As in Rome (and on Coruscant), democratically elected representatives had voted for a dictator. People began to refer to the new German state as the "Third Reich," though this term was never the official name of the state.

The impact of the iconography of Nazi Germany on *Star Wars* is obvious. It is seen in the military of the Galactic Empire, most particularly in the uniforms worn by the Imperial forces, which resemble the uniforms worn by the Wehrmacht, the German armed forces, in World War II.

German Panzer officers during World War II.

Darth Vader and Imperial officers wearing uniforms with a very similar cut to the Panzer uniform. (*A New Hope*)

The Galactic Empire uses the term *stormtrooper* for its shock assault forces. The first storm troopers (*Sturm-truppen*) had been elite assault troops of the German army in World War I, and the name was later employed for the paramilitaries organized by the Nazi Party (known in German as the *Sturmabteilung*).

The impact of the iconography of Nazi Germany on *Star Wars* is obvious.

Imperial stormtroopers on the Death Star. (*A New Hope*)

German storm troopers, 1918.

Hitler is also, in some ways, the most like Palpatine of the three dictators discussed in this chapter. He is the closest in age to the mature galactic politician, being forty-three when he became chancellor (Napoleon was thirty when he became consul and thirty-four when he became emperor). More significantly, Hitler is popularly seen as evil and indeed as a symbol of evil. This makes him an appropriate model for Palpatine.

Palpatine even uses some of Hitler's rhetoric. In his address to the Senate inaugurating the Galactic Empire, Palpatine says, "I assure you [the Empire] will last for ten thousand years" (*Revenge of the Sith*). Such rhetoric can only make the viewer think of the "Thousand-Year Reich," the term used by Nazis to predict their domination of the world. Both Hitler and Palpatine were to be proved very wrong, their empires lasting for only a few decades. Again, however, it should be noted that it was external wars that brought Nazi Germany down, not internal rebellion (there were German resistance movements, but they were small and largely ineffective).

Palpatine also uses a similar rhetorical style to Hitler. Hitler was a master of rabble-rousing rhetoric, as he demonstrated, for example, when addressing the Nazi rallies at Nuremberg. Hitler had massive party rally grounds constructed there and used them for the annual Nazi Party Congresses from 1933 to 1938. Hitler spoke to masses of Nazi Party members, troops, and other Germans. These mass addresses were often filmed, most famously by Leni Riefenstahl for her 1934 documentary *Triumph of the Will*. Hitler was very concerned about the opportunities for exploiting media, such as the cinema, television, and newspapers, for propaganda purposes. The 1936 Berlin Olympics were turned into a spectacle that would endorse Germany, the Nazis, and Aryan supremacy (though the victories of the African American Jesse Owens proved to be an embarrassment to that ambition). Palpatine's address to the Galactic Senate will make many viewers think of the familiar footage of Hitler delivering speeches to his supporters.

Once again, one can see a connection between the importance of the military to Hitler and its importance to Palpatine. Unlike Augus-

The 1934 Nuremberg Rally. Adolf Hitler is the central of the three figures at the bottom center of the photograph.

tus and Napoleon, Hitler did not use a preexisting military force to bring him to power—the German armed forces had been significantly restricted under the treaty of Versailles, limited to a hundred thousand men, and denied heavy guns, armored vehicles, submarines, and capital ships. Hitler rebuilt these forces and rearmed Germany, a significant factor in the consolidation of his power. Similarly, Palpatine has to build his military forces up from scratch. By the time of *The Phantom Menace*, the Galactic Republic has no military of its own and depends on the Jedi Knights to keep peace. These forces are inadequate in the face of the Separatists, so Palpatine is able to persuade the Senate to accept the creation of clone troopers to serve in the Army of the Republic. As noted previously, he subsequently uses that army to destroy the Jedi Knights.

Other similarities between the rise of Palpatine and the rise of Hitler suggest themselves, too. As in Germany, the leader of the Galactic Senate is given the title of "chancellor." And just as Hitler's rise to power was facilitated by other politicians who thought that he could be controlled and who did not understand the full extent of his plans, so Palpatine was able to persuade politicians such as Queen Amidala and Jar Jar Binks to support proposals that would resolve immediate dangers, but that also served to advance his own interests. Finally, like Palpatine (but unlike Augustus), Hitler eventually dispensed with his parliamen-

Palpatine's Clone army. Compare the massed ranks of soldiers to those seen in the photo of the 1934 Nuremberg rally. (*Attack of the Clones*)

tary body, the Reichstag, removing all legislative power and, after 1942, postponing its reconstitution (though he did not formally dissolve it).

"The Last Remnants of the Old Republic Have Been Swept Away"

This chapter has discussed some of the ways in which Lucas's *Star Wars* galaxy reflects the historical precedents set by past dictators and their overthrowing of democracies. Some of this use is obvious—elements lifted from Nazi Germany and Rome can be easily identified

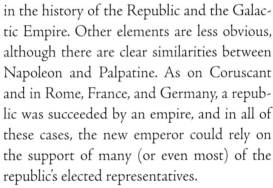

in the history of the Republic and the Galactic Empire. Other elements are less obvious, although there are clear similarities between Napoleon and Palpatine. As on Coruscant and in Rome, France, and Germany, a republic was succeeded by an empire, and in all of these cases, the new emperor could rely on the support of many (or even most) of the republic's elected representatives.

The reason that these exemplars are not always obvious is, of course, that Lucas is not simply repeating real history in space. Rather, the *Star Wars* galaxy uses elements taken from various periods of history, which Lucas selected and modified to fit. The result is a rich and believable Galactic history that can be adapted to the requirements of a saga without destroying its credibility. This richness has been welcoming visitors since 1977 and will continue to do so for many years to come.

"I was not elected to watch my people suffer and die."

—Padmé Amidala, *The Phantom Menace*

6

Teen Queen

Padmé Amidala and the Power of Royal Women

Janice Liedl

Long ago, a young woman asserted her right to rule a prosperous paradise against a stiff opposition that temporarily prevented her from ruling. The youthful queen benefited from the support of powerful military men, however, who helped restore her to power. She disastrously pursued a romantic relationship with one of these fabled fighters, an intense man who was not free to marry her. The queen died tragically, never to see her children grow up.

This sad story parallels the rise and fall of Padmé Amidala, but it's actually the story of Cleopatra. That Egyptian queen's life demonstrates how much power and peril royal crowns brought to the women who dared seize them. Padmé's problems are also mirrored in the lives of

151

other historical queens, from Maria Theresa of Austria and Hungary to Catherine the Great of Russia, and even the doomed British Boudicca. From ancient times up to the recent past, history abounds with examples of extraordinary royal women whose public and personal lives encompassed a range of triumph and disaster, just as Padmé experiences.

The irony is that although many women were queens, few actually ruled. Law and tradition meant that the queen who held the title only because she was the wife of a king was rarely in a position to assert equal power. These queen consorts might even be royalty by birth—a princess from another country who married a fellow ruler—but that foreign birthright didn't translate into their new realm. Only rarely did such a woman make a leap to wielding power independently, as happened when German-born Catherine, the wife of Tsar Peter II, engineered a coup against her own husband and took over the rule of the Russian Empire in the eighteenth century. Sometimes, even when a woman was in the direct line of succession, she couldn't receive the crown, due to traditions that either gave preference to a younger boy or ruled out women altogether.[1]

In other cases, women inherited royal or noble titles independently: ruling by themselves (as did Elizabeth I and Victoria, both in England) or jointly with a spouse, as did Isabella of Castile and Ferdinand of Aragon, who created the new kingdom of Spain through their marriage. These queens still didn't have an easy time of it, because custom, if not law, made it difficult for women to wield political power—something that Rebel Alliance figures such as Mon Mothma and Princess Leia never face in *Star Wars*' more egalitarian galactic culture. In times of

---

Our history and the history of the *Star Wars* universe preserve many stories of strong women rulers who, against great odds, fought for their people, their nation, and their right to rule.

---

war, queens rallied troops and inspired nations, just as Boudicca did against the Romans.[2] When medieval popes were hounded by the Holy Roman emperors in the eleventh century, it was a noblewoman, Matilda of Tuscany, whose troops and strategies saved the day. Our history and the history of the *Star Wars* universe preserve many stories of strong women rulers who, against great odds, fought for their people, their nation, and their right to rule.

"You Think a Princess and a Guy Like Me . . . ?"

Queens were both political leaders and women. Their private emotions and personal relationships often became part of their public lives in ways that few kings ever had to justify. Han Solo and Princess Leia show that love can cross boundaries of rank. A generation earlier, Padmé and Anakin's star-crossed love stretches across an even broader gulf of social class, when the one-time slave boy from Tatooine marries the former Queen of Naboo. Love and relationships complicated the lives of historical women sometimes even more so than they did in the time of the Republic and the Empire.

Consider the case of Cleopatra VII, who was born long ago but not in a galaxy far, far away. This powerful woman came into the world sometime during the winter of 69 BC. Cleopatra was part of the Ptolemaic dynasty, descendants of the general who accompanied Alexander the Great in his 332 BC conquest of Egypt. The country had been frequently torn by vicious battles for power between husbands and wives, brothers and sisters (sometimes one and the same, because Egyptian rulers tended to marry their own siblings in order to keep the bloodlines pure). When Cleopatra's father, Ptolemy XII, died in 51 BC, Cleopatra was only eighteen and the coruler of Egypt with her oldest brother and husband, ten-year-old Ptolemy XIII. Their new-won realm was bitterly divided, drowning in debt, and a tempting target for

Padmé Amidala is already an experienced politician by the time she becomes Queen of Naboo. (*The Phantom Menace*)

Cleopatra was only eighteen when she claimed her throne and not even forty when she committed suicide.

the powerful mercantile and militaristic state Rome.[3] Unlike Padmé's confrontational relationship with the Trade Federation, young Cleopatra welcomed Rome's intervention, which supported her as a ruler of Egypt against her annoying younger brother.

Cleopatra's greatest problem at that time was her brother and his courtiers. Ptolemy XIII wanted to eliminate his sister and coruler, and in the cutthroat politics of Ptolemaic Egypt, this meant having her killed. At least when Leia fights her own father while seeking to destroy the Empire, neither knows they are related! Ptolemy was supported by the great Roman general Pompey, who declared the youngster sole ruler of Egypt. In early 48 BC, Cleopatra therefore fled Alexandria, the royal residence, and sought refuge farther up the Nile River, near the historic heartland of Egyptian royal tradition, Thebes. Similarly, Queen Amidala flees her capital city of Theed, winding up in the Outer Rim world of Tatooine when the Trade Federation's guns damage her escaping starship. Her goal, however, was Coruscant, seat of the Galactic Senate, where she hoped to find support for her planet against the invaders.

When Cleopatra left Alexandria, the queen was only twenty-one and in a desperate situation. She moved on to rally an army in Syria, but an even more significant battle loomed across the Mediterranean in Greece. Pompey was at war with another Roman and his former ally Julius Caesar. After Caesar's victory at the Battle of Pharsalos, in August 48 BC, Pompey fled to Egypt. Instead of Pompey's finding refuge at Ptolemy XIII's court, the Egyptian courtiers killed him out of hand, while the young king watched. This move didn't endear Ptolemy XIII and his government to the victorious Caesar, as the Egyptian child-king had hoped. Instead, the Roman decreed that the brother and the sister should settle their differences before him. This invitation was all that Cleopatra needed to turn Caesar to her cause.

It doesn't matter whether Cleopatra had herself rolled up in a bed-sack (not a carpet!) and smuggled into Caesar's residence, as Plutarch described, or if she simply asked to speak to Caesar. Either way, the young queen presented her case with the charm and skill for which she would be renowned. What is important is that Cleopatra allied herself with the man who was rising to power, not only in Rome but wherever that state had influence. Caesar fought a war to defend Cleopatra's right to rule. When it was over, a year later, her siblings were dead or captured and Cleopatra gave birth to a son by Caesar, Caesarion, whom she would eventually adopt as her coruler.[4]

It's interesting that despite not having a son by his Roman marriage, Julius Caesar never acknowledged Caesarion, instead willing his fortune to his grand-nephew Octavian. Many Romans doubted Cleopatra's claim that Caesar was the boy's father, and rumors about the boy's parentage dogged the queen, rather as the secret of Padmé and Anakin's marriage helps shroud Luke and Leia's parentage in mystery. In both cases, pregnancy did not prevent these women from wielding political power. Padmé Amidala, even though she is pregnant and no longer the Queen of Naboo, still works as a Senator with Bail Organa and others to resist Palpatine's destruction of the Republic. Cleopatra's pregnancy was celebrated in Egypt, if not in Rome, and helped her retain her throne, even while Caesar brought her valuable state more securely under Roman control.

In 44 BC, Caesar was brutally assassinated by a number of high-ranking conspirators. Cleopatra commanded her own fleet to assist in avenging Caesar's death the following year. After the conspirators were routed, Cleopatra made a successful play for the most powerful of the trio of Roman rulers: Mark Antony. The two soon became lovers and enjoyed a scandalously lavish lifestyle together in Alexandria. Antony was Rome's greatest military leader, and Cleopatra's Egypt grew in wealth and influence under his protection. The ancient historian Plutarch confidently asserted that Cleopatra cold-bloodedly seduced and corrupted the Roman general, but he was just one of many to try to discredit the Egyptian queen as Rome's enemy. The reality of their relationship was likely more complicated: Cleopatra welcomed Antony's protection and the generous provisions he made for their children, who were given sizable kingdoms of Roman territory in the eastern Mediterranean; Antony probably preferred Alexandria's freedom of action over Rome's more restraining political system.

Antony's standing in Rome declined, however, due to rumors of his slavish devotion to a foreign queen, and he was soon defeated by his former coruler, Octavian, Caesar's grand-nephew and a cunning politi-cian who likely managed the propaganda campaign that discredited

Antony.[5] Just as Chancellor Palpatine orchestrates the downfall of the Republic, Octavian brought down the Roman Republic from within: Antony and Cleopatra were two of the casualties, although both chose suicide, rather than the humiliation of being paraded as captives before a Roman crowd. Their children were carried off by the triumphant Octavian to be paraded in Rome in their parents' place, including the twins, Alexander Helios and Cleopatra Selene.[6]

For all that Cleopatra is considered a figure of romantic tragedy, this queen was very careful in her love life. Cleopatra's relationships with Julius Caesar and Mark Antony appear more calculated than Padmé's desperate love for Anakin, and, unlike Padmé, Cleopatra never married her lovers. She was married, in name only, to her corulers: first her brother, and then her son. Both Caesar and Mark Antony were married to women from powerful Roman families, while they were involved with the Egyptian queen. This may have been to Cleopatra's advantage. She ruled for twenty-two years without having to hand over control to any man in her life. This degree of freedom was almost unimaginable for women in the classical world; few other queens ruled in the ancient Mediterranean world, and none of them enjoyed Cleopatra's independence, wealth, and power.[7] All of that came to nothing with Cleopatra's death. Egypt's riches were absorbed into Octavian's new empire, just as Naboo is folded into Palpatine's Imperial Empire.

> Just as Chancellor Palpatine orchestrates the downfall of the Republic, Octavian brought down the Roman Republic from within.

"The Queen Will Not Approve"

In disguise as a handmaid and on the run with Jedi Qui-Gon Jinn and Obi-Wan Kenobi, Padmé can hardly issue a royal decree when the Senate does not help her in her plight. At least, no one thinks it inappropriate that the queen will have opinions or wield some sort of power. The Calvinist preacher John Knox complained about European women rulers in a sixteenth-century book. Faced with three Catholic women in power, he argued that women's rule was unnatural: a "monstrous regiment of women."[8] His language may have been extreme, but his attitudes were hardly unusual. Historically, many kingdoms barred women entirely from ruling, while others practiced primogeniture, giving lands, power, and the royal title only to the oldest male child of the previous king—even if that heir had one or many older sisters.

Refreshingly, the *Star Wars* galaxy exhibits no prejudice against women rulers or leaders, whether during the Republic, when women serve as leaders in all levels of government, or in the fraught years of the Clone Wars. Although being young and female might have been two strikes against a candidate for the throne in ancient and medieval history, on Naboo, those qualities are positively celebrated. There, public service is mandated for youngsters. Citizens as young as eight years of age even contribute to the planet's government, apprenticing in the legislature. One such civic-minded and serious citizen is Padmé Naberrie, who can boast of six years' political experience when she is elected queen at fourteen years of age. Young Padmé takes a new name, Amidala, when she accepts the crown, but that doesn't mean she distances herself from her family. Indeed, Padmé keeps a close relationship with her parents and her older sister throughout her career as first Queen of Naboo and then, when her term as monarch is over, as that planet's Senator.[9]

If acceptable on Naboo, elective monarchy was exceedingly rare in Earth's history, especially for women. The Holy Roman Empire of medieval Europe might be the most famous example, and, even then, it was far from a free choice. Candidates needed to be leading landholders, as well as male. The tradition of primogeniture sidelined many women

> Refreshingly, the *Star Wars* galaxy exhibits no prejudice against women rulers or leaders, whether during the Republic, when women served as leaders in all levels of government, or the fraught years of the Clone Wars.

over the centuries, although, in some rare cases, a woman made for a useful compromise candidate. This was the case for Catherine of Brandenburg, who was elected Prince of Transylvania in 1629 on the death of her husband, who had previously held the title. Her power as prince, however, was severely limited, and charges that she was both extravagant and immoral helped push her out of office. These attacks were as politically motivated as those that Palpatine engineers to bring down Chancellor Valorum. The following year, Catherine was forced to abdicate in favor of the Hungarian nobleman Georg Rakoczi, a favorite of many of the Transylvanian courtiers.[10]

This avoidance of women rulers sometimes destabilized dynasties, as daughters (or *their* sons) might seek the throne despite the rule, which could lead to war with their male cousins (who often stood to inherit if the king's daughters were barred from the throne). This sort of conflict between cousins ignited the Hundred Years' War between England and France, for example.[11]

Women also couldn't succeed to rule in the Holy Roman Empire, which included much of central and Eastern Europe during the Middle Ages and beyond. The empire was an elective monarchy where bishops, dukes, and other nobles, known as prince-electors, chose the heir to the imperial throne. After the fifteenth century, the imperial title was almost exclusively a privilege of the Hapsburg family. When Charles VI died in 1740, there was a crisis. The only Hapsburg heirs were women: Charles's daughter Maria Theresa and her older cousins, daughters of the previous emperor. Yet women couldn't be elected to become emperor, and this situation led to a political crisis.

That wouldn't stop Maria Theresa from eventually taking power, although she had to work hard to earn her place. Her father spent his fortune bribing other kings and the electors to agree that Maria Theresa and her husband should inherit his position. These agreements, known as the Pragmatic Sanction of 1713, achieved little for Maria Theresa and Francis because most of the other kings and princes ignored their promises. In some respects, this resembles the promises of Chancellor

Palpatine to use his Emergency Powers only temporarily to fight the Clone Wars.

Unlike Padmé, who is both well-educated and experienced in politics, Maria was untrained to lead the state she ruled. Even more worrisome, she was almost without resources. As she later noted, her father had exhausted the empire's wealth in his attempt to secure her position as his successor: the new queen was "without money, without credit, without army."[12] Her Austrians had something in common with those who defended Naboo in the *Star Wars* galaxy against the endless wave of Trade Federation droids: those soldiers she could afford to pay had to make do with old and outdated materials, while facing a much more sophisticated opponent, the king of Prussia, who had relatively unlimited resources.

Maria Theresa rallied the Austrian people for her rule and against the Prussians in 1740.

Princess Leia presides over the celebrations and the awards ceremony after the Battle of Yavin. (*A New Hope*)

In some ways, Maria Theresa's first months on the throne were as perilous as those of newly crowned Padmé Amidala facing down the Trade Federation or Princess Leia smuggling battle plans for the Death Star out from under the Emperor's nose. Austria may have been a great state, but it was no match for the Prussians in 1740, just as Naboo is no match for the might of the Trade Federation at first. Prussia declared war on Maria Theresa's Austrians and won Silesia in the War of the Austrian Succession. In this conflict, the young queen was forced to defend herself against an opponent almost as crafty and cunning as Palpatine: Frederick the Great.

Maria Theresa had to work hard to fight off further conquests eating up her weakened realm. Although she was immediately crowned archduchess of Austria on her father's death and confirmed as queen of Hungary the following year, she never became Holy Roman empress in her own right. After Maria Theresa spent years building up the position of her husband, Francis, the electors finally chose him as the emperor in 1745. He held the title, but Maria Theresa exercised the real power as empress during his lifetime and later, when she shared power with her son, Joseph.[13]

Make no mistake: although she never held the imperial title on her own, Maria Theresa was the true power in the empire. She fought fiercely to gain and maintain her empire against some of the greatest powers of her age, including fearsome Frederick the Great of Prussia, whom she utterly despised. The Austrian empress also reformed the tax system to collect revenues from nobles and churchmen, as well as peasants, and significantly revised the law code that finally brought the witch-hunts to an end within the empire.[14] Despite all of these achievements, the Holy Roman Empire's traditions meant that Maria Theresa issued these decrees only in concert with a man, first her husband and then her son.

In England, women could inherit the throne, but that still didn't make it easy for them to rule. A civil war broke out in the twelfth century between supporters of King Henry I's only surviving heir, Matilda, and her cousin Stephen, in part because many English noblemen doubted a woman's fitness to rule. The nineteen years of conflict between the two sides that followed were so bad that people called it the Anarchy, a time "when Christ and his saints slept." Henry VIII felt the same way about female rulers, which is part of the reason he tried so desperately for a son, setting aside his first wife, Catherine of

Aragon, and executing his second, Anne Boleyn. The principle of primogeniture meant that Edward, a younger son by Henry's third wife, became the next ruler of England.

Only Edward's untimely death at sixteen years of age made his sisters' succession to the English throne possible. Mary, Henry's older daughter, followed after Edward, but her troubled reign lasted only five years. After Mary's death, her half-sister Elizabeth ruled for almost a century as an unmarried woman. Remaining single may have solved the concerns about sharing power with her husband (as Maria Theresa had to do), but it raised another problem that elective monarchs such as Padmé never face: the question of who would follow the queen on the throne. Until her death, Elizabeth avoided naming a successor from among her many distant relatives and instead played all of the possibilities, as any good politician would.

"She's a Politician, and They're Not to Be Trusted"

Obi-Wan wants Anakin, as a Jedi, to be wary of Senator Padmé Amidala: not because of romance, but because of her political interests. Politics might have been thought a man's game before the last century, but almost every queen in history had to play the game simply to survive. Many queens had to be ruthless and cunning in identifying and resisting their rivals. Padmé might be a strong supporter of the Jedi while she is Queen and during the period when she serves as Naboo's Senator, but that doesn't mean she is above the subtle work of politics. She out-maneuvers the Trade Federation through a combination of political appeals and military resistance. The same can be said of many historical queens who needed all of their wits to survive and thrive in the cutthroat world of court politics.

Consider the Russian Empire, where a series of women ruled for most of the eighteenth century. Anna was a Romanov tsarina who ruled the vast country from 1730 to 1740, but there were many who felt she was too much under the direction of her advisers. Her cousin Elizabeth seized the throne in 1742 and ruled for a further twenty years. Like England's Elizabeth, she never married and so could provide no legitimate heir to the throne. Tsarina Elizabeth worked hard to

Catherine the Great seized power from her husband in 1762 and ruled Russia until her death in 1796.

secure the royal succession. She adopted her nephew Peter as her heir, raised him, and arranged his marriage to a German princess, Sophia of Anhalt-Zerbst. The young bride was rebaptized in the Orthodox Church as Catherine: later she was known as Catherine the Great.

Catherine's transformation from young German princess to autocratic Russian ruler is a tribute to her political skills. Although her husband was heir to the throne, when his aunt died in 1762, the state was divided. Peter was impulsive and impractical, wildly unpopular at his own court. Catherine gathered support from the Russian army with the help of her lover, Grigory Orlov, and his brother, both officers, who drove Peter out of office. At thirty-three years of age, Catherine was proclaimed empress and ruled Russia until her death in 1796.

Rather than ruling in her son Paul's name, Catherine governed Russia without any male figurehead. She seemed quite comfortable with wielding power in her own right. Well-read, Catherine reformed laws and the educational system, while also leading Russia in successful wars against Poland and the Ottoman Empire. As empress, she promoted religious toleration, going so far as to endow two mosques for the Muslim minorities in her state. Catherine wrote that "one should do good and avoid doing evil as much as one reasonably can, out of love of humanity."[15]

Catherine loved humanity and not only in the abstract. Twelve men were openly recognized as her lovers during her sixty-seven years of life. She had at least two illegitimate children from her relationship with Count Orlov. In her memoir, Catherine indicated that an earlier lover was the father of her official son and heir, Paul. To be so open about her sexuality made Catherine a figure of scandal. Rumors about her sexual habits circulated after her death, suggesting all sorts of depravity.[16]

Here is another way in which the *Star Wars* galaxy's culture differs dramatically from those in Earth's history. Padmé's relationship with Anakin is forbidden only because he, as a Jedi Knight, is expected to avoid personal attachment. For a Jedi to profess romantic love or to

the Romans were dissatisfied with receiving half of the king's goods on his death. They took their anger out on the Iceni, beating the queen and raping her daughters. Demanding vengeance, Boudicca rallied a force of almost a quarter of a million Britons, women and men, against their Roman overlords. Her army sacked London and other great Roman settlements before the Britons were defeated and the queen ended her own life.[18]

About a thousand years later, a resolute Italian noblewoman roused her subjects to war against the might of Emperor Henry IV. Countess Matilda of Tuscany defended the church's independence against the empire during the Investiture Controversy of the eleventh century. She left her husband and cut off his access to her land and power, in order to provide support to the church leader. Her support was so successful that she was ultimately able to broker a reconciliation between the emperor and the pope at her stronghold of Canossa. Sadly, that peace lasted for only a short time, but Matilda continued to defend the church against the imperial army. As one of her chroniclers wrote, "Truly she acted nobly and magnificently, in a manner to which women are not accustomed; more I say, than manfully, she feared almost no danger. For whoever led her powerful army as she did?"[19]

Although Matilda may have provided the troops to defend the church, she never took up arms herself. Her military contributions were more akin to those of Mon Mothma, a politically skillful leader organizing the Rebellion against a powerful and entrenched force. The same could be said of Queen Melisende of Jerusalem. This twelfth-century queen battled indirectly against her husband and coruler, Fulk. The king attempted to rule without her and smeared her reputation by suggesting she had an affair with her cousin, the noble leader Hugh of Le Puiset. Melisende reportedly made life in the palace so dangerous for Fulk that he was forced to retract the charges and concede her right to rule in 1134.[20]

Royal women often rallied their supporters when danger threatened, as did Elizabeth I during the Armada crisis of 1588. She addressed the troops at Tilbury wearing a warrior's breastplate and vowed that she had the "heart and stomach of a king" to lead them against the enemy.[21] Sometimes such service was less public and more practical, as when the future Elizabeth II served as 2nd Lieutenant Elizabeth Windsor, a driver in the Auxiliary Territorial Service during World War II.[22] Princess Leia's hands-on role in the evacuation of

Queen Elizabeth's greatest achievement was defending England against a planned Spanish invasion in 1588.

Hoth or the assault on the Imperial bunker on Endor would have been entirely in character for any of these royal women, who were used to taking charge in times of war or crisis.

"Are You an Angel?"

A queen had an image to maintain, though perhaps not as high a standard of beauty as the angels of Iego, whom Anakin mentions to Padmé. Yet the image of a queen is bound up with the ceremony and the regalia of rule. Queen Amidala, burdened with heavy robes of state and pale under formal court makeup, appears a very different person from Padmé Naberrie, the royal attendant who escapes Naboo with Qui-Gon and Obi-Wan. In truth, the two women are the same person. Stories abound of kings and princes escaping notice and palace life, dressed as ordinary subjects. Sometimes these disguises failed utterly, as in the case of King Louis XVI of France, fleeing the French Revolution. His profile's clear resemblance to that stamped on his coins gave the fugitive king away.[23] How much easier would it have been for a queen whose rare public appearances were so marked by ceremony and heavy, formal styles to adopt a different identity away from hers at court?

In the fifteenth century, European queens and noblewomen wore torturous court fashions: headdresses of wire mesh molded into unnatural shapes and stiffened gowns lined with fur made them seem almost inhuman. Under that formal finery, a very different person could be found. Just as Padmé makes her escape from the Trade Federation's confinement in the guise of an ordinary handmaiden, Jacqueline or Jacoba, Duchess of Bavaria and Countess of Holland, literally threw off formal fashion to win her freedom during the Netherlands' Hook and Cod War. Jacqueline was only a teenager in 1418 when her uncle forced her to marry a spoiled and boorish younger cousin, John of Brabant.

Padmé Amidala escapes the Trade Federation's blockade only after abandoning her formal court dress and makeup.

Countess Jacqueline of Hainault disguised herself as a man and escaped imprisonment in 1426 with the help of two brave knights.

Jacqueline fled to England, where she repudiated the marriage. At only a little more than twenty years of age, the young duchess married King Henry V's younger brother, Humphrey, Duke of Gloucester, who briefly championed Jacqueline's cause. Tiring of the campaign against John of Brabant and his ally, Philip, Duke of Burgundy, Humphrey abandoned Jacqueline and renounced their marriage.

Just as Padmé makes her escape from the Trade Federation's confinement in the guise of an ordinary handmaiden, Jacqueline or Jacoba, Duchess of Bavaria and Countess of Holland, literally threw off formal fashion to win her freedom during the Netherlands' Hook and Cod War.

Jacqueline refused to despair, even when Philip captured her and put her under house arrest in the castle of Ghent. Rather like Padmé fleeing Naboo in disguise, Jacqueline made her second escape in 1426 with the help of two loyal knights, as daring as Qui-Gon and Obi-Wan. The nobles smuggled men's clothing in for their duchess to wear, in order to slip past her unsuspecting guards. Unfortunately for Jacqueline, her good fortune ended two years later, and she was forced to sign an agreement granting the Duke of Burgundy all power over her territories.[24]

For all that most of these historical cultures agreed that women didn't truly belong in the public world of politics, royal women were expected to be part of the public ceremonies of monarchy. In the sixteenth century, Hapsburg empresses and princesses in Spain and the Holy Roman Empire lived lives defined by public ceremonies. They accompanied their fathers, husbands, and brothers in grand processions and sometimes carried out these public events on their own. Most common and significant were weddings, but queens were also celebrated with grand entry pageants and parades when they visited subject cities or on occasions when their great service to the church resulted in an award of the Golden Rose from a grateful pope.[25]

Ceremony and grandeur may have been useful for political power plays, but ceremonies also helped people cope with loss. Royal women were often given elaborate funerals that were as much a comfort to their subjects as to their immediate family. Consider the death of the seventeenth-century Thai princess Krom Luang Yothathep, who was seized by one of her father's rivals and taken as a wife, in hopes of providing legitimacy to his rule. After her husband's death, Yothathep retired to a monastery, where she stayed until her death in the eighteenth century.

Even though she no longer held power, Yothathep was widely mourned. Her passing was marked by "a dramatic display of what a study of Renaissance England calls the 'theater of death.' Borne in a gold palanquin, the urn containing her ashes was carried up a gold tower built in the shape of the sacred Mount Meru. As many as ten thousand monks officiated in the rituals, which lasted for three days."[26]

When former queen Liliuokalani died in 1917, Hawaiians mourned her death with a grand funeral.

Many other royal women's deaths were marked with great public mourning. Liliuokalani was the last queen of Hawaii, who fought helplessly against powerful settlers in the late nineteenth century. Deposed in 1893, she was tried for treason by the new government in 1895 and spent much of the rest of her life under watchful guard, for fear other Hawaiians would rise up in her cause.[27] When she died in 1917, a state funeral featuring endless processions and stately Hawaiian decorations made a grand, if belated, tribute to the former queen. Padmé Amidala's magnificent state funeral on her home world of Naboo also involves thousands of mourners who knew her as queen, Senator, and fellow-citizen, including her successor, Queen Apailana. Although Padmé is no longer there to inspire her people, her image continues to exert a powerful influence on those in the galaxy who believe in the ideals of the Republic, just as Liliuokalani's memory was celebrated, particularly through the popular song that she composed: "Aloha 'Oe" (Farewell to Thee).

When Padmé Amidala dies of a broken heart, her former subjects on Naboo mark her passing with a solemn ceremony. (*Revenge of the Sith*)

"Look, I Ain't in This for Your Revolution, and I'm Not in It for You, Princess."

Although history is filled with stories of men as rulers and leaders, occasionally women filled these roles. Many women fought for power as fiercely as any men: Cleopatra used her troops and treasury, as much as her feminine allure and her wits, to seize and hold power in the ancient world. While law and custom severely limited women's right to rule in many countries, even when an heiress such as Marie Theresa couldn't hold the imperial power in her own name, she still ruled effectively. Catherine the Great's life demonstrates that even when a woman wasn't born into a ruling family, if she was ambitious and driven, she could rise to great heights and rule a great nation. Others, such as Boudicca, driven by the desire for vengeance, rallied their people into war against great empires and their armies.

The royal women of the *Star Wars* universe aren't in it for the power, let alone the money that Han Solo suggests is his motivation in *A New Hope*. He correctly identifies Leia's interests as revolutionary. Padmé Amidala and her daughter are both driven by dreams of improving their people's lives and saving the galaxy from tyranny. Queens in our history may not have faced the challenge of a Sith Lord, but they battled formidable opponents in war and diplomacy, often against overwhelming odds, much in the same way that their counterparts did, long ago in that far-away galaxy.

"You have restored peace and justice to the galaxy."
—Emperor Palpatine to Darth Vader, *Revenge of the Sith*

7

"There's Always a Bigger Fish"
Power, Politics, and the Rule of the Ruthless

Kevin S. Decker

Just when science fiction movies were "deader than dead," *Star Wars* succeeded in reinvigorating space opera by using cultural themes from the past, but within a fantastic setting.[1] When it comes to politics, history, and *Star Wars*, a number of puzzles present themselves: Why did the venerable Republic crumble? What roles did behind-the-scenes manipulations, war, corruption, and a lack of public feeling play in its demise? Does political success require wise and virtuous leaders?

Our own history's tyrannical regimes have been elevated not only through consolidation of power, but also by playing on the fears of the public and the desire of elites for glory and honor. Yet tyrants and dictators are elevated to authority because of special virtues the populace believes they possess. Imbalanced political authorities such as these often emerge from two political forms that contrast strongly with absolute rule, democracy, and republicanism. Although absolute power is by no means a Western invention, all four of these types of governance—tyranny, dictatorship, democracy, and republicanism—are legacies of the Greek and Roman heritage of Western civilization.

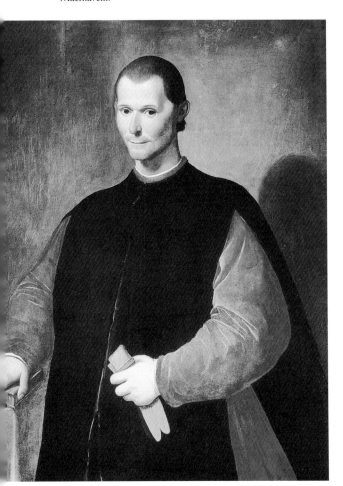

Palpatine's inspiration? A portrait of Niccolò Machiavelli.

Similarly, Palpatine's christening of a new Galactic Empire set up a political system that was not entirely unique in the history of the *Star Wars* universe. Power in Lucas's cosmos typically fluctuates between participatory republics and iron-fisted empires, where shifts in influence are often determined by court intrigues or military superiority. These large power shifts were also characteristic of Renaissance and Reformation Europe. A new way of thinking about politics emerged from the factionalism and incessant warring of the small northern Italian republics in the Renaissance and from the ideas of a man who puts a name to this pain, Niccolò Machiavelli of Florence (1469–1527). Is Palpatine genuinely "Machiavellian"? Is it possible for a supreme political authority to escape the power of the dark side? The answers are complex and require our careful attention.

Longer Ago, Farther Away

The meaning of "republic," one form of governance, originates from the Latin phrase *res publica*, or "public thing." So, whatever is public—the resources of a state, its judicial and legislative institutions, its system of education, among others—is not only the property or jurisdiction of a single monarch. The "public" can also be contrasted with the *private* good of citizens. A republican form of government is supposed to balance public and private goods, erring on the side of protecting the masses for the happiness of all—overseeing security, education, and labor practices, for example. When a republic falls, it is as much due to the inability of its supposed defenders to distinguish between the public and the private good as it is to the desires of a tyrant to wield singular power.

History's actual republican governments have been built on the idea that liberty can't be secured without each citizen taking a vital part in government. The active political life, as a civic or moral duty for every citizen, is taken very seriously. Self-government requires not only time and commitment, but also the civic virtue of its citizens.[2] One interpretation of Socrates's downfall in ancient Athens is that he lacked civic virtue. By contrast, the Renaissance political genius Leonardo Bruni believed that "the citizen is he who can develop as many forms of human excellence as possible and develop them all in the service of the city." *Versatility* and *patriotism* were, for Bruni, virtue's chief constituents.[3] The ideal of the virtuous citizen is wound throughout the strands of political thought in Western history.[4]

Tyranny and dictatorship, on the other hand, have always been seen as aberrations from "normal" government. In its oldest Greek use, *tyrannos* simply indicates the sovereign power of a wealthy monarch. Aristotle (384–322 BC) was a stolid critic of tyranny. Prizing as he did common good of the political community, he called tyranny the "arbitrary power of an individual which is responsible to no one," associating

Aristotle once said, "Man is a political animal."

it with the abuse of legitimate power.[5] Ancient political practices allowed concentration of ultimate power in the hands of one citizen, but only temporarily, perhaps in the case of a military emergency.

The Roman position of *dictator*, voted to Julius Caesar by the Senate five times within four years, was also a legitimate political tool, "limited in its exercise during emergency circumstances by allotted time, specified task, and the fact that the dictator had to restore the previously standing political-legal order that had authorized the dictatorship."[6] Yet what might be called "sovereign" dictatorship seeks to perpetuate itself and construct an entirely new political order. It results from abuse of the powers of legitimate dictatorship, and it's precisely the slide from the first type to the next that we see occur in the events of *Attack of the Clones* and *Revenge of the Sith*. In the former, Palpatine seems to grudgingly accept radical "emergency powers" to combat Count Dooku's Separatist movement. To do so, he embraces the Military Creation Act, calling into action the Grand Army of the Republic. About three years after the battle on Geonosis that begins the Clone Wars, the situation has intensified enough for Force-lightning-scarred Palpatine (now ugly enough that even other Sith Lords might avoid him!) to declare himself supreme leader with precious little opposition.

Tyrants: Light or Dark?

It seems that Sith who openly practice the rites of the dark side make bad tyrants. Here's why. The "first historian," Herodotus, spoke of one of the earliest tyrants, Kypselus of Corinth (who ruled from 655 to

625 BC).[7] His rise to tyranny set the precedent for gaining power by appealing to the politically marginalized, the same folk who ended up suffering banishment and seizure of their property by Kypselus. Aristotle warned, "History shows that almost all tyrants have been demagogues who gained the favor of the people by their accusation of the notables."[8]

Later Athenian tyrants had to reckon with the legacy of Solon (ca. 630–ca. 560 BC), who assumed the responsibilities of "virtual dictator" in order to respond to widespread crises in Athens and the surrounding regions. Called "the savior of his country and the ideal lawgiver" by Aristotle, Solon freed poor farmers and landless men who had been turned into debt-slaves, as well as turning food production and trade to favor local need, rather than profit.[9] Most important, Solon was responsible for breaking down ancient tribal affiliations, a crucial element in the movement toward democracy.

The role of Solon is comparable to the Republic's Chancellor Tarsus Valorum, who around 1000 BBY completely renovated the shattered confederation's government, dismantling its standing army, giving greater control to planetary systems and sectors over even his own authority, and even bringing the Jedi into the judicial wing of the government. Yet Valorum's "Ruusan Reformations" saved the Republic at the cost of paving the way for the slow creep of corruption and bureaucracy that was to lead to the Republic's end.

Solon brought law to a polis long ago and far away.

Rivalry in the Galactic Senate would presage this end, just as aristocratic rivalries led to a breakdown of Solon's Athenian constitution. The most dramatic story of one-man rule in Athens centers on Pisistratus, who first seized control in 561 BC. He took power by cunningly exiling some aristocrats and taking the sons of others hostage. Pisistratus may also be history's first master of propaganda: he

the Jedi and the Republic.[13] As the leader of the Separatists, the count seems to gain his power not only through his apprenticeship to Sidious, but also through his charisma and powers of persuasion. In *Attack of the Clones*, Dooku uses these powers to forge an alliance of powerful and rapacious corporate powers, taking advantage of their indignation at the facts that "star systems are starving under heavy taxation[,] pirates plague the spacelanes, corporations consume worlds, bureaucracy stifles justice—and yet the Senate can do little."[14] Even insightful Jedi such as Mace Windu and Ki-Adi-Mundi are fooled into believing he is a "political idealist, not a murderer." In the long run, a force far darker than mere tyranny betrays Dooku.

"For a Safe and Secure Society . . ."

Some have claimed that "the idea of Rome and the idea of power are inextricably linked."[15] To back up this claim, historians point to the Roman creation of a military machine that was unparalleled in the ancient world.[16] While the Greeks were ready to elevate to the status of "political hero" leaders who would reorganize society in their own image, Romans were proud of the political institutions of both the Roman Republic and their military and wanted leadership to conform to their "established conventions and settled expectations."[17] Their experience offers us two different senses of what political *power* consists of.

The monopoly over power in Roman society was typically divided between two distinctive kinds of institutions. *Potestas* was the power of executives, such as consuls, magistrates, and military leaders. It represents the coercive power not only to wage wars but also to impose sanctions against lawbreakers. The other type of power was *auctoritas*, vested in Roman jurists and in the Senate. It was a subtle thing, "more than advice and less than command, an advice which one may not safely ignore."[18] These two types of power correspond to two types of coercion, or political violence. The coercion of *potestas* is used in the *foundation* of a legitimate order and, in Rome's case, the expansion of its empire; the "conservation" of that order is *auctoritas*.[19]

The Roman Senate clearly invites comparisons with the Senate of the Republic, which meets in its vast, lavender, bowl-shaped Senate chamber at the center of Coruscant. The ruling body of the galaxy is, in many ways, less powerful: it can only issue "constitutional conventions," which some systems treated as nonbinding. This Senate was also less exclusive in its membership than its Roman counterpart. Leaders of member worlds had the right to vote and introduce legislation, as Queen Amidala does in *The Phantom Menace* when she calls for a vote of no confidence in Chancellor Finis Valorum. The "Rights of Sentience," perhaps the most radical clause in the original Galactic Constitution, protect the society and customs of nonhumans from encroaching humanocentrism. This is an important contrast with

Queen Amidala calls for a vote of no confidence. (*The Phantom Menace*)

Chancellor Palpatine addressing the Galactic Senate. (*The Phantom Menace*)

the later Empire, which is unabashedly speciesist in excluding all but human species from service, whether stormtroopers or officers.[20]

Patriotism was a key virtue gaining popularity and swaying public opinion among the Romans. Stemming from the Latin root *patria*, or "fatherland," patriotism for the Romans channeled the original power of loyalty to close kin for political survival. Patriotism is hard to find in a galaxy far, far away, where "the galactic representatives have become distanced from their people and now the entire system is degenerating." Not only is there no common agreement on the good that the *res publica* represents, but Republican politics have devolved into a tool for personal or planetary gain. There is no better example of this than the Neimoidians, who ignore both law and ethics in an effort to turn politics to their own profit.

Yet patriotism still retains the ability to persuade in the Republic. With the perfect vision of hindsight, we can appreciate the irony of Supreme Chancellor Palpatine's words to the Senate in *Attack of the*

Clones: "It is with great reluctance that I have agreed to this calling. I love democracy. I love the Republic. The power you give me I will lay down when this crisis has abated. And as my first act with this new authority, I will create a Grand Army of the Republic to counter the increasing threats of the Separatists."

Yet why do the Republic's Senators applaud this turn of events, when so many of them were previously opposed to the Military Creation Act? Perhaps they agree with Anakin in his exchange with Padmé from the same film:

Anakin: I don't think the system works. We need a system where the politicians sit down and discuss the problem, agree to what's in the best interest of all the people, and then do it.

Padmé: That's exactly what we do. The problem is that people don't always agree.

Anakin: Then they should be made to.

Padmé: By whom? Who's going to make them?

Anakin: Someone . . .

Padmé: You?

Anakin: No, not me.

Padmé: But someone . . . ?

Anakin: (nods) Someone wise.

Padmé: I don't know. Sounds an awful lot like dictatorship to me.

Anakin: (*after a long pause*) Well, if it works . . . ?

In turn, perhaps the script is alluding to someone such as Julius Caesar, elected to Roman dictatorship after dictatorship and showered with honors far beyond any sense of proportion. Caesar had been voted forty days of thanksgiving after stunning military victories in Gaul, Egypt, Asia, and Africa. Traditionally, a consul such as Caesar would be elected dictator for only six months, but for him, the Senate had ratified a ten-year position; the next year, he would be voted *dictator perpetuo*. Caesar won these votes because he had packed the Senate with supporters and co-opted many potential opponents, but the reasons for his rise extended beyond his enormous political gifts:

> The conventional view is that a large empire from time to time necessitated huge military commands, which had the effect of putting strong, personally loyal armies into the hands of men such as Sulla and Caesar who could not resist the temptation to use them. Empire undoubtedly had two effects of huge political significance: it necessitated the recruitment of impoverished soldiers who had little reason to support the political status quo; and it created an enormous (by ancient standards) capital city—incomparably wealthy and grand, and also well endowed with slums—that by the 60s [BC] . . . was no longer willing to acquiesce in conservative aristocratic control. One-man rule was the logical outcome.[21]

In a familiar refrain, the Roman Republic's model allows a model citizen to be named a *temporary* dictator, acting out of virtue to restore equilibrium. Yet when Caesar gained the post of censor for life—with direct control over the naming of senators, he was literally flirting with godhood. The people "addressed him outright as Julian Jupiter and ordered a temple to be consecrated to him and to his Clemency," claimed Cassius Dio.[22]

While Caesar dreamed of divinity, Senator Marcus Tullius Cicero (106–43 BC) argued against this concentration of power. His reasoning would not be easily reconciled with our own democratic aversion to tyranny today, for Roman senators stood for the essentially aristocratic values of their own personal freedom from "the dominance of others" and their own liberty to "exercise authority and dignity, while retaining 'equality' among their own peer group."[23] It's the loss of this type of

Cicero's political oratory was unequalled.

freedom, and not the peril posed to the liberties of ordinary Romans, that was Cicero's greatest worry in 49 BC as Caesar crossed the Rubicon. As the Empire replaces the Republic in *Revenge of the Sith*, Padmé Amidala's own woes would not have seemed out of place in Rome. "So this is how liberty dies, to thunderous applause," she grimly declares.

> "So this is how liberty dies, to thunderous applause."
> —*Padmé Amidala*

Cicero was also right to be concerned in his own case: despite Caesar's assassination on the Ides of March, 44 BC, his adoptive heir, Octavian, became the first proper emperor of Rome in 27 BC and began the 180-year Pax Romana.[24] The constitutional balance of power shifted from the Senate's *auctoritas* to the emperor's *potestas*, and the control of the former by the latter was absolute. In spite of this, Cicero's vision lived on at the heart of republicanism, an ideal that survived the waning of the Roman Republic.

The beginning of the end for the Republic. (*Revenge of the Sith*)

"The Dark Side Clouds Everything"

Although republican government was to remain submerged in European society for more than a thousand years, the Middle Ages were still intimately shaped by the legacy of the Roman Empire. A new layer was added to medieval kingship and the feudal economy by the application of Christianity and its distinctive morality. Rulers and the ruled became more concerned about the legitimacy of regimes than ever before, and Christian virtues overtook secular ones in defining the public good. St. Augustine believed that just civic arrangements followed two rules: "do no harm to anyone" and "help everyone whenever possible."[25] From St. Augustine's point of view, the overweening desire for secular political power could be traced back to the Fall, which starkly contrasted with the peacefulness of Augustine's "City of God."

In the medieval era, the devious ins and outs of court culture defined much of the constellation of politics orbiting kings, queens, and princes. The picture is of a coterie of "officials, clerics, and nobles who attended the king more or less regularly in both informal and formal capacities," pusillanimously seeking patronage or access to the head of state.[26] In response, the twelfth-century Englishman John of Salisbury spent hundreds of pages in his book *Policratius* decrying flattery. "Success, implacable foe of virtue, applauds its devotees only to harm them, and with its ill-starred prosperity escorts them on their joyous way to bring about their ultimate fall," he wrote.[27] John was echoing the views of Aristotle and Cicero. For him, courtier culture inevitably inspired avarice, pride, vanity, competitiveness, envy, and hatred, in both rulers and the ruled. In such a situation, the Sith Code would dictate that we should be a manipulative courtier, rather than the self-deceived monarch. Indeed, this is one possible interpretation of how Darth Sidious ingratiates himself with so many different forces—the Neimodians, Count Dooku, Anakin Skywalker. Each is powerful in his own right, but also flawed in a way that Sidious is clever enough to exploit. One wonders whether his own pasty-faced lackeys in *Return of the Jedi* were trying to turn the same trick on him.

Machiavelli, breaking away from this tradition in the Renaissance, would have us be neither of these. If anyone has followed the dictates of the man whom Shakespeare has Richard III admiringly refer to as "the murderous Machiavel," it must be Darth Sidious. Sidious is a true Sith pioneer, avoiding direct confrontations, yet working to destroy the Republic from within. Palpatine's bid for power is a wedge between a manufactured external threat—Dooku's Separatist Confederacy, backed by the Trade Federation's Droid Army—and internal corruption and loss of a common center in the galactic polity. His strategy shrewdly exploits the rational self-interest of the Senators and their constituents, promising protection from the Separatists, but not until the situation is at its most dire. By actively engineering a formidable threat to the Republic (as Sidious) and slowly but surely taking the reins of military and political control (as Supreme Chancellor), Palpatine embraces the ominous dictum that "the ends justify the means."

Machiavelli immortalized this dictum in his book *The Prince* (published in 1532). In its pages, he famously claimed that since "men love

Does it really make sense to make deals with Sith? (*The Phantom Menace*)

> Sidious is a true Sith pioneer, avoiding
> direct confrontations, yet working to
> destroy the Republic from within.

at their own will and fear at the will of the prince," it is "far safer to be feared than loved."[28] Machiavelli demonstrates here the acute understanding of human psychology and its application to effective ruling that has earned him his place in history as one of the inventors of modern political theory. His "political science" was, in many ways, ahead of its time.

Yet Machiavelli is also a man *of* his time, in his interest in using the models of classical Greece and Rome as guides: Renaissance humanism of Machiavelli's age used historical cultures and actors as sources of inspiration for the present. If it seems odd that *The Prince* is a book that emerges from humanism, consider that its genesis also lies in an Italy torn apart by the European powers, its former republics rent by the antagonism of factions, while the liberties of the people withered in the face of the growth of private wealth.[29] In 1494, Charles VIII of France forced Florence and Rome into submission and pillaged the countryside. His successor, Louis XII, mounted three more invasions, "generating endemic warfare throughout Italy."[30] Not to be outdone, the Holy Roman Emperor Charles V invaded as well, turning Italy into a bloody battleground for thirty years.

Machiavelli was an adviser to the powerful who died in poverty.

The Prince confronts this kind of political violence as a new fact of life. The charismatic and ruthless Cesare Borgia (1476?–1507), the bastard son of Pope Alexander VI and *gonfaloniere* of the papal states, was one of Machiavelli's inspirations. It was not merely Borgia's means, but his ends that attracted Machiavelli: Borgia put an end to the cruel and ineffective governance of the petty lords of the region of the Romagna, thus lifting a long-standing burden from the shoulders of its people.[31] Machiavelli admired Borgia—as he did the classical leader Hannibal—and concluded that both rulers' "inhuman cruelty" was the key to their glorious success. Machiavelli insisted that we must accept that "if a ruler is genuinely concerned to 'maintain his state,' he will have to shake off the demands of Christian virtue, wholeheartedly embracing the very different morality which his situation dictates."[32]

Cesare Borgia takes a break from poisoning old allies.

It's not surprising, then, that Machiavelli didn't dare to publish *The Prince* during his lifetime, and when it was printed after his death, *The Prince* was put on the Church's *Index Librorum Prohibitorum*, its list of officially prohibited books in 1559. The book, first printed in 1532, "found very few discerning readers who understood its value. At the same time, it found a host of enemies who saw it as an evil work, inspired directly by the devil, in which a malevolent author teaches a prince how to win and keep power through avarice, cruelty, and falseness, making cynical use of religion as a tool to keep the populace docile," wrote a recent biographer of Machiavelli.[33]

Yet as much as readers of *The Prince* focus on its callous demand to choose fear over love, it also has many illustrations of entirely moral principles, such as the one that rulers should temper their worst impulses in dealing with their subjects. This advice would have been quite acceptable to the ancient Romans whom Machiavelli admired so much. With it, he is recommending that princes consider putting aside the indiscriminate use of coercive *potestas* in favor of well-thought-out *auctoritas*, that is, the "soft" power that relies on understanding of, and respect from, one's subjects. As we'll see, Palpatine relies on the mastery of the first of these, but only the semblance of the second.

"A Pathway to Many Abilities Some Consider to Be *Unnatural*"

We have already seen the parallels between two histories: one of Greek tyranny and Roman dictatorship, the other of the rise and fall of the Galactic Republic. How much blame for the demise of a great civilization can we lay at the feet of its primary architect, Darth Sidious? Or—not quite the same question—how Machiavellian *was* Palpatine? Machiavelli might have admired Palpatine more for his highly organized, long game of seizing power than for what Palpatine does once he *has* power.

On the one hand, the Emperor recognizes that the successful Machiavellian ruler must commit his regime to constant war. Heeding Machiavelli's often-repeated advice, Palpatine puts no trust in mercenary armies, even hardwiring into the program of an entire clone army various orders.[34] Despite this, he has often had use for bounty hunters, particularly Cad Bane, whom he employs in a number of episodes of *The Clone Wars*. Machiavelli warns "the Prince" that because mercenaries have no fealty to those who employ them, their devotion to protecting property and persons should always be suspect. Despite her ruthless devotion to fulfilling her contracts, Aurra Sing's intense hatred of the Jedi threatens to distract her from her work for her employers. We see evidence of this when she teams up with the young Boba Fett to assassinate Mace Windu in *The Clone Wars'* "Death Trap."

> Machiavelli might have admired Palpatine more for his highly organized, long game of seizing power than for what Palpatine does once he *has* power.

Learning from the best: Aurra Sing and Boba Fett. (*The Clone Wars*)

Throughout history, these Machiavellian lessons have been taught well outside of Renaissance Italy. Similar to early China's brutal "First Emperor," Qin Shi Huangdi (246–210 BC), Emperor Palpatine enforces a strict "resistance is futile" policy through the construction of a totalitarian New Order in the galaxy.[35] Imperial industries produce deadly engines of battle, such as the colossal Star Destroyers and the nimble TIE fighters. This New Order encourages the growth of a new type of rapacious individual. One of these, the Grand Moff Tarkin, is put in charge of the Death Star, a crystallization of the Empire's technological terror. Like Palpatine, Tarkin is someone whom impetuous young Anakin Skywalker looks up to for his criticisms of the inefficiency of the Jedi during times of war. In *The Clone Wars'* "Counterattack," Tarkin mirrors Machiavelli's disdain for conventional morality and religion when he tells Anakin, "I find [the Jedi's] tactics ineffective. The Jedi Code prevents them from going far enough to achieve victory, to do whatever it takes to win, the very reason why peacekeepers should not be leading a war."

On the other hand, as a Sith Lord, Sidious violates Machiavelli's principle that cruelty must not be used indiscriminately. We see his cold-blooded nature onscreen, commanding Trade Federation troops on Naboo to "wipe them out. All of them." He proves there's no honor among Dark Lords when he sacrifices Darth Tyranus to his desire for a more powerful apprentice in *Revenge of the Sith*, compelling Anakin to execute his former apprentice. Off-screen, his crimes are even more remarkable: he murders his Master, Darth Plagueis—required by the Sith "Rule of Two," but nonetheless a reminder to an aspiring Sith Lord to put off taking an apprentice until the last possible moment!

Darth Sidious, despite his immense power, still doesn't want to reveal his hand until absolutely necessary. Yet for Machiavelli, part of the "virtue" of the successful prince was that he was publicly seen to be possessed of great mercy and great cruelty, of both magnificence and ruthlessness. In his role as a politician, Palpatine employs the publicly acceptable force of *auctoritas* to get things done, and here he is an ideal

Machiavellian, "using his grasp of psychology and bureaucracy to stifle justice" and bringing about successive crises for the Republic, each of which helps build his political and military powers.[36] Against the background of an increasingly corrupt Senate, Palpatine has both unethical, manipulative means and legitimate institutional channels to achieve his unscrupulous ends. He has learned the central Machiavellian lesson well:

> I will even be so bold as to say that it actually does a prince harm to have those good qualities and always observe them. But appearing to have them will benefit him. Of course, it is best to both seem and be merciful, loyal, humane, upright, and scrupulous. And yet one's spirit should be calculated in such a way that one can, if need be, turn one's back on these qualities and become the opposite. . . . He must have a spirit that can change depending on the winds and variation of Fortune, and as I have said above, he must not, if he is able, distance himself from what is good, but must also, when necessary, know how to prefer what is bad.[37]

Yet not until he becomes Emperor does Palpatine seem to be able to employ wholesale the central Machiavellian tool of direct application of fear, "held in place by a dread of punishment, which one can always rely on."[38] The asymmetry in the Sith "Rule of Two" between Master and Apprentice means that Vader is used as a "blunt instrument" of Palpatine's policy, often being kept in the dark himself about the Emperor's ultimate goals. Former allies such as the Trade Federation are simply absorbed into the Empire, dissidents are sent to the spice

Power play: Supreme Chancellor Palpatine tricks Anakin Skywalker into becoming his new apprentice. (*Revenge of the Sith*)

mines of Kessel, and the only programming available on the HoloNet is Imperial propaganda. Palpatine does away with the Senate in *A New Hope*, working most effectively with the governors of planetary systems who are willing to use the same terror tactics and ultimately using the Death Star to instill fear throughout the galaxy.

The asymmetry in the Sith "Rule of Two" between Master and Apprentice means that Vader is used as a "blunt instrument" of Palpatine's policy, often being kept in the dark himself about the Emperor's ultimate goals.

And Yet . . .

Overheard in the Mos Eisley Cantina: "Say what you will about Palpatine, at least he made the Corellian freighters run on time."[39] It's hard to believe that there are some who will actually *miss* his totalitarian rule after his death, but history has demonstrated this does happen in the cases of dictators such as Stalin and Mao Zedong. Therefore, it's important to keep in mind that the rule of the ruthless, in our galaxy or any other, can't be credited merely to the scheming of one man. Conditions of cultural decadence, political amoralism, and unrestrained, all-consuming commerce and industry paved the way for the Empire. As Padmé observes, liberty died not with a whimper, but to thunderous applause.

Although Machiavelli told us how to manipulate the public in *The Prince*, he conceded in his *Discourses* (1531) that absolute power should not be concentrated in the hands of one corruptible individual. Instead, "the willingness to do what is necessary to advance the common good, and thereby acquire glory for the city, is virtue (*virtù*), which for

Luke and Anakin, face to face. (*Return of the Jedi*)

Machiavelli explains why monarchies cannot compete with republics."[40] The *Discourses* imagined government along the lines of the Roman Republic, not the absolute dictatorship of the Empire. It returned to the examples of Aristotle, Cicero, and John of Salisbury in extolling the ideal of the virtuous citizen supporting a free republic. Machiavelli's ideal republic in the *Discourses* "maintain[s] a free constitution under which every citizen is able to enjoy an equal opportunity of involving himself actively in the business of government."[41] So although the onscreen work of the Rebellion against the Empire is shown mainly in the hands of X-wing pilots and forest-moon commandos, we should not forget the serious, if less flashy, roles of Bail Organa, Mon Mothma, and Leia Organa in preparing for a new and, it is hoped, more virtuous estate after the Empire's fall.

Similar to the *Star Wars* universe, Machiavelli's world of warring Renaissance Italian city-states—like the Roman Empire—was "a political universe inhabited at its very center by magic."[42] For Sidious, this magic is the Force; for the Romans, the emperor himself was divine; for Machiavelli, the power of *Fortuna* (fortune), often symbolized as an inconstant woman or an ever-turning wheel. The need to outguess and outmaneuver fortune is one of the important lessons in political history and the hardest to master. Its test is one that Emperor Palpatine ultimately fails, because of an unexpected, yet highly fortunate bond: that between a father and his son.

On May 25, 1983, *Return of the Jedi*, the highly anticipated final installment of the original *Star Wars* trilogy, premiered in the United States. Anticipation had been building for months, and, not coincidentally, 1983 was also the year of *Star Wars* imagery in U.S. politics. On March 8, President Ronald Reagan gave a speech to the National Association of Evangelicals, in which—obviously referring to the USSR—he talked of "the aggressive impulses of an evil empire."[2] Two weeks later, Reagan publicly proposed the Strategic Defense Initiative (SDI), which aimed at creating a space-based missile defense system. The very next day, Senator Kennedy mocked it as "Star Wars." The *Washington Post* quoted him, *Time* magazine did a cover story using the term, and SDI soon had a very popular nickname. It was perhaps inevitable that the pet project of a former movie actor president would spawn a film analogy.[3] These speeches show how much *Star Wars* had already become a part of American culture, but they also tell us how the American viewers of the time directly linked what they had seen in *Star Wars* to their country's experience of the Cold War.[4]

Senator Edward Kennedy, who first christened SDI "Star Wars."

President Ronald Reagan denouncing the "evil empire" of the Soviet Union.

In particular, we should note how Kennedy immediately connects *Star Wars* with the idea of military technology. Certainly, military technology (its limitations and its morality) is a major theme of the original *Star Wars* trilogy, with the Death Star—or, rather, the two Death Stars—serving as the most important example. Named that way because of its ability to obliterate an entire planet, this space station is the supreme weapon of mass destruction and one whose objective is to maintain the Galactic Empire's dominance of even the most far-flung outposts. In the original *Star Wars* film from 1977 (now known as *A New Hope*), it is described as "the ultimate power in the universe." Grand Moff Tarkin uses it to annihilate the planet Alderaan—very clearly establishing its terrifying capacity and its deadly threat, as well as the utter ruthlessness and evil of the Empire.

Grand Moff Tarkin and Darth Vader force Princess Leia to watch the destruction of Alderaan, her home planet. (*A New Hope*).

American servicemen watch a mushroom cloud blossoming in the distance as the United States tests thermonuclear weapons in the South Pacific during the 1950s.

Much of the plot of the first *Star Wars* revolves around the Rebel Alliance's attempts to destroy the Death Star. Indeed, by the end the Rebels have managed to find a weakness that enables Luke Skywalker to do just that—although he is finally able to succeed because he turns off his computer and uses the Force. A second Death Star appears in *Return of the Jedi*, only to meet the same fate in an even more dramatic fashion. This time, it is the primitive Ewoks, attacking with spears and logs, who help bring down the protective shield, making its destruction possible. The strength of "people power" and the ultimate inadequacy of purely military and technological power are thus graphically shown.

The greatest worry during the Cold War was that of nuclear annihilation. The Death Star provides an obvious manifestation of this fear.

For obvious reasons, the Death Star does not have the same central position in the prequel trilogy. Its plans, however, are shown in *Attack of the Clones*, while it actually appears in an early stage of construction at the end of *Revenge of the Sith*. The Death Star and the Galactic Empire are thus associated from the very start.

As Kennedy's and Reagan's speeches show, *Star Wars* is a product of its time (or times) and so reflects many of its hopes and anxieties.[5] Undoubtedly, the greatest worry during the Cold War was that of nuclear annihilation. The Death Star provides an obvious manifestation of this fear, but it is also one example of more general worries about the evolution of the arms race and the fragility of democracy.

This chapter examines the influence that the very real atomic bomb had on the creation of a fictional super-weapon, the Death Star, and the parallels between them. The development of such a weapon required an enormous expenditure of resources and expertise, as the historical Manhattan Project—the secret World War II research project that developed the first atomic bombs—demonstrates. The twentieth century saw the emergence of other super-weapons used to intimidate whole populations, such as the neutron bomb or biological and chemical weapons. In comparing these real weapons of mass destruction with the Death Star, we should consider the fear generated by such arms and how they can become a focus for espionage and paranoia. How do super-weapons change the balance of power in each case, and how does fear of the "ultimate weapon" affect populations threatened with them? Finally, we should examine the military-industrial complex that grew out of and further promoted the creation of new super-weapons. A close analysis of *Star Wars* films shows how much they have been affected by the very real events of George Lucas's lifetime, which find a reflection there. *Star Wars* is not an isolated fantasy world but one heavily influenced by the major issues of its time—and, indeed, influencing them.

> *Star Wars* is not an isolated fantasy world but one heavily influenced by the major issues of its time— and, indeed, influencing them.

A nuclear explosion, conducted as a test by the United States in Nevada, April 1953.

The Death Star explodes. (*A New Hope*)

"This Station Is Now the Ultimate Power in the Universe. I Suggest We Use It."

Sixteen hours ago an American airplane dropped one bomb. . . . That bomb had more power than 20,000 tons of T.N.T. It had more than two thousand times the blast power of the British 'Grand Slam' which is the largest bomb ever yet used in the history of warfare. . . . It is an atomic bomb. It is a harnessing of the basic power of the universe. The force from which the sun draws its power has been loosed against those who brought war to the Far East.

—Harry Truman[6]

Clearly, the Death Star is a military arm but one that has a predominantly political function. In a certain sense, weapons of mass destruction (WMD) exist, paradoxically, so as not to be used—or used only once, to provide an example. As we have already noted, Tarkin talks of the need "to make an effective demonstration" of the new weapon.[7]

Admiral Motti in a Death Star conference room. (*A New Hope*)

Of course, the search for the ultimate weapon has played a role in very real conflicts far from the universe of *Star Wars*. More than one commentator has noticed the resemblance between the Death Star and the atomic bomb.[8] A great deal of time and expense were put into the fabrication of the first atomic bomb by British, Canadian, American, and other scientists working on the Manhattan Project. Though the bomb was used only against Japan at the end of World War II, its destructiveness terrified the very men who had ordered its detonation. For President Harry Truman, the atomic bomb was an apocalyptic weapon—one that inspired fear and terror—and to be employed only as a last resort.[9] Yet he refused to officially rule out its use, as this excerpt from a press conference during the Korean War shows:

Question: Mr. President, I wonder if we could retrace that reference to the atom bomb? Did we understand you clearly that the use of the atomic bomb is under active consideration?

Truman: Always has been. It is one of our weapons.[10]

President Harry Truman saw the atomic bomb as an apocalyptic weapon but refused to rule out a future use.

This became, of course, official U.S. and NATO policy, which refused to rule out the possibility of striking first.[11]

President Dwight Eisenhower, who had been a military man and therefore knew a great deal more about the subject, had a somewhat different attitude.[12] In October 1953, Eisenhower signed National Security Council document NSC-162/2, which became the government's basic document on American security policy: it insisted that the nation must be able to inflict massive retaliation against any attack.[13] Deterrence—the theory that the threat of overwhelming military retaliation by one country would prevent another from attacking it—became the foundation of U.S. and NATO policy. During the next years, a new field of study developed—that of nuclear strategy. Interestingly enough, though, it was not the military but civilian academics who developed some of the most controversial theories associated with it. In particular, Herman Kahn of the Rand Corporation and later one of the founders of the Hudson Institute and Henry Kissinger of Harvard wrote books with provocative titles such as *On Thermonuclear War* (Kahn, 1960), *Thinking the Unthinkable* (Kahn, 1962, the same year as the Cuban Missile Crisis), and *Nuclear Weapons and Foreign Policy* (Kissinger, 1957).[14] Even more worrying, government officials talked in a similar way: John Foster Dulles, Eisenhower's secretary of state, spoke of "the further deterrent of massive retaliatory power" and developed the idea of "brinkmanship."[15] Robert McNamara, in 1967, while secretary of defense, went so far as to affirm,

> It is important to understand that assured destruction is the very essence of the whole deterrence concept. We must possess an actual assured-destruction capability, and that capability also must be credible. The point is that a potential aggressor must believe that our assured-destruction capability is in fact actual, and that our will to use it in retaliation to an attack is in fact unwavering. The conclusion, then, is clear: if the United States is to deter a nuclear attack in itself or its allies, it must possess an actual and a credible assured-destruction capability.[16]

This idea became known as mutual assured destruction or, more simply, MAD.

Although the U.S. government played down the threat from nuclear weapons in the early 1950s with programs such as the "duck and cover" campaign (which taught schoolchildren that they could protect themselves from nuclear attack by ducking down and getting under some kind of cover, such as a desk or even a tablecloth), by the end of the decade, anxieties about nuclear warfare were being freely expressed in popular culture. Novels such as Nevil Shute's *On the Beach* (1957) and Peter George's *Red Alert* (1958) were imagining atomic disaster. End-of-world fears reached their high point in the dark parody of *Dr. Strangelove or How I Stopped Worrying and Learned to Love the Bomb* (Stanley Kubrick, 1964, based on *Red Alert*), where we see mushroom clouds exploding across the Earth at the conclusion. Not coincidentally, perhaps, the greatest crisis of the Cold War occurred during this period. The Cuban Missile Crisis of October 1962, the greatest example of brinkmanship, brought the world right to the edge of mutual assured destruction.

The debate about super-weapons was now in the open, which meant that new developments were bound to cause heated debate. One of the most controversial of the later super-weapons was the neutron bomb, technically known as an enhanced radiation bomb: it is a thermonuclear device that emits large quantities of lethal radiation but only reduced levels of heat and blast. In theory, these bombs would kill human and animal life, while allowing some structures to survive.

The news that the United States had developed a neutron bomb set off a massive debate around the time the first *Star Wars* film opened, with its Death Star. On June 6, 1977, the *Washington Post* published an article titled "Neutron Killer Warhead Buried in ERDA Budget," which revealed that the Carter administration was planning to install neutron warheads. Its author wrote, "The United States is about to begin production of its first nuclear battlefield weapon specifically designed to kill people through the release of neutrons rather than to destroy military installations through heat and blast."[17] In other words, people would be killed while buildings would be left standing. The article strongly but not entirely accurately implied that this was a new and particularly frightful development, and these charges quickly spilled across the pages of the world's press. The Soviet propaganda machine soon weighed in with a massive campaign in Europe against this ultimate capitalist weapon.[18] The controversy that resulted led to

Carter's decision to cancel the deployment of neutron bombs, although President Reagan reversed this decision in 1981.[19]

Biological and chemical weapons have been a more immediate concern in recent years, especially after the still-mysterious anthrax attacks in the United States in 2001. Certainly, they have a long and tragic history, notably with the use of mustard gas in World War I. A number of nations have used them since then. Saddam Hussein employed them in the Iran-Iraq war of 1980–1988 (having first obtained them from Western countries), notably against the Kurds in the Halabja attack of 1988. This fact, combined with his often belligerent attitude to UN inspections, provided the justification for the 2003 invasion of Iraq. Leading figures in both the U.S. and British governments drew terrifying pictures. Tony Blair, for example, told Parliament,

> When the inspectors left in 1998, they left unaccounted for 10,000 litres of anthrax; a far-reaching VX nerve agent programme; up to 6,500 chemical munitions; at least 80 tonnes of mustard gas, and possibly more than 10 times that amount; unquantifiable amounts of sarin, botulinum toxin and a host of other biological poisons; and an entire Scud missile programme. We are asked now seriously to accept that in the last few years—contrary to all history, contrary to all intelligence—Saddam decided unilaterally to destroy those weapons. I say that such a claim is palpably absurd.[20]

Note how Blair plays up fears by his use of words such as *toxin* and *poisons* and how he lists anthrax first, in order to play on memories of the earlier attacks in the United States. Yet, of course, no WMD were found once Iraq had been conquered and thoroughly searched.

The so-called Star Wars SDI plan proposed by Ronald Reagan, and in a very modified form continued by later U.S. administrations, as a "defense" against attack can also be seen as a "super-weapon": if successful (which is far from certain), it would destroy the entire premise of mutual assured destruction, which had prevented war between the superpowers for decades. The nation that possessed it would not have to worry about being annihilated and could presumably launch nuclear attacks without fear of retaliation—which is precisely what the Russians have repeatedly objected to. Its nickname of "Star Wars" undoubtedly came about due to the highly complicated descriptions of SDI's lasers presented in the press, which in some ways do resemble the Death Star's laser. And so we see how the mirrored parallels between real history and the *Star Wars* universe came to be: the *Star Wars* films were so strongly influenced by an awareness of the threat posed by nuclear weapons that their name actually became associated with one of the new "super-weapons."

An artist's conception of the SDI, 1984.

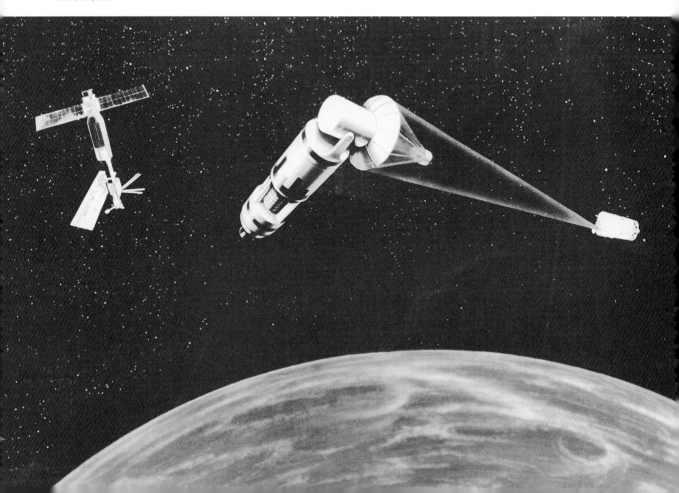

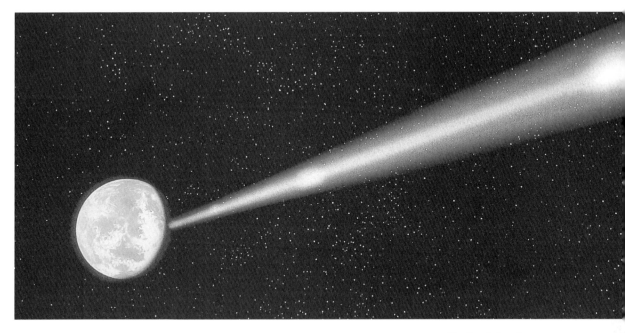

The Death Star fires on Alderaan. (*A New Hope*)

These highly controversial weapons and projects all received immense attention in the world's press. The original trilogy of *Star Wars* also offers a devastating criticism of WMDs. As we have already observed, the Rebel Alliance, the heroes of the first films, seek simply to destroy the Death Star, rather than build their own. The ways in which they destroy it—and other weapons such as the AT-AT Walkers of *The Empire Strikes Back*—are often very basic.[21] Of course, the Rebel Alliance is not a group of pacifists—they do use ordinary weapons to win their victory. Yet the Rebels clearly reject a never-ending arms race: the moral high ground belongs to those who refuse to use such weapons.

Star Wars . . . offers a devastating criticism of WMDs . . . the moral high ground belongs to those who refuse to use such weapons.

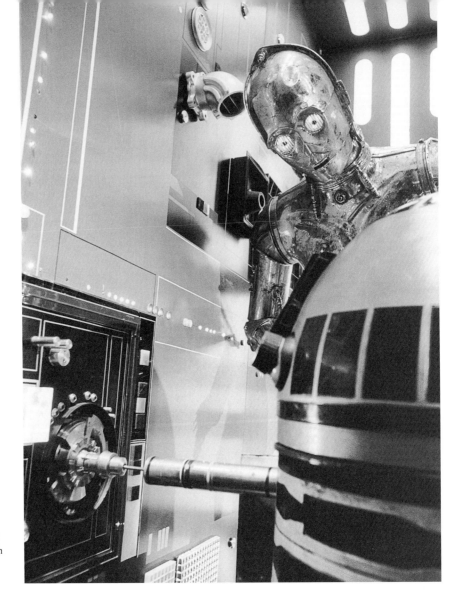

R2-D2 saves the day with his ability to interface with technology—yet again. (*A New Hope*)

Star Wars also demonstrates the advantages of technology. The droids C-3PO and R2-D2 appear in every single film and certainly figure among the heroes. In particular, R2-D2's expertise and abilities repeatedly save the human heroes.[22] In the first trilogy, the rebels use technology, as do the Jedi in the prequel films. The good guys are not antitechnological Luddites who want to return to nature (even if the presence or absence of natural scenery on a planet does reveal something about its inhabitants).[23] *Star Wars* history only warns us against destructive technology—and most particularly focuses on the super-weapon of the Death Star. Built with the sole purpose of keeping the Emperor's regime eternally in power by intimidating any dissent, it fails dramatically both times.

"Fear Will Keep the Local Systems in Line. Fear of This Battle Station."

> Of primary military concern will be the bomb's potentiality to break the will of nations and of peoples by the stimulation of man's primordial fears, those of the unknown, the invisible, the mysterious. We may deduce from a wide variety of established facts that the effective exploitation of the bomb's psychological implications will take precedence over the application of its destructive and lethal effects in deciding the issue of war.
>
> —1947 report by the U.S. Joint Chiefs of Staff Evaluation Board[24]

In the universe of *Star Wars*, the Tarkin Doctrine, expressed in a message from the future grand moff to Palpatine, states that the most effective way of maintaining order in the Empire is through fear and that this requires the creation of a super-weapon possessing massive destructive capability: the Death Star. In *Star Wars*, Tarkin explains its purpose: "Fear will keep the local systems in line. Fear of this battle station." He threatens Alderaan, Princess Leia's home planet, with annihilation unless she reveals the secret Rebel base. When she (falsely) identifies it as Dantooine, however, Tarkin proceeds with the attack on Alderaan anyway, explaining that "Dantooine is too remote to make an effective demonstration." His fundamental goal is clearly to provide an example that will so terrify the galactic population that the rebellion will end of itself. As he says afterward, "No star system will dare oppose the Emperor now."

Grand Moff Tarkin,
a champion of fear.
(*A New Hope*)

Fear has played a major role in many conflicts and, although it may seem paradoxical, has often been stronger before a war than during it. For example, fear undeniably influenced public opinion in Europe between the wars—in particular, because of the infant weapon of air power. Introduced at the end of World War I, many military experts believed that air power would be decisive in a future conflict. Certainly, fear of devastating aerial bombing played a major role in the peace and disarmament initiatives of the 1920s and the 1930s.[25] Later, the terror bombing of Guernica during the Spanish Civil War had a profound influence on public opinion (in that war, the German and Italian air forces experimented with massive aerial bombing, causing many civilian casualties).[26] One can get a good idea of the terror engendered by air power from a speech by then British prime minister Stanley Baldwin to the House of Commons in 1932:

> The speed of air attack, compared with the attack of an army, is as the speed of a motor car to that of a four-in-hand [a carriage pulled by horses] and in the next war you will find that any town which is within reach of an aerodrome [airfield] can be bombed within the first five minutes of war from the air, to an extent which was inconceivable in the last war, and the question will be, whose morale will be shattered quickest by that preliminary bombing? I think it is well also for the man in the street to realize that there is no power on earth that can protect him from being bombed. Whatever people may tell him, the bomber will always get through.[27]

The French were possibly even more afraid than the British, and a number of historians have cited this as a reason for France's defeat by the Germans in 1940.[28]

A London aircraft spotter watches for German bombers during the Battle of Britain in 1940. St. Paul's Cathedral can be seen in the background.

Obviously, fear was also a major weapon used by the Nazis, whether in Hitler's speeches, in violent attacks such as *Kristallnacht* or the "Night of the Long Knives" or by the deliberate targeting of the civilian population in bombing campaigns such as the Blitz of British cities. The Soviet Union also relied on fear to maintain order, both within the USSR and in Eastern Europe. The list of examples is endless, and, certainly, Western countries, including the United States, have not been immune from using this tactic. As the opening quote to this section shows, the Joint Chiefs of Staff were very much aware of the terror potential in the atomic bomb.

"Fear is the path to the dark side. Fear leads to anger, anger leads to hate; hate leads to suffering."
—*Yoda*

Interestingly enough, it was the United States that experienced a massive panic after the Soviet Union exploded its own bomb in 1949. No longer the only nuclear power, the nation discovered that the Soviets' new weapons, combined with the development of rocket technology, left it vulnerable. The creation of the "Iron Curtain" in parts of Eastern Europe and the communist victory in China in 1949 reinforced this disquiet. American anxieties intensified the following year with the revelation that the German scientist Klaus Fuchs, who had worked on the Manhattan Project, had given atomic secrets to the USSR. Many worried that there were other, still hidden, spies. A little-known senator from Wisconsin, Joseph McCarthy, immediately picked up on this widely shared fear:

> The reason why we find ourselves in a position of impotency is not because our only powerful potential enemy has sent men to invade our shores . . . but rather because of the traitorous actions of those who have been treated so well by this Nation. It has not been the less fortunate, or members of minority groups who have been traitorous to this Nation, but rather those who have had all the benefits that the wealthiest Nation on earth has had to offer . . . the finest homes, the finest college education and the finest jobs in government we can give.[29]

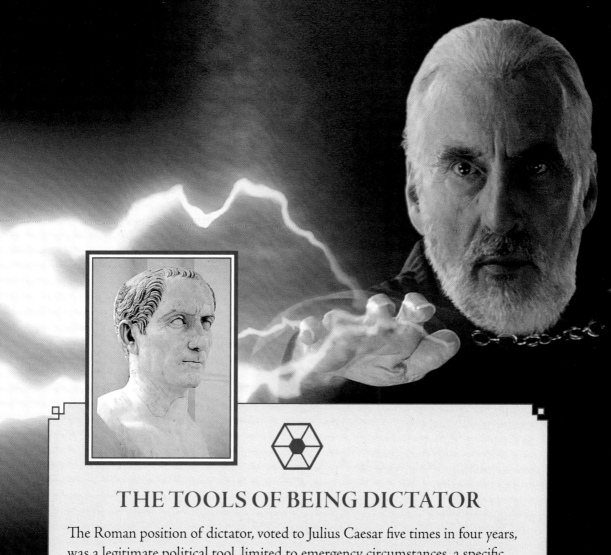

THE TOOLS OF BEING DICTATOR

The Roman position of dictator, voted to Julius Caesar five times in four years, was a legitimate political tool, limited to emergency circumstances, a specific task, and an allotted time. The senate gave Caesar this tool because it trusted him to turn it over once the emergency had passed. What Supreme Chancellor Palpatine seeks is something much different, "sovereign" dictatorship, which seeks to perpetuate itself and construct an entirely new political order.

The tools of becoming a dictator are very different, though, from the tools necessary to be one. In this respect, Count Dooku would have been more effective than Palpatine. As the leader of the Separatists, his power derives not just from his apprenticeship to Darth Sidious but also through his charisma and powers of persuasion. Like Adolf Hitler, he forges an alliance of ambitious and rapacious corporate powers, taking advantage of their indignation at taxes and bureaucracy while the Senate does nothing. Even the insightful Mace Windu and Ki-Adi-Mundi are fooled into believing Dooku is a "political idealist, not a murderer."

UNCIVIL DIVISIONS

The American Civil War is sometimes referred to as a war that pitted "brother against brother." This war not only divided a country, it divided families and loved ones. Sometimes this division was literal, as in the case of brothers Alexander and James Campbell, who fought on either side at the Battle of Secessionville in June 1862. Families in the border states were often divided, even as Anakin and Padmé ultimately choose different sides in the Clone Wars.

When Luke Skywalker joins the Rebel Alliance, he doesn't know that he will face his own father. This resembles the reality of some families in the Civil War. The battle of Malvern Hill in 1862 was a tragic event for Sergeant Driscoll, a sharpshooter in the Irish Brigade. He discovered he had shot his own son, who had gone south before the war. Maddened with grief, Driscoll led the next charge and ensured his own death.

REPUBLIC OF SLAVES

Just as slavery pervades human history, it's the demon distorting both the democratic Republic and the dictatorial Empire, even if Padmé Amidala is shocked it still exists on Tatooine.

No aspect of slavery is crueler than its destruction of families for power, punishment, and profit. In *Incidents in the Life of a Slave Girl*, Harriet Jacobs depicts a mother who saw seven of her children being sold in North Carolina before the Civil War: "Her wild, haggard face lives to-day in my mind. She wrung her hands in anguish, and exclaimed, 'Gone! All gone! Why don't God kill me?'"

Shmi and Anakin try to be brave when he leaves with Jedi Master Qui-Gon Jinn, who won him in a bet; however, the pain of their forced separation and Anakin's fury at Shmi's fate after she's sold too is what turns him to the dark side.

Until the Civil War exorcised slavery from America's body, it was a nation whose claim to be "the land of the free" rang hollow. It's this same freedom that the Rebels are ultimately fighting for in the end.

SEX SLAVERY

In almost every slave society, as on Tatooine, masters draw sexual satisfaction from their slaves. Jabba chains Oola to his throne so he can watch her dance. Her defiance is swiftly punished: he feeds her to the rancor. Her replacement is Leia, who uses her chain to exact the vengence Oola couldn't.

Women have been targeted for the sex trade since recorded history began, and immigrant women have always been particularly at risk. More recent Victorian vice laws only contributed to this problem. The U.K.'s Contagious Disease Acts and the U.S. Page Act both presumed that immigrant women were prostitutes. Driven out of respectable society, women forced into the sex trade received little help from the law.

THE DEATH STAR AGE

Like nuclear weapons, the main purpose of the Death Star isn't to destroy planets. It is to make people afraid their planet could be destroyed. Just as the U.S. attack on Nagasaki confirmed the results of Hiroshima and convinced the Japanese to surrender in 1945, destroying Yavin 4 would have confirmed Alderaan and convinced every planet both inside and outside of the Empire to submit.

The Soviet Union raced to develop its own atomic bomb, and during the Cold War that followed, both sides competed to produce nuclear and biological weapons so fearful that the other side would be intimidated. If an attack did occur, a doctrine of "mutual assured destruction" would guarantee the near total eradication of the other side's civilian population. Attempting to survive the (probably) unsurvivable, children spent forty years doing air raid and "duck and cover" drills. Backyard nuclear bomb shelters became a new fad, and families that couldn't afford their own practiced sheltering inside basements and closets. American popular culture regularly pondered the likelihood of total destruction in films such as *Fail-Safe*, *War Games*, *On the Beach*, and *Dr. Strangelove*.

The subjects of the Empire would have only practiced planetary evacuation drills—and laughed ruefully at their futility the way Americans were amused by *Dr. Strangelove*.

McCarthy's right-wing populism accused the federal government and the elites of the nation of espionage and betrayal. Because the Korean War began only a few months later, the panic that ensued is perhaps understandable. Many people argued that danger threatened from within, as well as from without, and that anyone, even the nation's leaders, could be a communist.[30]

These fears found their expression in the popular culture of the time.[31] George Lucas himself grew up in the shadow of the bomb and remembers the drills where children had to hide under their desks at school. Certainly, in his own lifetime he saw an explosion of panic that led to often appalling overreactions. Perhaps we can see this behind Yoda's statement in *The Phantom Menace*: "Fear is the path to the dark side. Fear leads to anger, anger leads to hate; hate leads to suffering." In the councils of government, we must guard against the acquisition

"Remember Back to Your Early Teachings. 'All Who Gain Power Are Afraid to Lose It.'"

of unwarranted influence, whether sought or unsought, by the military-industrial complex. The potential for the disastrous rise of misplaced power exists and will persist.

—Dwight D. Eisenhower[32]

Why did a great Sith Lord such as Emperor Palpatine need the Death Star? The simplest answer is that one person alone—even someone so powerful—cannot control an entire galaxy. For that, a strong military force is necessary, and army leaders want the latest and best weapons. In a technological age, this means the existence of industries that supply the weapons and other necessary tools. These industrial groups, in turn, seek to maintain their position and continue receiving government contracts (and so a second Death Star is built, even though a first one has failed) and solidify their political power. In this, *Star Wars* reflects one of the chief debates of the Cold War, which revolved around what then president Eisenhower termed in his farewell address "the military-industrial complex." The expression is defined by *Merriam-Webster* as "an informal alliance of the military and related government departments with defense industries that is held to influence government policy."[33]

In the United States, the military-industrial complex began to grow in earnest with World War II. A noticeable sign of this was the construction of the Pentagon—one of the largest office buildings in the world—which was opened in 1943. The advent of the Cold War entrenched both the military and its civilian suppliers. During the next decades, the two superpowers tried to outdo each other in military technology, building ever more powerful and accurate nuclear weapons. The United States generally had the lead, but the USSR scored some important triumphs, such as the launching of the world's first satellite, *Sputnik*, in October 1957. *Sputnik* provoked something of

Supreme Chancellor Palpatine. (*Revenge of the Sith*)

a panic in the United States and started both the Space Age and the Space Race.[34]

On one hand, however, the 1970s were a time of détente, a policy that sought to reduce international tension. A series of events and agreements showed that the friction between the United States and the USSR and China was gradually easing. First, there was the winding down and the disastrous conclusion to the Vietnam War, as well as Nixon's visit to China in 1972. The Strategic Arms Limitation Talks the same year resulted in the SALT I agreements (including the Anti-Ballistic Missile Treaty), which controlled and limited armaments in both the superpowers. So the original *Star Wars* film came out during a period of détente. Indeed, the very year of its appearance saw the signing of a nuclear nonproliferation pact by fifteen countries (including the United States and the Soviet Union).

On the other hand, the 1970s saw something of a low point in confidence in the executive branch's honesty. In June 1971, the *New York Times* began publication of what are known as "the Pentagon Papers"—a secret history of U.S. involvement in the Vietnam War prepared by the Department of Defense, leaked to the *Times* by military analyst Daniel Ellsberg. The newspaper later wrote, "They demonstrated, among other things, that the Johnson Administration had systematically lied, not only to the public but also to Congress, about a subject of transcendent national interest and significance."[35] The Watergate scandal followed, which would ultimately bring down the Nixon government, as did revelations about the U.S. government's continuing lies regarding its interventions in Indochina, such as the so-called secret bombing of Cambodia. Indeed, Lucas apparently based the Emperor on Richard Nixon.[36] Corruption in the highest places within the United States and the power of the military-industrial complex seemed all too obvious to many at the time.

In the prequel trilogy, naturally, we see only the origins of the Death Star. It seems that a dictatorship, once established, feels it must resort to fear and intimidation in order to maintain its hold on power. Yet if the earlier trilogy can be seen as a reflection of and about the Cold War, so the later trilogy reflects the worries of more recent history. At the end of *Revenge of the Sith*, the Death Star looks surprisingly near completion—in fact, it's hard to imagine why it took another twenty years to make it fully operational. Perhaps this is beside the point, though, and the real purpose is to show parallels with more current events such as the September 11, 2001, attacks and the Afghanistan and Iraq wars. Certainly, a massive panic seized America after the 9/11 attacks, and this fear was exploited to justify the invasion of Iraq. The threat of terrorists armed with super-weapons has cropped up continually. *Revenge of the Sith* was made while much of this debate was

The Emperor and Darth Vader view the Death Star, still under construction. (*Revenge of the Sith*)

occurring. It makes the point of showing the Galactic Republic being destroyed from within and with popular support. Indeed, Padmé Amidala comments, "So this is how liberty dies . . . with thunderous applause." Will Brooker has commented that

> this is the pattern suggested by Lucas' saga as a whole—not a straight clash between good and evil, or even the character arc of Anakin Skywalker's rise, corruption and salvation, but a cycle between apparently oppositional but in fact worryingly similar social structures, the Empire and Republic. Corruption, within Lucas's model, does not appear from outside, but festers within, emerging when a complacent society allows it to flourish; it can rise again if it is not checked and controlled, as Luke does with his urges towards hatred and revenge, or it can be exorcised, as Luke does, by saving his father and destroying the Emperor.
>
> Indeed, the only super-weapon in *Star Wars* belongs to the government. The vision of the Death Star at the end may be a warning to us all about the dangers to our own liberty of a new military-industrial complex.[37]

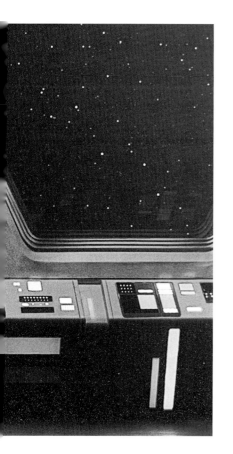

The Death Star at the end may be a warning to us all about the dangers to our own liberty of a new military-industrial complex.

What had been the city of Nagasaki, Japan, after the United States dropped a nuclear weapon in August 1945. A Roman Catholic cathedral can be seen in the distance. A Japanese report described Nagasaki as "like a graveyard with not a tombstone standing."

Appearing in four of the *Star Wars* films and central to two of them, the two Death Stars, the ultimate weapon of the Galactic Empire, are examples of the evil of absolute power, which inevitably seeks to preserve itself at all costs. Defeated by the simplest of weapons, the Death Star shows the futility of any regime seeking to perpetuate its power eternally. In this sense, it is a highly critical and yet optimistic commentary on the ultimate futility of the arms race, of much of the Cold War, and, indeed, of much recent history. It is also a reflection of the terror engendered by atomic power. Ultimately, *Star Wars'* message here is that we should be focused on controlling ourselves and our own base desires (looking within for the source of our troubles), rather than on controlling others, and this is true for nations, as much as for individuals. Or, as Yoda tells Luke in *The Empire Strikes Back*, "Control, control, you must learn control!"

PART III

"Excuse Me, Sir, but That Artoo Unit Is in Prime Condition, a Real Bargain"

ECONOMY AND SOCIETY IN A GALAXY LONG, LONG AGO

"I can't believe there is still slavery in the galaxy."
—Padmé Amidala, *The Phantom Menace*

9

From Slavery to Freedom in a Galaxy Far, Far Away

Paul Finkelman

Slavery is both a condition and an institutional arrangement.[1] This was true in the ancient world, in the New World, and in the galaxy where *Star Wars* takes place. In the *Star Wars* movies, we find the public institutional operation of slavery, individual bondage, people in slavelike conditions, and examples of the modern state slavery similar to those created by totalitarian regimes in the middle third of the twentieth century. To the extent that *Star Wars* is a metaphor about human history and society, as well as a philosophical musing about humanity, it is not surprising that we find slavery in the galaxy, just as we find it in human history and in our time.

Although the substance of slavery has varied from place to place and over time, systems of slavery include most, or all, of the following conditions: people are owned by others and can be sold, traded, or given away; the status of slave is inheritable, usually through the mother; formal legal structures or informal agreements regulate the capture and return of fugitive slaves; slaves have limited (or no) legal rights or protections; and slaves may be punished by slave owners (or their agents) with minimal or no legal limitations, and masters may treat or mistreat slaves as they wish. Although some societies banned the premeditated murder of slaves and certain extreme or barbaric forms of punishment and torture, Rome, Greece, and other ancient cultures considered slaves to be "socially dead," and thus it was not a crime to kill them.[2] Masters also have unlimited rights to sexual activity with their slaves. Slaves have very limited or no appeal to formal legal institutions, they are not allowed to give testimony against their masters or (usually) other free people, and in general their testimony is not given the same weight as a free person's. The mobility of slaves is limited by owners and often by the state, as well. Owners are able to make slaves into free persons through a formal legal process (manumission), but often these freed persons are not given full legal rights after manumission. Finally, slave ownership is supported by laws, regulations, administrative activities, courts, and legislatures, including provisions for special courts and punishments for slaves, provisions for the capture and return of fugitive slaves, and provisions and rules for regulating the sale of slaves.

In addition to formal systems of slavery, in the twentieth century massive

A slave in ancient Rome combing the hair of her mistress.

systems of state slavery developed in the Soviet Union, Germany, and Japan. In the 1930s and the 1940s, millions of people were forced into unpaid labor, not as chattels to be bought and sold, but as workers to be controlled by the state, working either for state enterprises or assigned to private work places by the state. In our own time, slavelike conditions have emerged for millions of people, usually migrants or refugees, who are exploited (often illegally). Most of this type of exploitation is found in the nonindustrialized world, but some people are also held against their will in modern, developed democracies, as they try to migrate to Western nations.

In *Star Wars*, we see many of these elements played out, including the buying and selling of slaves; the sexual exploitation of slave women; the torture and killing of slaves; the manumission of some slaves; and even free people accepting bondage as a way of moving or improving their lives, often with disastrous results.

The Universality of Human Bondage

At the American Constitutional Convention in 1787, the delegates had heated debates over the power of Congress to abolish the African slave trade. The debate was not over whether Congress could actually end slavery—no one imagined that possibility. Rather, the debate was over the power of Congress to regulate international commerce in general and this specific form of commerce in particular. Not surprisingly, the debate led to arguments about the morality of slavery itself. In responses to attacks on the slave trade and slavery, Charles Pinckney of South Carolina offered a spirited defense: "If slavery be wrong, it is justified by the example of all the world." Citing "the case of Greece Rome & other antient [sic] States; the sanction given by France, England, Holland & other modern States," Pinckney declared that "in all ages one half of mankind have been slaves."[3]

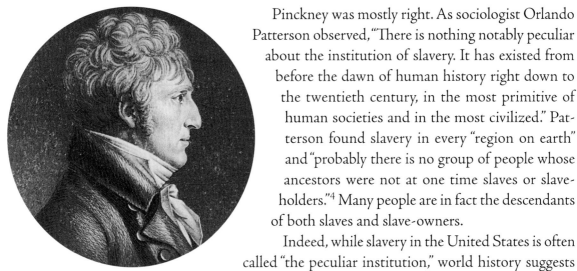

Charles Pinckney,
governor and senator
of South Carolina and
defender of slavery,
ca. 1800.

Pinckney was mostly right. As sociologist Orlando Patterson observed, "There is nothing notably peculiar about the institution of slavery. It has existed from before the dawn of human history right down to the twentieth century, in the most primitive of human societies and in the most civilized." Patterson found slavery in every "region on earth" and "probably there is no group of people whose ancestors were not at one time slaves or slave-holders."[4] Many people are in fact the descendants of both slaves and slave-owners.

Indeed, while slavery in the United States is often called "the peculiar institution," world history suggests that universal *freedom*—that is, an absence of slavery—is far more unusual. Slavery is one of the oldest known human institutions. Evidence of slavery is found in archaeological sites and in ancient legal records. With a few minor exceptions, slavery has existed throughout the world, in all cultures and societies. Slavery was one of the first legally defined statuses of human relationships and was justified in virtually all ancient legal codes, including the Mesopotamian, biblical, Babylonian, and Roman. An unsuccessful appeal for freedom by twelve Mesopotamian slaves more than 4,000 years ago is the oldest known freedom suit. Contract disputes over slaves and records of manumission date from around 2,500 years ago. Before the late seventeenth century, there were almost no visible opponents of slavery. Plato assumed there would be slaves in his Republic; Sir Thomas More provided for slaves in his Utopia, and John Locke saw no inconsistency between opposing inherited royalty and supporting a system where slaves inherited their status. To the extent that the *Star Wars* galaxy tracks human history, it would be hard to imagine that slavery would not appear on various worlds and even have the tacit support of those who proclaimed their belief in freedom. The first *Star Wars* movie—*A New Hope*—begins by telling us that there is a civil war "to restore freedom to the galaxy," but as we learn in subsequent movies, slavery was always present in the galaxy and even in the Republic. This mirrors human history, where slavery has often existed in "free societies."

Slavery is one of the oldest known human institutions. Only in the eighteenth and nineteenth centuries—after more than four millennia of human history—did slavery come under significant political and cultural attack. The late eighteenth-century opposition to slavery, which became the international abolitionist movement, was not immediately successful. On the eve of the American Revolution, slavery was legal everywhere in the New World, everywhere in Africa, in most of Asia, and throughout the Mediterranean basin. Only in Northern Europe had slavery disappeared. Slavery as a system did not exist in France, but slaves from Haiti and other French colonies were regularly brought to the metropolis and held there.[5] There was no system of slavery in Great Britain, and by the time of the Revolution, it was no longer legal for colonial residents or absentee British planters to bring their slaves into Britain. In 1772, in the case of *Somerset v. Stewart*, the Court of King's Bench ruled that slaves could not be kept in Great Britain against their will.[6] Lord Chief Justice Mansfield held that "the state of slavery is of such a nature, that it is incapable of being introduced on any reasons, moral or political; but only positive law, which preserves its force long after the reasons, occasion, and time itself from whence it was created, is erased from memory, it's so odious, that nothing can be suffered to support it, but positive law."[7]

Although slavery would not be allowed in Britain, Mansfield had no interest in interfering with the lucrative African slave trade or the vast fortunes being made in the American colonies—where slave labor produced sugar in the Caribbean and tobacco, rice, and indigo on the mainland colonies. Thus, Lord Mansfield also declared that "contract for sale of a slave is good here; the sale is a matter to which the law properly and readily attaches, and will maintain the price according to the agreement."[8] Thus, the British were heavily involved in the African slave trade, and thousands of wealthy Britons owned slaves in the

Caribbean, as absentee sugar planters, even if they could not bring their slaves home to London or Liverpool. During and immediately after the American Revolution, the New England and Middle Atlantic states either ended slavery directly or set it on the road to extinction in those states through gradual emancipation laws. Still, the institution remained firmly established in the new American Republic, just as it could be found in the galactic republic of *Star Wars* on Outer Rim worlds such as Tatooine and other planets under Hutt control.[9]

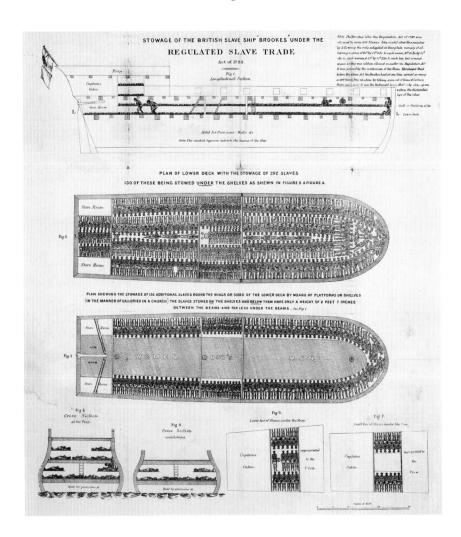

An etching showing the stowage of slaves on the British slave ship *Brookes*, c. 1788.

After the Revolution, slavery remained secure in the American South. The new American nation, the world's first successful republic and the first place to provide political rights for substantial numbers of citizens, was a slaveholder's republic. The irony of American slave-owners such as Washington, Jefferson, Patrick Henry, and George Mason fighting to gain their liberty was not lost on British Tories, who mocked the American revolutionaries: not a few Englishmen read the Declaration of Independence, mostly written by Thomas Jefferson (who famously owned about 150 slaves at the time), and wondered, as did Samuel Johnson, "How is it that we hear the loudest *yelps* for liberty among the drivers of negroes?"[10] The irony, of course, is that political liberty, democratic elections, and a republican form of government are not necessarily incompatible with slavery.

Nineteenth-century England and France had limited suffrage and were hardly democratic in any meaningful way. Perhaps because the power of the voters was limited, these nations were able to abolish slavery in their New World colonies. In the American republic, however, the vast majority of free men could vote. The Americans created a written constitution that supported civil liberties, due process of law, private property, and peaceful political change. Yet this constitution made it impossible to end slavery through the political process.[11] Indeed, the end to American slavery came through a Civil War and the loss of some 630,000 lives (the equivalent of about 6.5 million people today).

The abolition of slavery in the United States (1865) and the end of serfdom in Russia (1861) set the stage for the final abolition of slavery in the New World. Not until 1890—with the adoption of the Brussels Act—was there a comprehensive multilateral treaty directed specifically against the African slave trade. This international agreement really only affected Europe and the Western Hemisphere, however. It did not end slavery in Africa, the Middle East, or the rest of Asia, where slavery continued openly and vigorously well into the twentieth century. Moreover, slavelike conditions continued, especially in the African colonies controlled by the "civilized" nations of Western Europe.

Dozens of captives
rescued from a slave
ship in 1884.

At the end of the nineteenth century, European nations hurried to colonize most of Africa, in what was called the "scramble for Africa." These Europeans agreed that colonization was necessary to bring civilization to what they called the Dark Continent, and that one clear mark of civilization was the abolition of slavery. In their rush to control vast chunks of Africa, European imperialists agreed that slavery should be abolished under their tutelage and rule, but they all understood that "beyond the line" of Western society, slavery and other forms of forced labor would be eliminated slowly and only "as far as possible." The nations signing the Brussels Act pledged to bring civilization to Africa, but this did not preclude violent conquest of additional territories in pursuit of ending the slave trade. Nor did the act either discourage or prevent, within the colonized areas, massive use of coerced native labor that resembled slavery.[12]

After World War I, the League of Nations organized a new international effort to finally abolish slavery. The Slavery Convention of 1926 was designed to pursue slavery and the slave trade into every corner of what Europeans considered to be the uncivilized world. The convention also committed the signatories to attack slavery "in all its forms," including child trafficking, concubinage, debt-bondage, and forced labor.[13] Slavery was now defined as "the status or condition of a person over whom any or all of the powers attaching to the right of ownership are exercised." The world community thought that slavery was on its last legs, but in fact it was not.

Less than a decade after the leading nations of the world pledged to end slavery "in all its forms," the institution reemerged in new forms: Soviet gulags, German concentration camps and slave labor battalions, and Japanese POW camps and brothels run by the imperial army, where "comfort women" from all over Asia, as well as captured Australian nurses, were turned into sex slaves for the benefit of Japanese soldiers. In the six years between 1939 and 1945, Germany imported nearly as many slaves from other European nations as the New World plantation regimes imported from Africa in the nearly four hundred years between the discovery of the New World in 1492 and the final end of the African slave trade at the end of the nineteenth century. After World War II, German and Japanese leaders were tried and executed for "crimes against humanity" that included enslavement. Not surprisingly, enslavement was the first violation of human rights listed in the Universal Declaration of Human Rights in 1948.

In the modern world, slavery has been formally abolished in almost every country. Yet real slavery—the buying and selling of people—exists in many places outside the Western world. Slavelike conditions—including forced labor, forced prostitution, and illegal working conditions—can be found throughout the world.

"There Is Still Slavery in the Galaxy":
Star Wars and Slavery

To some extent, the *Star Wars* movies replicate the history of human bondage. The *Star Wars* galaxy is dominated by a modern, civilized Republic, yet it also has vestiges of the ancient and medieval worlds. Clothing often resembles modern notions of Roman garb; democracy exists, but there are still noble titles and royal families. Slavery should have been thoroughly abolished in the futuristic Republic that we enter at the beginning of *The Phantom Menace*, yet bondage is found in a variety of ways.[14] On the "Outer Rim" of the galaxy, slavery flourishes—just as it did "beyond the line" of civilization in the European conquest of America and Africa. The planet Kashyyyk, home to the Wookiees, is a hunting ground for slavers.[15] Han Solo's Wookiee partner, Chewbacca, was a slave he rescued. In some ways, this resembled the behavior of English adventurers (the Spanish would have called them pirates), like Francis Drake and John Hawkins, who liberated Spanish slaves in the sixteenth century Caribbean and then incorporated the former slaves into their crews. Drake and Hawkins, who sailed the Spanish Main seeking plunder and liberating slaves, might be seen as models for Han Solo, the smuggler, pirate, but ultimately the liberator.

> Slavery should have been thoroughly abolished in the futuristic Republic that we enter at the beginning of *The Phantom Menace*, yet bondage is found in a variety of ways.

On other planets in the world of *Star Wars*, people are bought and sold, and enslavement is open and unchallenged. We encounter a young Anakin Skywalker as a slave, and yet almost no one is dismayed by his bondage. It is a fact of life on the Outer Rim of the galaxy, "beyond the line" of true civilization. However, the naive Padmé Amidala, in *Attack of the Clones*, encountering the unambiguous slavery on Tatooine, declares, "I can't believe there is still slavery in the galaxy."

Yet forms of slavery also appear in the more civilized portions of the galaxy. This is not surprising, because, as art imitates life, even where slavery is banned, bondage often appears. Although slavery was not legal in England in the late eighteenth century, more than ten thousand slaves were probably in the realm on the eve of the American Revolution, serving mostly as household servants, as coachmen, and occasionally as cabin boys on ships. In the galaxy of *Star Wars*, slavery was similarly possible, even if not legally sanctioned.

Working our way through the six movies, we find slavery in the Republic and in the Empire. We find it on the rim of the galaxy, on small out-of-the-way planets, and in the heart of the galaxy.

Anakin Skywalker, Slave

In *The Phantom Menace*, we encounter obvious and familiar forms of slavery. Slavery is illegal in the Republic, but it exists in the Outer Rim, where the Republic has influence but no direct power. This is much like the world in the late nineteenth century. At the Berlin Conference of 1884 and the Brussels Convention of 1889, the major powers of Europe, as well as the United States, agreed to a complete end to the African slave trade and to end human bondage wherever these Western powers had influence. Yet in reality, slavery, bondage, and "slavelike conditions" proliferated in the European colonies of Africa, because the colonizing powers tacitly agreed that there would be little investigation of actual conditions "beyond the line" of civilization. At meetings in Europe, the representatives of republics and constitutional monarchies could agree to bring civilization to Africa, but on the ground, human freedom was fragile and often nonexistent.

Such is the case on Tatooine, where Shmi Skywalker and her young son, Anakin, are slaves. Shmi had been born free but was captured by pirates (along with her family) and sold into slavery; she and her son are eventually acquired by Gardulla the Hutt.[16]

Just as slavery on the periphery of civilization resembles the world of the nineteenth century, Shmi's own story is familiar to all scholars of slavery. At various times in human history, capture by pirates or slave hunters was common and accepted. The very word *slave* comes from the word *Slav*, a reference to the Slavic peoples of the Baltic region, who were so commonly captured and enslaved by the Vikings that being a Slav became synonymous with lifetime servitude—slavery. Thus, Shmi was similar to the tens of thousands of Slavs who were seized by pirates, Viking raiders, and others and carried off to the Mediterranean basin, where they were sold into a lifetime of bondage. When these Slavs arrived in medieval Italy, France, or Greece, no one questioned their status; no one wondered or asked how they became slaves. Their status was simply taken for granted.

The same process also applied to Africans, kidnapped from their homes by other Africans who operated as slave catchers. The captives were marched to the coast and sold to European traders, who then brought them to the Americas, where they were sold and often resold. No one in Brazil, the Caribbean, or the American South questioned the provenance of slaves who were brought from Africa. As with medieval Slavs, their chains were proof enough of their status. So, too, with Shmi. She appears on the planet Tatooine as a slave available for purchase, so Gardulla the Hutt buys Shmi and her son, as she apparently buys other slaves brought to the planet.[17]

Gardulla later loses Shmi and her son, Anakin, to Watto the Toydarian in a bet over a Podrace. This is typical of the nature of slavery. Slaves in the ancient world, the medieval world, and the American South were property, to be bought, sold, given away, and used as collateral for debt or even to settle a wager.

When Qui-Gon Jinn, a Jedi Master, lands on Tatooine to repair his ship, he comes to the junkyard of Watto, looking for spare parts. There Jinn meets the young Anakin and, later, his mother, who are Watto's slaves. Anakin has dreamed of becoming a Jedi, and in one of his dreams he "came back" to Tatooine as a Jedi "and freed all the slaves."

On meeting a real Jedi, the child Anakin thinks his dream will come true. He will be emancipated by Jinn, and then he can become a Jedi and return to free the slaves. Thus, the seemingly naive Anakin asks Jinn if he has come liberate him. Jinn honestly replies, "I didn't actually come here to free slaves." This is surely beyond the powers of a Jedi Knight, even though the Jedi are dedicated to justice. Slavery might be wrong and in violation of the laws of the Republic, but in a remote place such as Tatooine, it is a reality.

Yet on this trip to Tatooine, Jinn does free Anakin. Almost immediately after he encounters Anakin, Jinn realizes that this is an unusual child, with power and a connection to the Force. Jinn tests Anakin, discovering that he has an extraordinary high level of midi-chlorians, indicating that he has the potential to be a great Jedi. Yet Anakin is a slave, and Jinn does not have the money to buy him. Instead, he makes a wager with Watto that Anakin will win the Boonta Eve Podrace. If Anakin wins, then Jinn will become his owner. If Anakin loses, then

Qui-Gon wagers with Watto to win Anakin's freedom. (*The Phantom Menace*)

Watto will take possession of Jinn's ship. Jinn also tries to gain Anakin's mother, Shmi, as part of the bet, but Watto has no interest in losing her. He can afford to lose a small boy in a bet over a race. Slave children are potentially valuable, but in the harsh world of Tatooine where life is fragile, a young child might never become a valuable adult slave. Shmi is pretty, however, young enough to bear children, and valuable. Watto will not risk losing her.

Anakin, of course, wins the race. The Force is with him. His victory is also his ticket to freedom, just as many slaves, such as the Charleston, South Carolina, bondsman Denmark Vesey, gained freedom by winning lotteries. But Anakin's freedom comes at a great cost. Anakin has to choose between freedom—and the chance to become a Jedi—and living with his mother. It is a cruel choice. In many ways, it reminds us of one of the great horrors of slavery in the United States, where families were often disrupted and broken apart by the whims of the masters. It was common to give small children as gifts for weddings or other special occasions. Children and parents were thus often separated by sale or movement. For example, the great black abolitionist Frederick Douglass saw his mother for the last time when he was seven, about the same age Anakin is when forced to choose between freedom and family. For most slaves who escaped bondage, the same choice was before them. They might escape on their own, but they could not take family members with them.

Shmi encourages her son to choose freedom. When he wins the Podrace and thus the chance to escape his bondage, his mother tells him, "You have given hope to those who have none." She then urges him to leave, even though he must leave her. "Now you are free, your dreams can come true" she tells him. So, Anakin leaves with Jinn and his Padawan (apprentice), Obi-Wan Kenobi. He is no longer a slave but a free person, soon to be an apprentice himself, learning to become a Jedi.

One might argue that Anakin is simply compelled to exchange one form of slavery—as the property of another—for a different kind of bondage, the ever-obedient apprentice in a strict monastic order, where selfishness and greed are submerged and, as much as possible, eliminated. Anakin will resist the obedience, break rules, and, of course, ultimately be seduced by the dark side of the Force. One key to this obedience is the elimination of anger and hatred. Yet for an ex-slave forced to abandon his mother, this might never be possible. He is free, but his mother remains in bondage. He can grow and excel, but only at a huge cost. The cost leads to both anger and guilt. Anakin must feel pangs of conscience that he gained freedom but his mother could not.

The theme of *Star Wars* is ultimately the struggle between good and evil—the struggle between the light side of the Force and the dark side. The crisis of the galaxy is exacerbated by the transformation of Anakin Skywalker from an agent of good into Darth Vader, the embodiment of evil. Ultimately, Anakin can be seduced by the dark side because of his enormous pent-up anger. The slave boy, free himself, can never forget that his mother is still in bondage. Eventually, he returns to Tatooine to find his mother. By now, he is a Jedi, powerful and skilled.

He goes to Watto, only to find that once more his mother has been sold, this time to Cliegg Lars, a rural farmer. Lars is not a typical purchaser of slaves. He fell in love with Shmi, therefore bought and manumitted her, then married her. This was not uncommon in slave societies. Even in the American South, where manumission was difficult, because laws on race made marriage between

Anakin preparing to leave his mother, Shmi, on Tatooine. (*The Phantom Menace*)

a master and a former slave illegal, the most likely person to be manumitted was a slave mistress. Some masters lived openly with their slave mistresses, proclaiming their love for them.[18] Shmi and Cliegg married for love. This happy ending does not last. Tusken Raiders capture Shmi, subjecting her to ritual torture. This is not dissimilar to the use of slaves for ritual killings in some cultures, such as the Aztec. Anakin returns to Tatooine about a month after his mother was kidnapped. He goes out to find her and rescues her, only to have her die in his arms. In anger and in violation of the rules of the Jedi, he slaughters the entire clan of Tuskens. This is his first big step toward the dark side of the Force and will lead to his transformation into Darth Vader.

The story of Anakin Skywalker is, in the end, a story about the corrosive nature of human bondage. Anakin's potential as a great man—as perhaps the "Chosen One" of Jedi prophesy—is undermined by his slave past. He is never able to overcome his anger over his bondage, his disrupted childhood, and the separation from his mother and ultimately her death at the hands of yet another band of kidnappers. A Jedi must be dedicated to the Order and to the rules of the Jedi, but

Anakin finds his mother at the Tusken Raiders' camp too late to save her life. (*Attack of the Clones*)

Anakin, a former slave, can never control his emotions or separate himself from them. Emotionally scarred by slavery, he cannot in the end be a true Jedi.

> The story of Anakin Skywalker is ... a story about the corrosive nature of human bondage

Throughout human history, slaves faced the hardships of bondage, separation, and not knowing their roots. We never know who Anakin's father was. Like so many slaves in human history, he can never fully know his lineage; like many slaves he is forced to choose between family and freedom. His anger and, ultimately, the disruption of the galaxy emerge from his bondage.

Slavery and Luke Skywalker

Luke Skywalker grows up on Tatooine, a world where slavery is legal and common. He is not a slave, but in important ways he experiences many things associated with bondage. He is raised by his "uncle" Owen Lars, never knowing that Owen is the step-brother of his father, Anakin Skywalker, and that there is no blood relation. Owen keeps from Luke the true nature of his lineage. In this way, Luke is like his father, Anakin, never knowing who his father is. More important, the young Luke, like the young Anakin, is prevented from seeking his destiny by those who control him. At the beginning of *A New Hope*, Luke is stuck on Tatooine, working on his uncle's moisture farm. He desperately wants to continue his education by entering the Academy, where he can become an officer and a starship pilot. His best friend, Biggs Darklighter, goes to the academy to become a fighter pilot, but Owen will not let Luke leave. It is not clear whether Luke can legally leave his guardian, but even if he could, he is trapped on the farm by Owen's persistent demand that he needs Luke for "just one more season." Luke is free to leave only after Owen and his wife, Beru, are killed by storm-troopers.

Luke Skywalker on his uncle's Tatooine moisture farm. (*A New Hope*)

In the context of labor and education, the early life of Luke, who is the "emancipator" of the galaxy, resembles the early life of the great emancipator of the United States, Abraham Lincoln. When Lincoln was a child, he loved books and thirsted for an education, but his father refused to allow him to get more than the most basic schooling. As a teenager, Lincoln read in his spare time, which angered his father. By age eighteen, he was more than ready to go out on his own, but he could not. Lincoln could not leave home until he turned twenty-one, and he was required to turn over all of his wages to his father until he

> The early life of Luke, who is the "emancipator" of the galaxy, resembles the early life of the great emancipator of the United States, Abraham Lincoln.

reached the age of majority. On the day he turned twenty-one, Lincoln left home, never to return. Later in life, he would express sympathy with slaves because he knew he had been treated like a slave by his father. For years, he was forced to labor for free, unable to seek his destiny elsewhere.

Abraham Lincoln, c. 1857.

Luke's guardian is not so harsh. As a youth, Luke learns to pilot skyhoppers and drive landspeeders, develops close friendships, and gains a basic education. Yet he cannot leave home, cannot go out on his own, and cannot achieve self-determination, even though, like the young Lincoln, he is old enough and skilled enough to make it on his own. Not quite slaves, Abraham Lincoln and Luke Skywalker were bondsmen, working for others and denied the most basic essential element of freedom: to go where they wished, learn what they wanted to learn, and make something of themselves beyond the narrow confines of their frontier homes. Age, for Lincoln, and the tragic murder of his guardians for Luke, allowed their emancipation and thus enabled them to achieve a destiny of emancipating others. Growing up, both men knew bondage firsthand; as adults, they hated slavery.

"You'll Soon Learn to Appreciate Me": Sex, Slavery, and *Star Wars*

Throughout history masters have sexually exploited their slaves. In almost every slave society, masters have had sex with their slaves. Indeed, in some cultures sex has been a prime motive for enslavement. The biblical Abraham had children with his slave Hagar, while his

Cassandra of Troy, kidnapped and raped by Ajax after her city fell, became an enslaved concubine.

wife, Sarah, was apparently unable to bear children. Later of course he had a child with Sarah as well. Abraham's grandson, Jacob, had a flock of children with his two wives and their "handmaidens"—slaves in the household. On the African coast, some slave traders refused to sell certain women to the European purchasers, preferring to keep them for their own slaves and concubines. In the colonial period, lonely planters isolated in New World colonies bought slaves to be their sex partners. In antebellum New Orleans, there was a thriving commerce in slave women who were sold to houses of prostitution.[19]

On Tatooine in *Return of the Jedi*, Oola is given to Jabba the Hutt, who chains her to his throne, where she is an ornament of his power, a diversion, an entertainer, and, when he wishes, a vehicle for his sexual pleasure. Stripped of her dancer's costume, she is dressed in flimsy netting, barely clothed, and on display for all.[20] She is eye candy for all who have an audience in Jabba's throne room. The room itself—indeed, his whole enterprise—is like that of a Mafia don removed to some "oriental" setting, with harems, dancers, prostitutes, and a constant mixture of business, corruption, pleasure, sexual exploitation, violence, pain, and death. It could be a fort on the African coast, set up for slave trading; a decadent pasha's palace in some far-off corner of the Ottoman Empire; or a similarly exotic palace, somewhere between Timbuktu and the Taj Mahal.

When Oola refuses his demands, Jabba the Hutt pulls her by her chain until she is over a trap door, which leads to his rancor monster. Jabba releases the trap door and Oola drops to the bottom, to be eaten alive. Her resistance—pointless, senseless, and without any chance of success—is motivated by fear, anger, and a sense of hopelessness. Life as Jabba's slave, chained to his throne, to be his plaything, is not worth living. It is better to die resisting bondage than to be slowly destroyed and then die. Examples of resistance such as Oola's can be found throughout the history of slavery, in every society, in every culture. Africans sometimes threw themselves overboard rather than endure the transatlantic crossing; slaves physically attacked masters, knowing they would be punished and even executed; in German slave labor camps, some inmates, facing death in any event, threw themselves at guards or barbed wire, knowing their acts would end their lives.

It is not clear that Oola knew her resistance to Jabba would lead to her death. She might have assumed he would not kill such a talented dancer and so beautiful a slave. Yet her resistance to his demands would, at the least, surely lead to painful punishment. Instead, she died, her chain still around her neck.

Shortly after the demise of Oola, Jabba obtains an even better slave as a replacement for Oola: Princess Leia. Captured while trying to rescue Han Solo, Leia is Jabba's new throne ornament, barely dressed, vulnerable to his sexual demands, displayed for all to gawk at, and

Although chained, Oola fights against Jabba the Hutt in his throne room. (*Return of the Jedi*)

Leia choking Jabba on his barge. (*Return of the Jedi*).

chained like a small animal to the immense throne of the gigantic Jabba. Jabba, however, never has time to enjoy Leia or to violate her. She is soon rescued by Luke Skywalker. During this chaotic battle, Leia is still chained to Jabba's throne, but she becomes the hero of all slaves— especially slave women—as she strangles Jabba with the very chain that holds her in bondage. The slave becomes the agent of her own liberation, and Jabba in turn becomes a victim of his own horrid greed, corruption, and lust. Like the slaves in Haiti who savagely took revenge on their masters in the 1790s, Leia takes revenge on Jabba, ironically killing him with his own tool of enslavement.

"We Don't Serve Their Kind Here": Beyond Chattel Slavery

So far, this essay has focused on slavery as a form of ownership of human beings. This has been the dominant form of slavery in world history and dates from ancient times. Yet there have also been public slaves: galley slaves in ancient navies, or the Hebrews dragooned to build ancient cities in Egypt, described in the book of Exodus. In the modern world, new versions of public slavery emerged in the mid-twentieth century: Korean comfort women and captured Western nurses, dragooned to provide sexual services for Japanese soldiers; political prisoners and captured German prisoners of war sent to Soviet gulags; millions of European civilians and captured Soviet prisoners of war, sent to German factories and concentration camps. In these modern slave regimes, those in bondage were often worked to death because they were expendable "subhumans" who had no true market value. They were indeed "less than slaves."

In the *Star Wars* galaxy, this form of bondage is found in a variety of ways. Clone armies are essentially slaves—persons bred to give their bodies and their lives to the authority that controls and paid for them. At a key juncture, the clone troopers are used by their Sith Master to slaughter the Jedi under the programming of Order 66. The Empire's elite forces, the stormtroopers, are neither volunteers nor conscripts, but are brainwashed members of an Imperial cult. Then there are the droid armies—machines—the ultimate slaves, unquestioning in the devotion to their task. The Empire relies on mindless droids, clones, and storm-troopers to obey commands without thought, in order to force everyone in the galaxy into a kind of universal bondage.

> *Star Wars* reminds us of the profound evil of slavery and the huge social costs that come with a denial of freedom.

That is where the *Star Wars* movies begin in *A New Hope*. There is a Civil War in the galaxy. The Rebels seek "to restore freedom to the

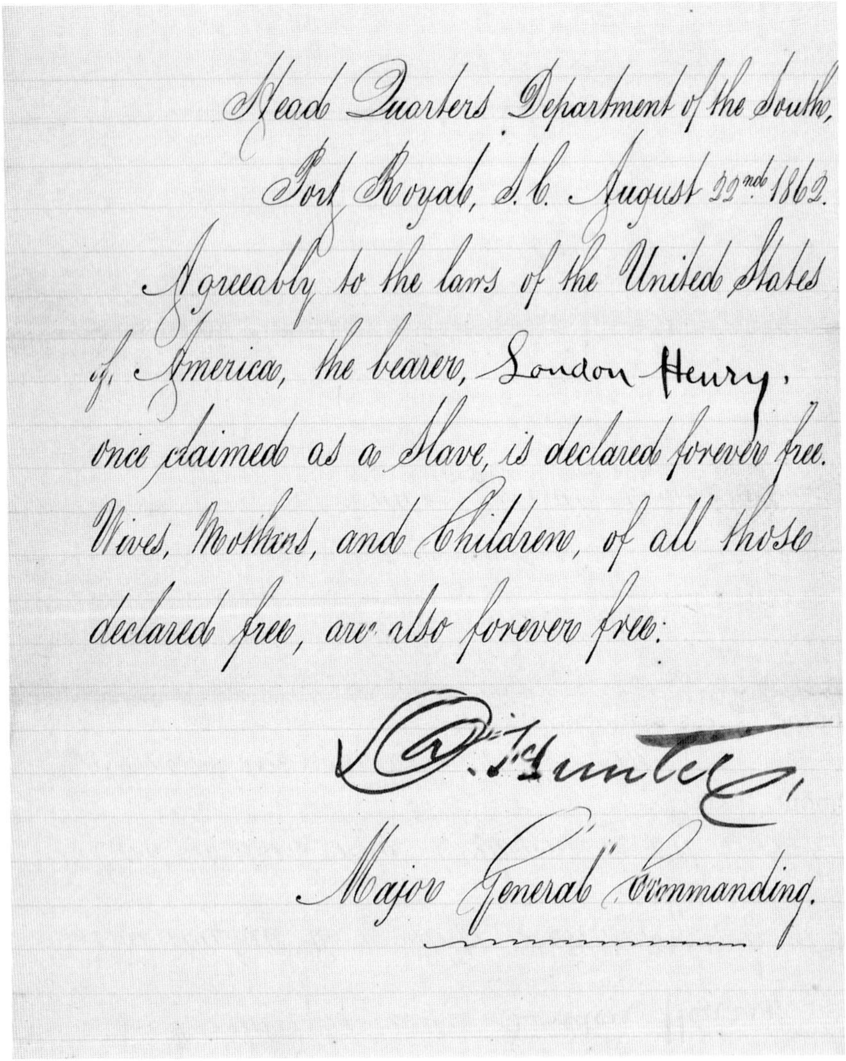

Head Quarters Department of the South,
Port Royal, S.C. August 22nd 1862.
Agreeably to the laws of the United States
of America, the bearer, London Henry,
once claimed as a Slave, is declared forever free.
Wives, Mothers, and Children, of all those
declared free, are also forever free.

D. Hunter,

Major General Commanding.

Free papers for former slave Henry London, signed by Major General David Hunter, Royal South Carolina, 1862.

galaxy." Freedom has multiple meanings. On one hand, freedom is the opposite of tyranny. Destroying the Empire and restoring a Republic will bring political "freedom" to the galaxy and get rid of the political "slavery" of the Emperor. Freedom is also the opposite of individual slavery. Emancipation brings "freedom" to those held in bondage. Yet on the other hand, freedom is the opposite of personal dedication (or enslavement) to an idea, a cause, a set of beliefs. A Jedi Knight is not "free" to choose his own direction but is constricted by a monklike obedience to the Order and the Force; a stormtrooper in service of the Emperor lacks freedom to choose on which side to fight; Darth Vader is, in effect, a "slave" to the dark side of the Force. Freedom and its opposites—tyranny, slavery, and selfless obedience—are in constant tension throughout the *Star Wars* movies.

All of these forms of slavery, or unfreedom, are present in the faraway worlds of the *Star Wars* galaxy. This makes sense because the movies are metaphors for human history. For most of human history, slavery and unfreedom have been the rule, not the exception. *Star Wars* reminds us of the profound evil of slavery and the huge social costs that come with a denial of freedom. It is true at the personal level of Anakin Skywalker, scarred for life by the utter unfairness of bondage, and Oola, who sought adventure and excitement, only to be enslaved, defiled, and destroyed. It is also true at the political level. The dark side of the Force is, in the end, the desire to have total control, even life-and-death control, over others. This, ultimately, is what slavery was always about.

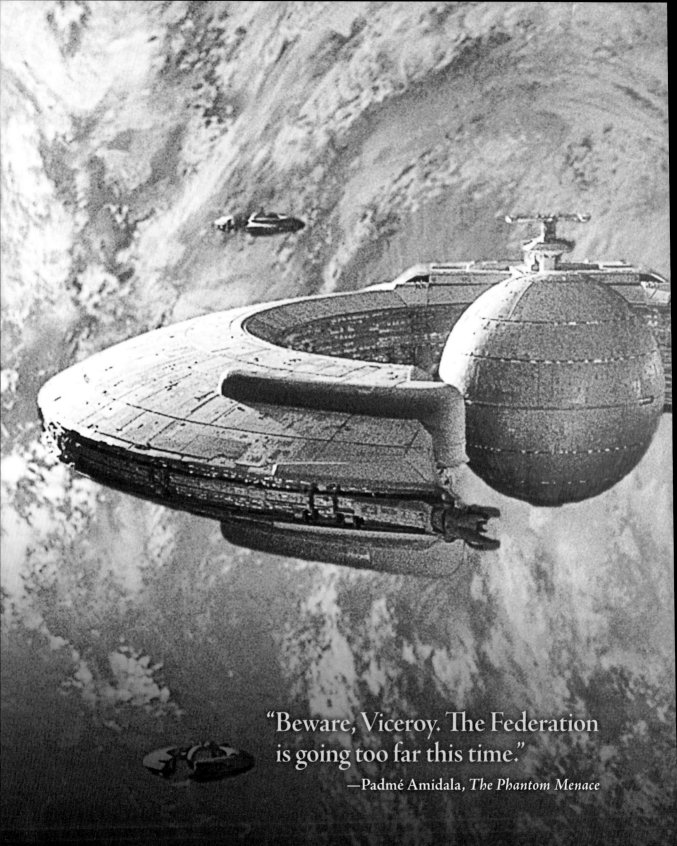

"Beware, Viceroy. The Federation
is going too far this time."

—Padmé Amidala, *The Phantom Menace*

10

"Greed Can Be a Powerful Ally"

The Trade Federation, the East India Companies, and Chaotic Worlds of Trade

Michael Laver

Without justice, what are kingdoms but great robberies? For what are robberies themselves, but little kingdoms? The band itself is made up of men; it is ruled by the authority of a prince, it is knit together by the pact of the confederacy; the booty is divided by the law agreed on. If, by the admittance of abandoned men, this evil increases to such a degree that it holds places, fixes abodes, takes possession of cities, and subdues peoples, it assumes the more plainly the name of a kingdom.

—Augustine of Hippo[1]

Fiction rarely springs from the head of its creator without being influenced by the events, characters, and often stranger-than-fiction narratives that make up what we collectively call "history." Certainly, this is true in the case of *Star Wars*: its pirates, merchants, and company officials had their counterparts in our history, as well. This chapter explores the parallels between the political and economic situation of the Republic and the Empire and the rather chaotic and fluid situation in the South China Sea region beginning in the sixteenth century. The actions of the Dutch East India Company and the British East India Company—multinational mega-corporations with trading bases throughout the Asian maritime world—showed striking similarities to the role played by the Trade Federation and other members of the Separatist Council in the transition from Republic to Empire, as illustrated in Episodes I through III of the movies.[2] The region's history also featured various eccentric figures, both Asian and European, who were at times pirates, legitimate merchants, company servants, or something wildly in between; some are oddly reminiscent of such shady or opportunistic figures as Jabba the Hutt, Lando Calrissian, Nute Gunray, Count Dooku, and indeed Han Solo himself. In other words, the question of where legitimate trade ends and piracy begins is one that depends very much on the circumstances and the economic situation. One person's pirate, it seems, can be another person's patriot. As Augustine observed in the fifth century, the line between a band of rapacious merchants and a sovereign government can also become blurred.

The actions of the Dutch East India Company … showed striking similarities to the role played by the Trade Federation and other members of the Separatist Council.

"You Old Pirate": Merchant Bandits on the Edge of Empire

One of the first scenes in which we are introduced to Luke Skywalker in *A New Hope* depicts him lamenting that his home planet Tatooine is, for lack of a better term, remote: "Well, if there's a bright center to the universe, you're on the planet that it's farthest from." This is a common lament of many young men and women, who long to be a part of something bigger than what their relatively isolated and sheltered youth has offered them. The quotation also demonstrates something more significant (and more literal), however, about the planet's place in the galaxy. Tatooine is very much on the edge of the galaxy spatially, but also politically and economically. It is on the edge of territory controlled by the Republic and later the Empire, so its location is ideal for activities of questionable legitimacy. We know that the planet is a haven for pirates, gangsters, and a mafia-like organization run by Jabba the Hutt. This is nowhere better illustrated than in the description of Mos Eisley spaceport, as well as its famous Cantina.

Overlooking Mos Eisley, Obi-Wan Kenobi states rather dramatically, "Mos Eisley spaceport. You will never find a more wretched hive of scum and villainy." He then ends with the somewhat gratuitous warning that "We must be cautious." Although the various ports along the South China Sea in the sixteenth and seventeenth centuries were not quite this dangerous, the region was nonetheless filled with piracy, naval battles, and characters who—through sheer charisma and business acumen—built up illicit commercial empires of trade. Although Lynn Pan was writing specifically about early modern trade in Asia, her words could also be applied to Tatooine: "It was difficult to know where piracy ended and contraband trading began. Indeed foreign trade was simply one vast smuggling operation."[3] Other parallels are found in the various ports of southeastern China, such as Xiamen and

Guandong, which were far removed from the center of Chinese imperial power in Beijing. At times, when the dynasty was experiencing turbulence and existential threats from corruption and foreign pressure, these ports were almost entirely outside of official control and became centers of illicit activity in an entirely extra-legal seaborne economy.[4] In the *Star Wars* galaxy, Outer Rim worlds such as Tatooine and the mining outpost of Cloud City resemble these early modern Asian ports, thriving on the fringes of established states.

Just as the Republic and the Empire exercise little real power over remote planets, so the Ming dynasty, which ruled China from 1368 to 1644, struggled to maintain control over peripheral areas such as the southeastern coastal ports. This was especially true in the sixteenth and early seventeenth centuries. To be sure, the dynasty tried its best to enforce trading bans against groups such as the Japanese, who were viewed as lawless pirates. These bans simply drove trade into the arms of merchant bandits, who used remote coastal ports as centers of international trade that spanned the entire region from the Indonesian archipelago in the west to the port cities of Japan in the east.[5] Although the Ming dynasty was occasionally able to crack down on piracy by defeating a fleet of pirate ships, this was a temporary victory. There was a seemingly endless supply of other merchants eager to take over the lucrative trading opportunities that these networks represented, just as Lando Calrissian quietly takes over the lucrative mining outpost of Cloud City two years after the Battle of Yavin.[6]

> Outer Rim worlds such as Tatooine and the mining outpost of Cloud City resemble these early modern Asian ports, thriving on the fringes of established states.

In the sixteenth century, China and Japan, the traditional powers in East Asia, were struggling for political and economic stability. Although the Republic falters due to internal threats, China's Ming dynasty entered a terminal state of decline as China suffered attacks from Mongol tribes to the northwest, pirate bands from the sea, and a large-scale Japanese invasion of Korea from 1592 to 1597: all of which were events that drained the treasury of funds and stretched military resources thin.[7] Corruption within the ruling elite, along with other factors, caused a popular rebellion that ultimately led to the fall of the Ming dynasty in 1644. During the same period, Japan was also in a chaotic state of endemic warfare known as "the Warring States Period." The country was fragmented into half a dozen large power blocks at this point, all competing violently with one another for supremacy within the archipelago. It would not be until the turn of the seventeenth century that a semblance of lasting political order would be enforced on the country by the warlord Tokugawa Ieyasu. The Tokugawa spent the next half-century trying to augment their power at the expense of the other warlords and foreigners who came to Japan in an effort to tap into the rich silver mines of the country.[8]

While power struggles flare at the center, opportunities open on the edges of a political system. We know from various clues interspersed throughout *Return of the Jedi* that Jabba the Hutt is a gangster who exploits the remote location of Tatooine for his own nefarious ends. He runs a smuggling operation, which apparently includes the smuggling of spice. Han Solo's loss of that cargo incurs Jabba's displeasure, which leads to Solo's encasement in a block of carbonite and his display, trophylike, on the wall of Jabba's palace, most likely as a warning to other would-be debtors. Also, similar to the bandits who dominated

Jabba's barge is as much a vehicle used for intimidation as it is for pleasure. (*Return of the Jedi*)

Pirates of the South China Sea employed grand ships identical to those of the authorities who tried to contain them.

China's lawless ports and the emperors they defied, Jabba boasts his own fleet, including an ostentatious pleasure barge.

Pirate bandits on the edge of China's empire took a similar approach and established their trade networks in the port cities of southeast China. They then used their extensive contacts, often with overseas Chinese kin, in the same way that Jabba uses his Hutt clan, to secure trade with places such as the Philippines, Japan, Taiwan, and the ports of Java. One such merchant was Li Dan, who was born in the city of Quanzhou in Fujian province. He ultimately immigrated to the port city of Hirado in western Japan, where he established a far-ranging merchant empire with contacts in Manila, Taiwan, and China. Li Dan is most famous for pulling a confidence trick on the head of the British East India Company, Richard Cocks, in Japan during the early seventeenth century, in which he took ever-increasing amounts of money from the poor Englishman in return for trade in China. What Mr. Cocks was unable to fathom, apparently, was that he was being duped, and that Li Dan had no real intention of allowing the English to cut into his lucrative trading operation.[9] Jabba wouldn't have shared well with others, either.

When Li Dan died in 1625, his operation was taken over by another Chinese merchant, Zheng Zhihlong.[10] In cooperation with the Dutch East India Company, Zheng engaged in unofficial trade in Taiwan and eventually in western Japan, which brought him into competition with the Dutch.[11] Although this trade by Chinese merchant bandits was tolerated in Japan, it was definitely and totally banned by the Ming dynasty. In that sense, people such as Li and Zheng were categorically considered pirates by Chinese authorities, although some might see them as entrepreneurial merchants. The story took a strange

turn when Zheng Zhihlong, after having defeated a large Ming fleet in 1628, switched over to the Ming cause and was awarded the title of admiral, in which capacity he fought for the Ming, while he continued to ply his own personal trade from Southeast Asia to Japan for some years, although he was later executed by the invading Qing dynasty. Zheng Zhilong's work as pirate and patriot continued with his son, Zheng Chenggong (Coxinga), who led the resistance against the invading Qing dynasty after 1644.

Like Zheng Chenggong, the seventeenth-century pirate and patriot, Lando Calrissian eventually takes up arms against the usurping Empire. (*The Empire Strikes Back*)

Zheng Zhihlong's career goes to show that where no particular government is able to exercise control, local actors will step in to fulfill the commercial needs of the region and to exploit commercial niches for their own often great profit. In that respect, Zheng's life most closely parallels the story of Lando Calrissian, a smuggler, a gambler, and an opportunist who runs Cloud City for a short time under the nose of the Empire until coming to Vader's notice. Lando's conversion to the Alliance cause is a wiser choice than Zheng's political experiments, as the former baron-administrator becomes one of the heroes of the Battle of Endor.

"Business Is Business": From Independent Traders to Multinationals

Zheng Zhihlong and Lando Calrissian were not the only morally flexible characters to spot business opportunities in areas that were vulnerable due to power struggles in the center: in Holland and England, seafaring merchants saw that there were rich pickings to be had in the South China Sea, as well. When Dutch and English merchants began to sail to the East Indies for trade in the 1590s, several small companies outfitted fleets to journey from Europe to Asia and bring back valuable cargoes of spice and other luxury goods that would fetch high prices on the European market.[12] These companies were essentially formed for the length of a single voyage, and when the voyage was complete, the profits were divided up among the investors, and the companies dissolved. If a voyage failed to return because the ships were lost or other problems arose, then the investors were simply out of their investment, which was often quite substantial. Another difficulty was that as European investors realized the potential profits to be made in the Asian trade, more and more companies were formed to pursue that trade. This surfeit of companies led to a glut of spices in the market and, consequently, a crash in their prices in Europe. For the Dutch, the solution was the creation of a singular body, the Dutch East India Company, whose acronym, VOC, actually means the United East India Company.[13]

The new company came about in 1602, after long and complicated negotiations among various merchants from across the Netherlands.[14]

Now, instead of several companies competing, there was only one company to control the supply, so as to manipulate the price of Asian luxury goods. Similar tactics are employed by the Commerce Guild and the Trade Federation in the run-up to the Clone Wars. Furthermore, to minimize losses and ensure the long-term survival of the company, the company mandated that investors would only buy "stock" in the company and would be obliged to keep their investment in the company for a fixed term in return for a yearly dividend.[15] A British equivalent, the British East India Company, came into being in 1600 but lagged behind the VOC for many years as a commercial and political success.

These two companies, the world's first joint stock companies, are often termed the first *multinational corporations* in world history. Both companies established a series of trading posts, called *factories*, across Asia: from India in the east to Japan in the west. They tied together capital from across Europe with the production and distribution of spices and other luxury goods in Asia. Like the Trade Federation, the VOC constructed a variety of its own ships, making up a large fleet used in pursuit of trade, diplomatic, and military goals.[16] Its British counterpart, the East India Company, rented out its ships, at least during the seventeenth century. Many of these great ships were actually built in India for company use, produced from local resources and dominating the lucrative trade route from India to the Chinese coast.

The Trade Federation's origins are similar to these companies' creation. Several commercial organizations apparently came together to create a more powerful and effective organization more capable of enforcing its trade policies and dominating trade routes.[17] Like the VOC and the British East India Company, the Trade Federation is not shy about using military force to pursue its own economic and political objectives, as it does on Alaris Prime, on Naboo, and in many systems.

The overall organization of the Trade Federation and the VOC also seem quite similar. The Trade Federation

> Like the VOC and the British East India Company, the Trade Federation is not shy about using military force to pursue its own economic and political objectives, as it does on Alaris Prime, on Naboo, and in many systems.

Trade Federation viceroy Nute Gunray has powers similar to those of the early trading company leadership. (*The Phantom Menace*)

JAN PIETERS ZOON.COEN
GOUV'.GENER'. VAN INDIA.

Jan Pieterszoon Coen felt that he answered to no one as governor general of the VOC.

is headed by a powerful viceroy, Nute Gunray. The VOC had a very similar structure, at least at the top of its hierarchy: the company was directed in the Netherlands by a group called the Herren Zeventien, or "Gentlemen Seventeen," which was responsible for setting company policy overall. In addition, the day-to-day governance of the company was undertaken by a group of councilors at a city called Batavia (present-day Jakarta) and headed by a powerful figure called the governor general. Powerful governors general, such as Jan Pieterszoon Coen, resembled Trade Federation viceroys such as Nute Gunray in that through sheer force of will, they were able to imprint their own political, economic, and military views on the company in Asia.[18]

"A Blockade of Deadly Battleships": Tactics of Isolation and Intimidation

The VOC was created not simply to carry out trade with far-flung regions of the globe, namely, South and Southeast Asia, but also as an instrument of war: the vessels that its shipyards built to carry cargo were also well armed.[19] The company's foundation during a prolonged war with Spain and, by extension, Portugal (literally named the Eighty Years' War) meant that one of the primary responsibilities of the fleet was to intercept Iberian shipping at every opportunity, both as a way to inflict damage on a hated rival and as an avenue to economic gain. In legal jargon, we would call the VOC's actions privateering, rather than outright piracy, because a state of declared war existed. Military action was important for the early VOC.[20] This violence soon became a normal and necessary part of the VOC's operations in Asia, directed not only against the Spanish and the Portuguese, but also against indigenous rulers and populations, as the Dutch sought to consolidate their position across Asia and to enforce their monopolies over the export of local spices.[21]

Just as the commercial entities of the *Star Wars* galaxy dominate small planets with their massive ships of war and commerce, the great East Indiamen, the vessels sent out from Europe to Southeast Asia, were ships of war, as much as they were of peace. These ships were exceedingly well armed, not simply for defense against would-be pirates, but for offensive action in the East Indies. The same situation can be observed in the Trade Federation: it is not simply an organization dedicated to the pursuit of filthy lucre, but is eminently willing and able to resort to warfare to further its economic aims.

Both the VOC and the Trade Federation used blockades to achieve their strategic goals. The *Star Wars* saga begins with the Trade Federation engaged in a planetary siege of Naboo in order to protest the Senate's taxation of trade routes. Similar tactics, albeit for different motives, were used by the VOC against its arch-enemies the Spanish and the Portuguese. The VOC's blockade of Goa, a port city on the west coast of India that served as the Portuguese headquarters in Asia, was an almost annual event in the seventeenth century. Although the blockades were never completely successful, they did manage to severely disrupt Portuguese trade in Asia.[22] In another instance, the Dutch East India Company attempted a massive invasion of the Portuguese settlement in Macao in southeastern China in 1622 that, because of poor planning and even poorer execution, resulted in a hasty withdrawal to the island of Taiwan. Finally, in an alliance with the English East India Company, the VOC imposed a blockade of the Spanish port of Manila in the early seventeenth century that succeeded in capturing several ships but ultimately failed to drive the Spanish out of the Philippines.[23]

The Dutch East India Company could pursue these militaristic goals because the charter that created the company in 1602 specifically allowed the company to act as a representative of the Dutch state in all

VOC warships imposed their rule on the coastal kingdom of Cochin in 1656.

Trade Federation tanks invade the peaceful world of Naboo. (*The Phantom Menace*)

foreign affairs in Asia. The company also made treaties with independent rulers in Asia, and it went to war without waiting for authorization from Europe, just as Nute Gunray orders the illegal occupation of Naboo. Some scholars have gone so far as to describe the Dutch East India Company as either a state within a state or a quasi-state.[24]

It is extremely difficult to separate politics from economics and both of those from war when dealing with the Dutch East India Company's activities in Asia, and the same could certainly be said for the Trade Federation, as it pursues its own policies through a combination of negotiation, manipulation, and, ultimately, war. The blockade of Naboo—as the Trade Federation attempts to force the Republic to accede to its wishes regarding the taxation of trade routes—is a complex dance of negotiation, given that the two Jedi sent to Naboo are supposed to negotiate on behalf of the chancellor. Like the Dutch and English trading companies, the Trade Federation practices gunboat diplomacy when it attempts to force the Queen to negotiate a treaty favorable to the Trade Federation and later uses outright force with a massive invasion to effect a fait accompli on the Senate.

The [Dutch East India Company] ... made treaties with independent rulers in Asia, and it went to war without waiting for authorization from Europe, just as Nute Gunray orders the illegal occupation of Naboo.

"The Oppression of the Trade Federation": Commercial Empires at Their Height

Just as many comparisons can be made between the Trade Federation and the Dutch East India Company, so are many similarities apparent between the Trade Federation and the English East India Company. Founded in 1600 with a charter from Queen Elizabeth I, the English company sent out its first fleet in 1601 and began to trade in several locations across Asia, although relatively soon the English East India Company focused its activities on the Indian subcontinent. In 1612, the English concluded a treaty with the emperor of the Mughal Empire, the Islamic government that ruled most of the subcontinent at the time, which allowed the English exclusive access to a port called Surat on the Indian coast in exchange for providing the emperor with European luxury goods.[25]

A seventeenth-century engraving of the Mughal emperor Aurangzeb, who fought against the East India Company. His successors were ultimately forced to accept British "protection" in 1803.

The company continued to enjoy the favor of subsequent Mughal emperors, resulting in 1712 in a treaty that allowed the English to trade in India completely free of the duties that applied to other foreign merchants. This increasing favor, combined with British victories over their European rivals during the course of the seventeenth and eighteenth centuries, made the East India Company the preeminent European presence in India. A turning point in the role of the company came as early as the 1670s, when King Charles II allowed the company to make war against its enemies and to gain control over territories in Asia. In this way, the British resembled its Dutch counterpart, in that the English East India Company also became a "state within a state," far from the European "center."

Just as the Trade Federation and the Corporate Alliance have seats in the Senate, the East India Com-

TRADE HATES
A VACUUM

When government can't regulate control over a region's trade, local actors will always step in to exploit the void.

Lando Calrissian may be a smuggler and a gambler, but he is also a savvy opportunist who runs Cloud City until Darth Vader takes notice. Whether Lando turns against the Empire because he is an idealist or because events force him into a corner with little choice is unclear.

History is full of Landos. John Hancock, one of America's founding fathers, was a savvy dealer who could be seen as either an entrepreneur or a criminal. Hancock inherited a Boston shipping business and expanded it greatly, but the British naval and customs officials saw him as a smuggler who flouted the Empire's laws. He offloaded his ships before they reached ports in order to avoid paying customs duties on a wide array of contraband—and profited handsomely. Like Lando, he ultimately joined the rebellion: in both cases, the bet paid off.

TRADE LOVES A MONOPOLY

When Dutch merchants began sailing to the East Indies for trade in the 1590s, the supply of luxury goods fluctuated too much for steady profits: there were often shortages of expensive spices, but sometimes new shipments would flood the market and drive down the prices temporarily. So the Dutch East India Company was created in 1602 to manage trade and keep prices stable, and high.

The Trade Federation had a similar origin. Several commercial organizations came together to create an alliance that could enforce its trade policies and dominate the galaxy's trade routes. And like the Dutch East India Company, as well as the rival British East India Company, the Trade Federation used military force to pursue its own economic and political objectives, as it did on the peaceful planet of Naboo.

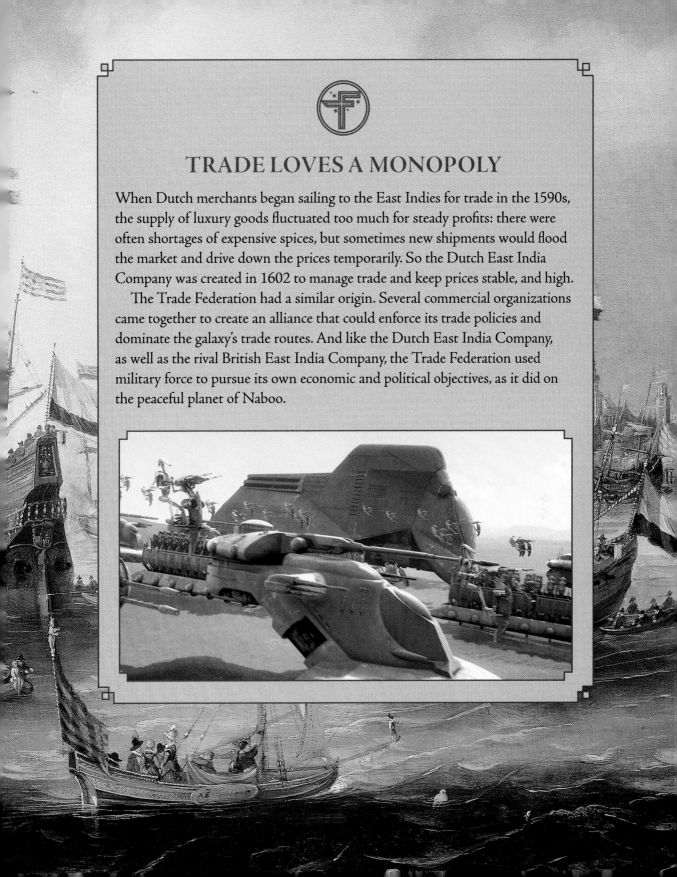

GREED IS A FICKLE ALLY

The Trade Federation and the two East India Companies met similar ends when they no longer served the needs of their imperial masters.

The Trade Federation was dissolved shortly after the formation of the Empire and its assets incorporated into Chancellor Palpatine's government. As a result of corruption and prolonged unprofitability, the Dutch East India Company was dissolved in 1800 by the Batavian Republic, a Dutch government that was a "client state" of France, and its overseas assets were reorganized as French colonies. The British company was dissolved by its government in 1874 after its brutal response to the Indian Sepoy Mutiny fatally weakened the company's image and embarrassed the empire in 1857.

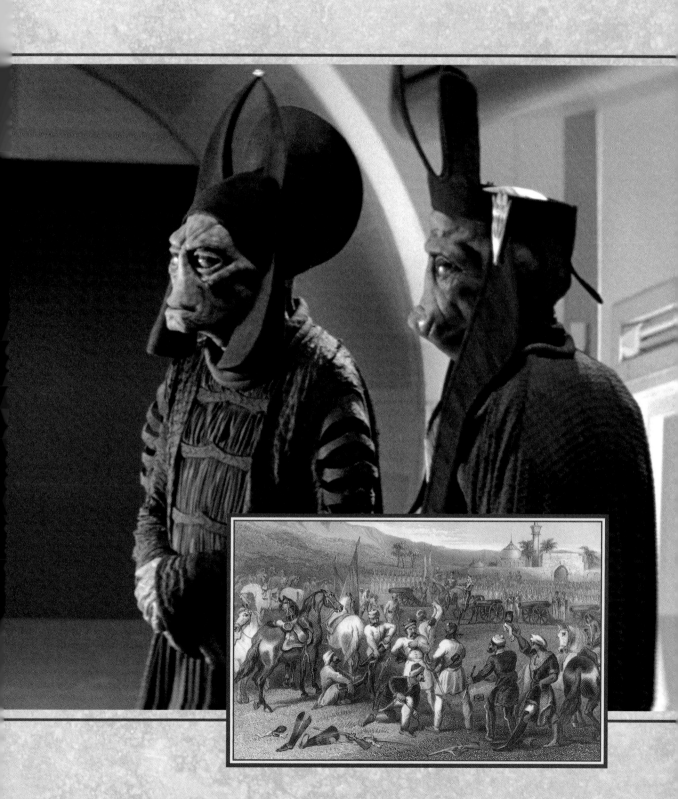

THEY DON'T DIE;
THEY JUST FADE AWAY

Coruscant was created as a symbol of the political and economic center of *Star Wars*, a seemingly eternal "great city" that serves as a universal hub of the galaxy.

In the sixteenth century, Antwerp was one of the world's great commercial centers thanks to the sugar and spice trades and its banks and stock exchange. Amsterdam replaced it in the seventeenth century when the Dutch East and West India companies made it the world's wealthiest city. A century later London stood atop the world, overseeing an empire on which the sun never set and powered by the Industrial Revolution. And in the early twentieth century, New York City became the center of world finance and trade.

THE POX

During the Clone Wars, a mad scientist named Dr. Nuvo Vindi re-created the Blue Shadow Virus, a waterborne plague that affected all species and killed anyone affected. He also created an airborne version, making its spread considerably easier.

There are many historical analogues to the Blue Shadow Virus. Bubonic plague and the mysterious "sweating sickness" that swept sixteenth-century Britain were similarly lethal. Like the Blue Shadow Virus, anthrax and glanders can be weaponized. And like polio, they could be eradicated. Smallpox offers strong historical parallel to the Blue Shadow Virus in all three respects.

About one-third of those infected with smallpox will die; the most virulent forms of the disease kill over 90 percent of those infected, and the survivors of even the less uniformly lethal varieties are often hideously scarred and disfigured for

life. Lord Amherst, for whom the Massachusetts town is named, was infamous for giving smallpox-infected blankets to Native Americans during Pontiac's Rebellion. After killing hundreds of thousands per year for centuries, it was finally declared eradicated in the wild in 1980 thanks to a two-decade global inoculation effort. It now exists only in two World Health Organization facilities. Destroying the last set of samples is hotly debated.

pany was a political force. The East India Company maintained a powerful "lobby" within the Parliament in London that allowed its wealthy
merchant directors to gain a tremendous amount of influence and to
persuade Parliament to continue to support its monopoly over trade
with India, similar to the monopoly over interstellar commerce held by
the Trade Federation. During the eighteenth century, the company
gradually moved from being a commercial organization that traded by
leave of the Mughal emperors to being a territorial power in its own
right in India, possessing its own private armies, large enough to defeat
and overthrow local Indian rulers. This process began in earnest with
the Battle of Plassey of 1757, which saw the entirety of Bengal placed
under East India Company jurisdiction, and served to essentially
destroy any vestige of cordial relations between the British and the
Mughal state. Thereafter, the British continued to gain power and territory in India until almost the entirety of the subcontinent, similar to

Queen Amidala has to
face similar challenges
from the Trade Federation.
She is as successful as
Aurangzeb in resisting
them, although in the long
run her realm succumbs to
Imperial control, as well.
(*The Phantom Menace*)

the planets under the Trade Federation's domination, came under either direct or indirect control of the company.

Commercial empire building wasn't a long-lasting endeavor. A big company became a big target or, as Qui-Gon Jinn would have understood: "There's always a bigger fish." In this case, the biggest fish was the government back home in Europe. In 1773, Parliament passed the East India Company Act, which asserted the government's supremacy over any territories that the company acquired. This led to the appointment of a governor general in territories controlled in India. Reforms continued well into the nineteenth century, until the Indian Rebellion of 1857 caused Parliament to finally strip the company of all administrative control in India.[26] The company was nationalized, and control of India passed to the Crown, although the East India Company continued to survive and supervise the tea trade with China. This "absorption" of the East India Company in India parallels nicely Palpatine's manipulation and eventual destruction of the Trade Federation leadership.

The VOC's rule over the areas it controlled became equally ironclad. Perhaps the most strategic port for controlling the bulk of interregional trade in Asia was the port city of Malacca and the narrow Straits of Malacca, through which most trade from the South China Sea to the Indian Ocean must pass. The Dutch took control of Malacca from the Portuguese in 1641. The VOC established *factories*, the early modern term for trading posts, at Batavia, Ayutthaya (near present-day Bangkok in Thailand), Taiwan, and Nagasaki in western Japan. In the west, the Dutch established factories in Ceylon (present-day Sri Lanka) and Cochin, on the southwest coast of India.[27] This network of trading hubs allowed the Dutch to both maximize their profits by shipping a variety of goods across Asia and to partly control native shipping in the region. To get a sense of the brilliant profits and power that accrued to the company through its control of these strategic points, we need only read an inscription on a clavichord created during the Dutch "Golden Age" titled "Allegory of Amsterdam as center of world trade:" "Did you think that, barred from the Spanish west, I would be lost? Wrong: Because with God's help I opened the way to Africa and India, to where exotic China stretches out, and to a part of the world that even the ancients did not know. Continue to favor us, God, and pray that they learn of Christ."[28]

Even then, Dutch control was not entirely complete: we know from contemporary journals that a fair amount of smuggling was a matter of course, as other Western nations tried to break the Dutch monopolies and local rulers eagerly played one power off against another.[29] Monopolies always invite a black market, and smugglers similar to Han Solo operated under the radar throughout the region.

> The Federation is not simply a commercial organization, but is also a major political force … similar to the two East India companies, the Federation makes fabulous profits out of doing so.

The Trade Federation follows a similar strategy for establishing economic dominance in the galaxy. We are told, for example, that the Trade Federation monopolizes many of the trade routes in the galaxy and presumably many of the hubs of production, although that must remain speculation. Similarly, we know that even though it is not a planetary power along the lines of Naboo or Alderaan, the Trade Federation nonetheless obtains a seat in the Senate by dint of the tremendous influence it wields in the galaxy. This means that the Federation is not simply a commercial organization, but is also a major political force: at least, as long as it serves the Sith's purposes. Similar to the two East India companies, the Federation makes fabulous profits out of doing so.

Clearly, the Trade Federation is not averse to entering into deals, however nefarious, to further its own interests. On several occasions, the viceroy and the Sith Lord are seen in consultation, although it is clear that the viceroy is very much in the inferior position. Nevertheless, one can imagine a certain casual disregard for morality (and transparency) as the viceroy makes his deals with the likes of the Sith—all, of course, in the service of the company. The lack of ethical concerns in corporate/government partnerships is not unique to the Trade Federation, of course—we see it today, as well—but the VOC offers one of the earliest historical examples.

The greed of the Trade Federation results in an uneasy alliance with the Dark Lords of the Sith. (*The Phantom Menace*)

Both the VOC and the British East India Company were intimately connected to their respective governments. They inserted themselves into local rivalries and commercial networks, making allies and fighting against enemies. Both eventually became the rulers of Asian territory: the subcontinent, in the case of the English, and the islands of the Indonesian archipelago, in the case of the Dutch. Just as the Trade

Federation and its Separatist allies blur the lines between war, politics, and commerce, so the East India companies used an entire arsenal of strategies, including the use of violence against the peoples they ruled, to further their aims.

Similar to the Dutch and the English East India companies, the Trade Federation routinely concludes agreements with various rulers, and of course, we know very well that in the first installments of the *Star Wars* saga, the Trade Federation is in league with a Sith Lord, for its own profit and advantage. We can see in the Trade Federation the same blurred lines between commercial, political, and military functions.

The Trade Federation's power doesn't lie in formal control of planets or systems, so much as in its monopoly on trade-route information and its heavy-handed use of political clout. Although the Trade Federation will stop at almost nothing to ensure its own success, it seems to resort to outright invasion and conquest only to obtain limited goals. This is clearly demonstrated in the case of Naboo, which the Trade Federation invades in order to remove a stubborn obstacle to its untaxed monopoly of trade routes in the Senate, although the omniscient viewer knows, of course, that the Trade Federation is being manipulated the entire time by the Sith. Aside from these ulterior designs of the dark side, however, it appears that both the Trade Federation and the Dutch East India Company pursued not a blanket policy of conquest, but rather the establishment of a commercial empire consisting of control over strategic trade hubs and corridors of commerce.

One of the signal symptoms of a decaying state is the rise of corruption, both at the top, among the political and economic elites, and throughout the whole structure, to the point where the state exists more or less for the personal and corporate profit of those who are in a position to exploit the resources at hand. This dismal state of affairs describes perfectly the systemic rot that characterizes the last years of the Republic and was endemic in the Dutch East India Company from the eighteenth century onward. In the case of the company, this pervasive corruption was evident not only in the Netherlands, but in the various offices throughout Asia.

A tight-knit group of top civil servants in Amsterdam, many of whom were related in a network of kinship, distributed the most important positions in the VOC among themselves and to their clients, who would then proceed to amass large personal fortunes.[30] The similarity between this situation and Palpatine's calculated rise to power in the Republic is staggering.

In Asia, accusations of corruption usually took a different form, that of company servants who spent their limited time in Asia amassing enormous personal fortunes at the expense of the company. Donald Keene painted a grim picture of VOC merchants as men whose "sole purpose was to make money, and to this end they devoted themselves with unbounded energy and complete ruthlessness. Even when measured by the eighteenth century yardstick of economic exploitation, the activities of the Dutch company in the Indies cannot fail to horrify us."[31]

This culture of corruption was certainly not limited to the Dutch, but these cases of corruption stand out in stark contrast to that earlier era of general prosperity. Just as the leaders of the Trade Federation and the Corporate Alliance put their interests above their companies' in the rise up to the Clone Wars, so did the officers of the East India Companies in their last centuries of operation and the international banking corporations of the twenty-first century.

"Make Them Suffer": Cruelty and Greed under the Rule of Commercial Monopolies

The ultimate goal of the Trade Federation and similar corporate entities in league with the Separatists, as with the Dutch and English East India companies, was monopoly: of both trade routes and products. We learn from *The Phantom Menace* that the Trade Federation fiercely protects the secret hyperspace trade routes, holding a sizable monopoly on interstellar trade. A similar policy was actively pursued by the Dutch East India Company in its dealings—particularly with smaller islands that produced the various spices that were so valuable on the European market.

In the blockade of Naboo, the Trade Federation is clearly trying to isolate the planet and its troublesome, if fabulously dressed, Queen from contact with the outside world. This is perhaps all the more effective a strategy because Naboo is a rather distant planet, far from the corridors of power and influence. Similarly, the natives of Naboo, certainly in the case of the Gungans, are perceived to be rather primitive in the face of superior technology. In the end, of course, that technology is not quite enough to secure a decisive victory for the Trade Federation. Combined with the fact that the Trade Federation is protesting the taxation of trade routes by the Senate—routes over which presumably the Trade Federation holds at least a partial monopoly—this reveals strong similarities to both the English and the Dutch East India companies.

The VOC pursued ruthless policies in what is today Indonesia, aimed at controlling the export of spices to the outside world, as well as the price of spices on the market.[32] One ingenious, if not inhumane, way of concentrating spice production in company hands was to eliminate any other type of agriculture—particularly, food crops—from the small Spice Islands, except for the production of products such as cloves, nutmeg, and mace. This allowed the VOC to manipulate the islanders in two ways: first, it maximized spice production, and second, it gave the VOC leverage in terms of providing the essentials of survival. The islanders were wholly at the mercy of the VOC for the provision of basic foodstuffs and clothing, and if they rose up against company rule, they could simply be starved. It is no wonder, then, that various native strongmen in the Spice Islands sought to play the Dutch off against their other European enemies, in order to get out from under the thumb of the VOC.

The English also used similar tactics of exclusion when it came to their increasingly monopolistic trade in India. They used the threat of violence and other coercive measures to prevent local rulers from coordinated action, the result being that by the eighteenth century, the British were able to effectively "divide and conquer" the subcontinent. Sometimes their schemes backfired, however, such as with the recruitment of local soldiers, who became known as *sepoys*. In 1857, the sepoys staged the rebellion that ended company rule in

Indian generals in the Indian Rebellion of 1857 deployed elephants and countless troops seeking to overthrow the British East India Company.

India, showing that local military forces, such as the Gungans, should never be underestimated.

The Trade Federation's invasion of Naboo in order to further its economic goals also resembles the British East India Company's attacks on various port cities of China in the Opium Wars of the 1840s and the 1850s. The East India Company marshaled the power of the Royal Navy to destroy the defenses of the city of Canton and to sail up the Yangtze River toward Nanjing, forcing the Chinese government to sign the first of what would come to be known as the "unequal treaties," which included the payment of reparations, the abolishment of the Chinese system of trade that the English saw as an impediment to their profits, and the surrender of the island of Hong Kong to the British. This wanton act of destruction and economic/military dominance was

Trying to save their home world, the Gungan Army utilizes large beasts to fight against the Trade Federation's battle droids. (*The Phantom Menace*)

The Trade Federation's invasion of Naboo in order to further its economic goals also resembles the British East India Company's attacks on various port cities of China in the Opium Wars of the 1840s and the 1850s.

simply the first in a long line of foreign engagements with China that would result, by the early years of the twentieth century, in Chinese sovereignty being severely compromised and the Qing dynasty becoming essentially a pale shadow of its former grandeur. The parallel is not exact, of course, because in the films, the Trade Federation is defeated in the invasion of Naboo, whereas the East India Company was eminently and decisively victorious over the forces of the Chinese. Yet in terms of economic policy and a ruthless pursuit of profit at the expense of any tenuous notions of justice, the parallel can be instructive: in each case, corporate barons did not hesitate to use military force to protect their monopolies and profits.

"Lord Sidious Promised Us Peace": The End of Commercial Empires

The Trade Federation, as depicted in the *Star Wars* galaxy, resembles both the Dutch and the British East India companies in their organization, in their economic and military policies, and, ultimately, in their respective demises. All three organizations, for example, came about out from a union of disparate commercial groups seeking to combine their aggregate might into a "super-company" better able to exploit trade (and natives along the way). All of them, though primarily commercial, also resorted to arms quite readily to obtain their goals. All three organizations were able, through the control of strategic hubs and trade routes, to establish monopolies on trade that resulted, at least for a while, in increased profits and greater regional power and influence. As Qui-Gon Jinn noted in *The Phantom Menace*, "greed can be a powerful ally." Yet greed could also lead to disaster. As with the Dutch and British

East India companies' overambitious expansion, the Trade Federation's greed leads to ruin as Viceroy Gunray and the Federation's droid army become unknowing pawns in Palpatine's rise to imperial power.

A final parallel between the Trade Federation and the two East India companies can be found in the manner in which they met their ends. The Trade Federation and the other economic bodies that drive so much of the Separatist cause are dissolved shortly after the formation of the Empire, and their assets are incorporated into the new government. Similarly, as a result of corruption and prolonged unprofitability, the Dutch East India Company was dissolved in 1800 by the Batavian Republic, a Dutch government that was a "client state" of France, and the VOC's overseas assets were then reorganized as colonies by the French. The British East India Company was dissolved by the British imperial government in 1874, after the large-scale native uprising in India had fatally weakened the company's image and authority in Britain. Similar to the Trade Federation, the British East India Company was discarded once it no longer seemed useful to the imperial government. All of these commercial organizations thus met their end with the drastic reorganization of the political scene after long and eventful histories, some aspects of which were clearly violent or morally questionable.

Often, when we think about Western imperialism in Asia, our minds jump to images of the British Raj in South Asia or perhaps French Indochina or even the Dutch East Indies. That is to say, we immediately tend to think of conquest on a massive scale or even "spheres of influence," as in nineteenth-century China. This picture, however, is accurate only after the mid-nineteenth century.

Western involvement in Asian cultures during the period when the great trade companies were emerging was very different and much more limited.[33] Western powers, led by Portugal and Spain and soon followed by the Dutch and the English, were able to establish only relatively small footholds in various strategic ports along the coastlines of South and Southeast Asia; their trading companies were the means by which they accomplished this. What measure of real control the Western powers did hold in Asia was determined not by great territorial possessions, but rather by occupying strategic centers of commerce, as well as port cities that happened to straddle commercially strategic waterways. In the same way, the Trade Federation also increases its economic and political power not by large-scale territorial conquest,

Even after the VOC was dissolved, its effects lingered, as evidenced by this depiction of Dutch ships and a Dutch family in nineteenth-century Yokohama.

but rather by monopolizing the strategic trade routes that criss-cross the galaxy.

This essay has pointed out the parallels between the *Star Wars* galaxy and the chaotic and dramatic commercial competition in the South China Sea region and the Indian subcontinent that began in the sixteenth century. Between the dramatic decline of the Chinese Ming dynasty and the chaotic, war-torn situation in the Japanese archipelago, there arose a group of pirates/entrepreneurs who took advantage of the chaos to carve out for themselves exceedingly lucrative networks of trade, which were later incorporated into the first of the great East India companies. This resembles the state of affairs described on remote planets such as Tatooine or Cloud City over Bespin, where the power of the center does not hold sway, gangsters and smugglers are free to operate with relative impunity, and even a giant, charismatic, slug-shaped smuggler can, with the right attitude and the right family background (the Hutts, in this case), get ahead in a cutthroat world of opportunity. In all of these settings, political instability and warfare could make for good business: opportunities that lured in groups of merchants from far away, who formed their own networks.

Just as the Trade Federation is an entity that blurs the lines between commerce, politics, and war, the British and Dutch East India companies were willing and able to employ a number of tactics to increase their power and profits in Asia. They gained enormous political influence "back home," while combining commercial strategies with questionable, often violent, tactics to gain a foothold in the "Outer Rim," manipulating local rulers and populaces—or using their own armies or armed ships—in a way that was advantageous to the company. Both companies, much as the Trade Federation did, began to resemble not so much a commercial enterprise but rather another territorial player in the unfolding history of South and Southeast Asia, becoming sovereign in the areas they controlled. In the long run, however, the metropolitan powers in the "center" ultimately absorbed the merchant states within a state: in all three cases, they had outlived their usefulness.

"I saw a city in the clouds."
—Luke Skywalker,
The Empire Strikes Back

11

Coruscant, the Great Cities of Earth, and Beyond

Katrina Gulliver

Cities have an important role in human society. They house our centers of education and government, become points of contact for diverse populations, and foster new cultural development. As one scholar wrote, "The city has thus historically been the melting-pot of races, peoples, and cultures, and a most favorable breeding-ground of new biological and cultural hybrids."[1] Cities generate their own culture, and their development in history has fueled advances in technology, education, and communication.

In the galaxy of *Star Wars*, we see a variety of townscapes, from Otoh Gunga, the luminous underwater city of the Gungans, to the elegance of Theed; from the low adobe houses of Mos Eisley, to the industrial Cloud City and the glittering diversity of Coruscant. Such bright urban centers have long been a lure for people from rural areas, especially young people looking to broaden their horizons—such as Luke Skywalker on Tatooine, wanting to leave and attend the Academy. In *A New Hope* he even says, "If there's a bright center to the universe, you're on the planet it's farthest from."

Although cities have lured people from the country who want to pursue opportunities, tales of urban danger for the unwitting rural visitor have also been common in cultural history. Even the earliest recorded cities had a tinge of danger, or sin, as Roman historian Tacitus (AD 56–AD 117) commented in his *Annals*: "All thing atrocious and shameless flock from all parts to Rome."[2]

> Bright urban centers have long been a lure for people from rural areas, especially young people looking to broaden their horizons—such as Luke Skywalker on Tatooine.

Part of a city's attraction is the freedom and range of options it offers. As urban theorist Jane Jacobs wrote, "The point of cities is multiplicity of choice."[3] Urban life can offer conveniences and access to services not available elsewhere. Cities can allow for freedom in other ways, in anonymity, as when Anakin Skywalker and Padmé Amidala hide their marriage while living in Coruscant. They are hiding in the crowd, safe in the knowledge that in a big city their relationship will not be noticed.

This is demonstrated on a smaller scale by Padmé's security practices in *The Phantom Menace*. Her makeup serves as a way to conceal her identity: she and her decoys all look similar, interchangeable. This allows her to accompany Qui-Gon Jinn and Obi-Wan Kenobi unrecognized, as at least one of them does not know what she looks like without the elaborate hairstyles and cosmetics. Her makeup and style of dress also mark her cultural affiliation. We later see her successor as Queen of Naboo wearing a similar costume. Indeed, she also shows how cities lead fashion. Queen Amidala and later her daughter, Princess Leia, demonstrate the fashions of elite women in their cities. Padmé's style of makeup and costume also bring to mind the geisha, whose elaborate costuming helped create the mystique geishas held in traditional Japanese society.

Going to Town

In medieval Europe, the biggest towns were often walled, built to be defensible against enemy attack. They would also be trading points, to which farmers and craftsmen would travel seasonally to sell their wares and buy their supplies. The calendar of such events followed the harvest year, and traveling to town could be a big event for a medieval peasant, just as traveling to Mos Eisley is an exciting prospect for young Luke. Major trading towns were often at the junctions of rivers or on coastal ports, allowing goods to be brought in and out. These trading customs were the forerunners of the modern financial network, when cities became centers of banking, as well as of commerce.

The medieval European custom of the "freedom of the city" also meant that residence in the city for a year and one day could make a man free, reflected in the German saying *Stadtluft macht frei*: "city air makes one free." At a time when peasants lived as vassals to landowners, this path to freedom was tempting and placed cities in a particular place in the cultural imagination. For slaves such as Anakin and Shmi Skywalker, such policies would have been welcome, but their frontier world's laws offer no such hope.

Cities were often sites of power, both secular and religious. They held the great palaces of kings and the most important religious buildings, which were designed to inspire awe in any who looked on them. They were also centers of knowledge and education. As the capital of the Republic, Coruscant holds a diverse population and offers services,

The Jedi Library on Coruscant. The Jedi Temple also has the scholastic role of the ancient universities, drawing its pupils from across the galaxy. (*Attack of the Clones*)

Radcliffe Camera, part of Oxford University's Bodleian Library.

entertainment, and business of all kinds. This includes education, just as medieval cities provided. The first universities in Europe were established in Bologna (1088), Paris (c. 1150), and Oxford (1167). These cities became cultural magnets in themselves, attracting not only scholars but all attendant support trades: tailors, bookbinders, vellum stretchers, and, later, paper makers and stationers. The kind of archive that we see in the Jedi Temple in Coruscant is like the great libraries of the ancient universities.

With the coming of the Renaissance, ideas of urban design changed. Whereas cities before this point had developed organically, with no central planning, Renaissance thinkers idealized their views of the classical city and ideas of symmetry and balance in urban design. Buildings were made symmetrical; grand plazas were built for public gatherings.

The beautiful Renaissance cities have long been part of the imagination of life in other parts of space in science fiction. Giovanni Schiaparelli and Percival Lowell, astronomers in the late nineteenth century, became known for their theories about the existence of canals on Mars—Lowell, in particular, felt this was evidence of intelligent life on the planet. His books—*Mars* (1895), *Mars and Its Canals* (1906), and *Mars as the Abode of Life* (1908)—helped spark the imaginations of a generation of science-fiction writers who envisioned life on the red planet. Illustrations were drawn of their fantasized Martian towns. Their influence can be seen in the way the creator of *Star Wars* conceived of his canal city, Theed, on Naboo.

Long before London rose to prominence, before Columbus headed for the Americas (thinking he was going to Asia), Venice was the most fabulous and exciting city in Europe, and it remains our closest parallel to Theed. Elegant palazzos demonstrated the wealth and taste of the city's residents. The canals were an engineering feat, providing transport. They shaped the expanding city to human needs, in keeping with a neoclassical aesthetic.

Theed's elegant architecture is reminiscent of Renaissance Italian cities. (*The Phantom Menace*)

Renaissance Venice, as depicted by Bellini.

Venice was also where some of our modern financial and banking concepts emerged, including share investment—partly as a tool for private merchants to help fund long sea voyages. Where previously someone might invest in a ship—and lose everything if that ship were lost—the notion of shares meant instead that it was possible to invest in a percentage of a fleet, rather than in one particular vessel. Whichever of the ships returned safely, the investors could get a return on their investment. This innovation helped spread risk and encouraged people to back such trading expeditions, which, in turn, contributed to Venice's wealth and economic importance.

Reaching for the Sky: Cities Go High

Cities were centers of production in the Industrial Revolution, and the introduction of factories led to massive urbanization during the nineteenth and early twentieth centuries, with people seeking work in the fast-growing towns. At the same time, technology was making agriculture less labor-intensive, so many rural agricultural laborers became urban factory workers.

The first skyscrapers began to appear in the last quarter of the nineteenth century, although they were not tall by today's standards: for instance, the Home Insurance Building, built in Chicago in 1885, was only ten stories high. Since then, such buildings have appeared all over the world, as badges of urban modernity.

The forerunners of skyscrapers were the multistory buildings that existed even in Roman cities, built from brick, stone, and cement. Yet technology limited how high masonry buildings could go. Walls had to be ever thicker to support the weight of the higher stories. The development of steel-frame construction allowed buildings to go higher than before, and the elevator made such buildings usable. Henry Bessemer introduced the Bessemer Process for steel production in 1858. This enabled the inexpensive production of steel in large quantities, and revolutionized the construction industry, shipbuilding, and the railways. Similar technological innovations must have enabled residents of the *Star Wars* galaxy to live in bubbles underwater in Otoh Gunga or among the clouds of Bespin.

The steel-frame building opened a way for architects to create upward, lifting the visual spectacle of the city toward the sky. The notion of the urban skyline contained both high-rise buildings to look at and such vantage points to look from. Before the invention of the elevator, the highest floors of a building were the least desirable and were associated with servants' quarters. The modern skyscraper with elevators changed this, with the appearance of the penthouse apartment as the ideal of urban luxury. The convenient downtown location and the view became the selling point for such homes, as we see in the view from Padmé Amidala's apartment in Coruscant. Besides offering a stunning view of vistas such as the Coruscant skyline, skyscrapers also projected modernity, ambition, and sophistication.

Skyscrapers increased both housing density and, by creating new workplaces in high-rise offices, drove demands for public transportation.

The view from
Padmé's apartment
on Coruscant.
(*Revenge of the Sith*)

These buildings radically changed a city's appearance and the ways people lived. Offices created different modes of working in cities and led to the rise of the commuter lifestyle. Factory workers had tended to live close to the factories—often in purpose-built housing owned by their employer or in tenements nearby, as with the workers on Cloud City. We have yet to reach the technology that allowed Cloud City to be built, miles above the planet's surface, as floating layers of urban cityscape housing five million people.

The growth in technology also helped create ideas of urban planning and ideal living arrangements: as one urban historian

notes, in the nineteenth century "enlightened planners wanted the city in its very design to function like a healthy body, freely flowing as well as possessed of clean skin."[4] This included the idea that cities should have circulation, as a human body does: circulation of vehicular traffic, railways, and subway systems, with green spaces to serve as the "lungs" for the urban center.

Besides offering a stunning view of vistas such as the Coruscant skyline, skyscrapers also projected modernity, ambition, and sophistication.

The traffic had taken different forms: initially horse-drawn, with buses and then streetcars that ran along tracks laid on the road. Later, the streetcars were electrified: the cars were powered by electrical wires strung above the roadway. Urban planners looked above (elevated railways), and below (subways), as they tried to find ways to move the increasing numbers of commuters through the city. These needs of growing urban populations produced some of the greatest feats of human engineering, such as the London underground system.

Cloud City resembles many crowded, modern commercial cities. (*The Empire Strikes Back*)

New York City began construction of its subway system in 1900.

The first underground railway was constructed in London in 1863. Other cities soon followed, adding underground systems that increased the volume of human traffic through the city. Subways changed the way of moving through the city by putting passengers in tunnels: they no longer saw the streetscapes they were traveling through. In London, the underground system later saved the lives of thousands of Londoners, who were able to use the underground stations as bomb shelters during the air raids of World War II.

City life not only changed how people lived and traveled, it has made us behave differently. Note how German sociologist Georg Simmel described the particular psychological effects of living in a city:

> With each crossing of the street, with the tempo and multiplicity of economic, occupational and social life, the city sets up a deep contrast with small town and rural life with reference to the sensory foundations of psychic life. The metropolis exacts from man as a discriminating creature a different amount of consciousness than does rural life. Here the rhythm of life and sensory mental imagery flows more slowly, more habitually, and more evenly.[5]

Urban life also created new figures, for instance, the private or undercover detective: such policing was possible only once towns were large enough for anonymity in crowds. The idea of being "undercover" depended on cities with large populations and the need for such detectives (whether private eyes or police plain-clothes detectives) to solve crimes, for which the pool of suspects could be in the thousands. It is the plain-clothes detective who is able to move through the juxtaposed spaces of the urban site. Indeed, in *Attack of the Clones* Anakin Skywalker and Obi-Wan Kenobi become, in a sense, private detectives as they pursue the would-be assassin of Padmé Amidala. Obi-Wan enters a bar and orders a drink, very much as that quintessential urban detective Philip Marlowe would do. The detective has to be able to operate at all levels of society and relate to a range of people. The Jedi's mind skills offer a shortcut to this talent, which otherwise depends on a particular ability to relate and build a rapport. In another scene in *Attack of the Clones*, Obi-Wan goes to meet a friend in a diner, in a setup that could have been in any 1930s hardboiled detective movie. The robot waitress uses old slang such as "Java juice" for coffee, part of a diner vocabulary that evolved in mid-twentieth-century America.

Diners specialized in being open long hours (often twenty-four hours), providing for the needs of shift-workers but also, in cities, for nightclub partiers, who wanted to get breakfast or a snack in the early hours. Occasionally, disused railway dining cars were turned into cafes, often near a railway station. This created a style of a long narrow room, with a counter and stools, much like that on a railway dining car. So popular was this aesthetic that prefabricated diners were built to resemble such carriages. Their streamlined shape, often accented with chrome, became an icon of the American landscape from the 1930s onward. This is the design of the diner in *Attack of the Clones*, suggesting a similar urbanizing process there, too.

Star Wars also shows us the layers of economic development that follow the rise of urban industrialization. The Jawas on Tatooine sell discarded or stolen droids, as they sell C-3PO and R2-D2 to Owen

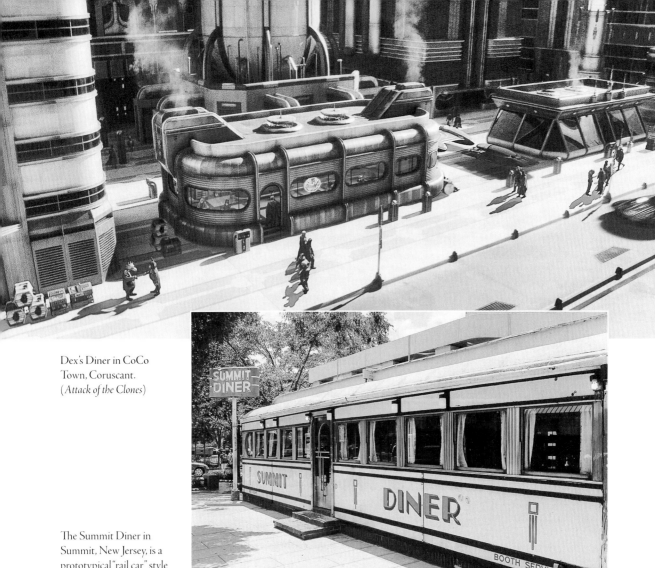

Dex's Diner in CoCo Town, Coruscant. (*Attack of the Clones*)

The Summit Diner in Summit, New Jersey, is a prototypical "rail car" style diner built in 1938.

Lars—and as in our world used cars, motorcycles, and other appliances are sold by entrepreneurial middle-men. We can compare them to the rag-pickers of nineteenth-century European cities and some of the slum dwellers of India today. Living on the fringes of cities, they collect discarded items to repair or resell. This kind of secondary economy has always sprung up around cities, especially in the Industrial Age, as the volume of manufactured goods means there are more things to be discarded or recycled.

London and Coruscant: Cities at the Center of It All

A long time ago in a galaxy not so far away, the first envoys of the East India Company were sent by Elizabeth I in 1601. Their goal was to make contact with the King of Aceh, to form a trading relationship for spices that were of high value in Europe. Companies such as this were given charters to trade and colonize certain parts of the world. As Michael Laver discusses in chapter 10 of this book, the East India Company, similar to the Trade Federation in *Star Wars*, had troops and ships, to defend (and enforce) their trade routes. As Venice had introduced share investment, the joint-stock company became key to British colonial expansion, with the East India Company, the Virginia Company, the Hudson's Bay Company (and others) allowing private investors to drive colonial expansion.

As trade grew, the need to improve geographical knowledge grew, too. The British government and its trading companies relied on accurate maps to delineate colonial territory, and ships needed precise charts to avoid heading off course. This resulted in a contest for a means of establishing longitude (allowing ships' navigators to accurately establish their location). Inability to establish longitude while at sea led to maritime disasters, as navigators miscalculated their locations and hit rocky shores or reefs. Clockmakers, astronomers, and mathematicians attempted to solve the problem. As long as they knew the time in one place (for instance, the home port), sailors could establish longitude by figuring the solar time where they were and calculating the time difference from home. The problem they faced was that clocks were unreliable on sea voyages. Given the importance of naval power and merchant shipping to London, it was there that this problem was solved.

The successful establishment of international longitudinal measures in 1884 placed London—specifically, the Royal Observatory at Greenwich—at the center of the world, longitudinally. The Prime

Meridian (or zero degrees west or east) is the reason we still observe Greenwich Mean Time, because all time zones are counted outward from London. Every time we set our watches to a new time zone, we are in a way acknowledging London's historic legacy and dominant position in the global economy of the eighteenth century. For the inhabitants of the galaxy in *Star Wars*, Coruscant fulfills this role, with its coordinates of 0,0,0. In both cases, the use of these coordinates reflects the fact that both London and Coruscant were the political and economic centers of their respective worlds at the time the systems were set up.

That Coruscant long endures at the center of the *Star Wars* galaxy stands in sharp contrast to our history. Great cities rose and fell over the centuries. As Fernand Braudel explained,

> Dominant cities did *not* dominate forever; they replaced each other. . . . When Amsterdam replaced Antwerp, when London took over from Amsterdam, or when in about 1929, New York overtook London, it always meant a massive historical shift of forces, revealing the precariousness of the previous equilibrium and the strengths of the one replacing it. The whole circle of the world-economy was affected by such changes and the repercussions were never exclusively economic.[6]

Like Coruscant, London from the sixteenth century onward was a center of commerce, if not always the greatest center for world commerce that it eventually became, which meant that ships carrying all kinds of goods would be at the docks at any given time. To many residents and visitors, the city itself was a wonder. William Dunbar wrote, "London, thou art the flour [flower] of cities all!"[7] By the time that London became the capital of the largest empire ever known, the city boasted residents hailing from all over the world. In the eighteenth century, traveling to London from the colonies was a primary ambition of those who wished to be worldly and educated (and who had the money to do so). It offered high life, low life, and all manner of cultural diversions.

London's financial services were also sufficiently developed—and trusted—that when France sold Louisiana to the United States in 1803, it was not a Paris or Philadelphia institution, but Barings Bank in London that handled the financial transaction. Even Napoleon and Thomas Jefferson respected London as the financial center of the world.

James Boswell, in his *Life of Johnson*, famously wrote, "When a man is tired of London, he is tired of life."[8] In the nineteenth century, Benjamin Disraeli described it as a "modern Babylon," and Ralph Waldo Emerson said, "London is the epitome of our times, and the Rome of to-day."[9] London could be all of these things, offering the best and the worst of life, as one historian has described it: "the modern city was increasingly to be seen as simultaneously Babylon *and* Jerusalem: a city of license (and potential disorder) was also a city of individual liberty; a city of toil was also a city of opportunity for self-betterment; one person's disorganisation . . . was another person's community."[10]

> London and Coruscant were the political and economic centers of their respective worlds.

Meanwhile, the image of the city was not aided by the popular perception of it as full of crime and danger. "Commonplace nineteenth-century popular imagery of the city states simultaneously that the city's streets are paved with gold and that the city is a snare and destroyer of youth."[11] Even Jane Austen admitted, "We do not look in our great cities for our best morality."[12] She was referring not only to urban life, but to political corruption, as we also see in the Galactic Senate on Coruscant.

Along with moral risk, a concern in such crowded cities historically was disease: large numbers of people in close proximity could turn an outbreak into an epidemic. The Black Death, for instance, ripped through the cities of medieval and Renaissance Europe. Potentially even more lethal is the Blue Shadow Virus, recreated as an airborne contagion by Dr. Nuvo Vindi in *The Clone Wars*. During the nineteenth century, major cities were still struck with diseases such as cholera and yellow fever. Such instances spurred scientific research into the causes and prevention of such diseases, as well as urban populations providing (unwittingly) perfect subject populations for studying how outbreaks had occurred, thus helping doctors trace the source.

New York: The Empire City

In what is known as the Gilded Age, the last quarter of the nineteenth century, New York began to overtake London as the world's cultural capital, and it is seen even now as the world's most important city. The center of gravity in the financial world began to shift from London to New York around this time, too, with the rise of firms such as J.P. Morgan making Wall Street the world's financial heart. This process was accelerated by World War I and was largely complete by the 1920s. This importance meant that the Wall Street crash of 1929 triggered a global economic downturn. Home of the United Nations Headquarters since 1952, New York is perhaps the most similar to Coruscant (home of the Galactic Senate) of our contemporary cities. Although obviously not a planet city, Manhattan is an island city, and indeed Manhattan is for many of us the quintessential "urban" space.

With its neon and beautiful buildings, asked Ezra Pound, is New York "the most beautiful city in the world? It is not far from it. No urban night is like the night there. . . . Squares after squares of flame, set up and cut into the aether. Here is our poetry, for we have pulled down the stars to our will."[13] The city itself was a great human achievement, an image of optimism for a capitalist age. Thomas Wolfe wrote that "New York blazes like a magnificent jewel in its fit setting of sea, and earth, and stars."[14]

Cities have always been centers of creativity and innovation, the opportunity to meet the like-minded. Artists and musicians have honed their crafts, often as entertainers for the diverse crowds in such cities. The musicians in the Mos Eisley Cantina are like so many who

The victory parade on Naboo. (*The Phantom Menace*)

developed different rhythms and new sounds while playing in the speakeasies of the Prohibition era.

Urban space has offered audiences and community for grand processions and display, as seen in *The Phantom Menace*, which shows a parade following the battle victory on Naboo. Although parades have long existed, the use of ticker tape (essentially, a waste product of modern communication technology) as a kind of confetti created a new kind of visual celebration medium. The corridors of tall buildings in Manhattan particularly lend themselves to this, with people able to throw tape and confetti from the windows of high floors. This allows for a level of group participation that would not be present in a parade that was simply watched, and it is also a tactile experience for those in the parade, being "showered" with the recognition of the city's residents and workers. The first ticker-tape parade was in fact spontaneous, after the opening of the Statue of Liberty in 1889, so there was no person or group being hailed, so much as a general group party atmosphere.

The musicians in the Mos Eisley Cantina are like so many who developed different rhythms and new sounds while playing in the speakeasies of the Prohibition era.

The celebration on Coruscant after the fall of the Empire. (*Return of the Jedi*)

A 1926 ticker-tape parade in New York City.

This is shown in the images of celebrating cities at the end of *Return of the Jedi*. In New York, ticker-tape parades quickly caught on, however, as a custom and were organized during the next century for major figures who were visiting the city. Parades and public events can also mark solemn occasions, as at the end of *Revenge of the Sith*, when Padmé Amidala's funeral is shown as a grand public event, attended by throngs of mourners. Her hearse is led through the city to be seen by all of the residents whom she represented in the Senate.

Yet the gilded urban surface often concealed an underbelly of crime or danger. Cities, or their dock areas, were often regarded as seedy or disreputable. Mos Eisley is the lawless space that many port cities have been, historically. Qui-Gon describes spaceports as "havens for those who don't wish to be found" in *The Phantom Menace*. Of Mos Eisley, Obi-Wan (who by that stage is a long-term resident of Tatooine) says, "You will never find a more wretched hive of scum and villainy," in *Star Wars: A New Hope*.

Bars in such areas were regarded with particular suspicion. These were often places where men would meet, and respectable women would not go near, as well as having a reputation as havens for criminals and social deviants. In port cities, they could be places to exchange information: sailors recently arrived would have the most up-to-date news of the ports they had come from. Port taverns were places to trade goods, make deals, and participate in gambling and other entertainment. We see this in *A New Hope*, where Obi-Wan knows that the Cantina will be the place to find someone who is willing to provide transport and who will not ask too many questions.

In the twentieth century, private transportation and the introduction of the automobile as an affordable commodity brought a new measure of freedom for many people, and the private vehicle is clearly playing the same role in *Star Wars*. We see on Coruscant traffic flowing at multiple levels in *Attack of the Clones*, obviously the result of particularly detailed planning of the population's needs.

The crowded city of Coruscant, a whole planet for a city, is much bigger than any of the mega cities we have on Earth today. The

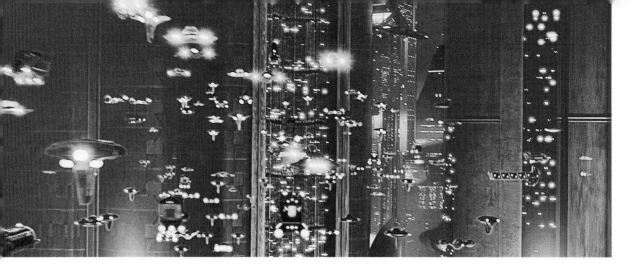

Airspeeder traffic lanes
on Coruscant.
(*Attack of the Clones*)

challenges faced, in terms of environmental pollution and public health, have obviously been resolved on Coruscant. Its traffic of airspeeders and taxis is much like the World of Tomorrow envisaged at the World's Fair in the 1950s. It demonstrates the planning of skyscrapers and dense urban populations.

The City of Tomorrow

Cities with aerial transport to the downtown area would be very different from cities today. In the early days of aviation, such personal air transport was envisaged. Although we now have large-scale long-distance aviation, the trend has been toward building airports farther out of downtown metro areas, making it less convenient than early planners had imagined. Indeed, original plans for the Empire State Building envisaged a docking site for zeppelins at the top.[15] Many images of the urban future anticipated downtown landing spots and personal aircraft, such as this one from science-fiction illustrator Frank Paul. The closest thing to the flying car in general use remains the helicopter, which is both impractical and uneconomic for most people. Rather, as cities have grown, we have seen a need for more public transport.

What can the worlds of *Star Wars* teach us about our own relationship with cities? It is apt that we should look to film to learn about cities. It was the medium of cinema in the early part of the twentieth century that first gave people a chance to see cities in different parts of the world, in movies and newsreels. Although photos were published in books and newspapers, the whirl of the urban experience is captured more fully on film. Indeed, some of the earliest footage still in existence shows us street scenes: horse-drawn carriages, bicycles, and pedestrians flickering past the lens.

One of the greatest urban theorists of the twentieth century, Lewis Mumford, wrote that cities themselves transcended reality:

> This metropolitan world, then, is a world where flesh and blood is less real than paper and ink and celluloid. It is a world where the great masses of people, unable to have direct contact with more satisfying means of living, take life vicariously, as readers, spectators, passive observers: a world where people watch shadow-heroes and heroines in order to forget their own clumsiness or coldness in love, where they behold brutal men crushing out life in a strike riot, a wrestling ring or a military assault, while they lack the nerve even to resist the petty tyranny of their immediate boss: where they hysterically cheer the flag of the political state, and in their neighbourhood, their trades union, their church, fail to perform the most elementary duties of citizenship.[16]

Flying cars and skyscrapers inhabit this 1942 vision of a futuristic city.

Science fiction has always been a way to explore our hopes and fears of the future— *Star Wars*, although set "a long time ago," exists in a different time from ours, past, present, and future. There are millions of observers of the urban space, in person and remotely through the media, and it is in fact the digital that has created the final layer of the city as spectacle. This has been associated with Tokyo, but we can see hints of it emerging in discussions of other Asian cities, such as Shanghai and Singapore. Tokyo is often the focus of the positive imaginings of future urban settlements and is associated with the notion of technology and economic success. Many of the popular images of Tokyo involve bullet trains or pod hotels, which represent the ultimate in social isolation or alienation. Cities offer anonymity, the chance to hide in a crowd and to explore new identities. The digital city of the future may remove human contact altogether.

> Science fiction has always been a way to explore our hopes and fears of the future—*Star Wars*, although set "a long time ago," exists in a different time from ours, past, present, and future.

Cities have given us freedoms and opportunities, as the contact of groups has sparked new creativity. Cities created problems to be solved (transportation, housing, sanitation) and then supplied creative solutions. Cities of our world have changed our lifestyle, our approach to socializing, our work and career opportunities. Yet we can make our own cities, too: as Shakespeare wrote, "The people are the city."[17] Our rural-urban relationships have varied over time and in different parts of the world. Overall, though, the trend has been toward urbanization. *Star Wars* manages to reflect some of these differences between capital and outpost, city and frontier.

The built environment of a city is "collectively consumed."[18] Our conceptions of urban space have changed with the means we use to travel through them. Cities change us, too. In cities, we live cheek-by-jowl with strangers, surrounded by the sights, sounds, and smells of thousands of other lives, unfolding right next to our own. Yet the anonymity of the urban offers its own privacy, as we saw on Coruscant and Cloud City. I may pass thirty people on the street where I live, but I know none of them. We became city people and continue to do so, as the world becomes increasingly urbanized. If you're reading this, chances are you live in a city somewhere, too.

THE JEDI COUNCIL

William J. Astore, a retired lieutenant colonel (USAF), is a professor of history at the Pennsylvania College of Technology. A *Star Wars* fan since 1977, he still has his collection of *STARLOG* magazines from his teen days. His doctorate in modern history is from the University of Oxford.

Kevin S. Decker is an associate professor of philosophy and the director of the philosophy program at Eastern Washington University, where he plays the role of Obi-Wan Kenobi on Halloween. His research interests include American pragmatism, ethics, and social and political philosophy, and his work has appeared in both scholarly journals and magazines such as *Wired* and *Inked*. He is the coeditor of *Star Wars and Philosophy*, *Star Trek and Philosophy*, and *Terminator and Philosophy*, and his work on philosophy and popular culture has appeared in books on the work of Stanley Kubrick and Tim Burton and on diverse films and television shows, including *30 Rock* and *Doctor Who*.

Paul Finkelman is the President William McKinley Distinguished Professor of Law and Public Policy at Albany Law School. He is currently the John Hope Franklin Visiting Professor of American Legal History at Duke Law School. His doctorate is from the University of Chicago, and he was a fellow at Harvard Law School (1982–1983). He has published about thirty books, including *Millard Fillmore* (2011), *Slavery and the Founders: Race and Liberty in the Age of Jefferson* (2001), and *A March of Liberty* (2011). The U.S. Supreme Court has cited his Bill of Rights scholarship. He has published op-ed pieces in the *New York Times*, *USA Today*, the *Washington Post*, and Huffingtonpost.com. He has appeared on PBS, on the History Channel, on C-Span, and in the movie *Up for Grabs*. He was an expert witness in the Alabama Ten Commandments Monument Case and also in the lawsuit over the ownership of Barry Bonds's seventy-third home run ball. In 2009, he gave the annual Nathan I. Huggins Lecture at the W. E. B. Du Bois Center at Harvard University.

Katrina Gulliver holds a Ph.D. in history from the University of Cambridge. She is the author of *Modern Women in China and Japan* and presents the podcast "Cities in History."

Mark Higbee is a professor of history at Eastern Michigan University, where he teaches courses in American and African American history. His Ph.D. is from Columbia University. He saw the first *Star Wars* film on the day it opened in 1977, in his hometown of Indianapolis.

Paul Horvath is an award-winning teacher of mathematics at Eastern Michigan University, where he also earned his graduate degree in mathematics. His love of *Star Wars* is exceeded only by (in no order of importance) mathematics, his children, fishing, and the most beautiful of wives.

Tony Keen teaches classical studies courses for the Open University in Great Britain, for which he has also taught film history. He is active in science fiction fandom as well. His book *Martial's Martians and Other Stories: Studies in Science Fiction and Fantasy and Greece and Rome* is forthcoming from Beccon Press in 2013. It was in a cinema in Buxton, England, in 1978 that an Imperial Star Destroyer first flew over his head.

Michael Laver is an assistant professor of history at the Rochester Institute of Technology, where he teaches East Asian history, as well as classes on European interaction with Asia. His research focuses primarily on the Dutch East India Company and, more broadly, on early modern Japan. His most recent work is titled *The Sakoku Edicts and the Politics of Tokugawa Legitimacy*, published by Cambria Press in 2011. Michael lives in Rochester with his wife, Annie, and his two boys, Bennie and Old Hambone, who are new and eager explorers of the *Star Wars* galaxy.

Janice Liedl is an associate professor of history at Laurentian University in Sudbury, Ontario. She has a doctorate from the University of Toronto and has published on English intellectual and women's history. The editor of Wiley's forthcoming *The Hobbit and History*, she's collected *Star Wars* memorabilia since she first spotted the novelization of *A New Hope*.

Terrance MacMullan is a professor of philosophy and honors at Eastern Washington University. He received his doctorate in philosophy from the University of Oregon in 2002 and has since published on a wide range of topics, including Latin American philosophy, the philosophical relevance of *The Daily Show*, and pragmatist solutions to racism. The Force is so strong in him that as a five-year-old, he persuaded his parents to take him to see *A New Hope* a total of twenty-six times in three different nations.

Lori Maguire, a professor of British and American studies at the University of Paris 8 (Vincennes-St Denis), received her doctorate at St. Antony's College, Oxford University, and her habilitation (advanced doctorate) at the University of Paris IV (Sorbonne). She has published a large number of articles and books on the political history of Great Britain and the United States, notably on their foreign policy. Professor Maguire has been a fan of *Star Wars* since she saw (even more times than her friends) the first film in 1977.

Nancy R. Reagin is the chair of the Department of Women's and Gender Studies at Pace University in New York City, where she is also a professor of history. She holds a doctorate in European history from Johns Hopkins University and has sundry publications in modern German history and European women's history; she is also the editor of Wiley's Pop Culture and History Series. She camped out in line for much longer than her parents thought reasonable, in order to see *A New Hope* the day it opened in Los Angeles in 1977; the moment the music started and the opening crawl began, she knew it was all worth it.

ACKNOWLEDGMENTS

Making History That Spans Galaxies

"A long time ago in a galaxy far, far away . . . ."

The words that open every *Star Wars* movie speak to historians: they tell you that here is someone who understands how history shapes worlds and lives. Consequently, our first and foremost acknowledgment is to George Lucas, whose creative force launched us all on this journey. He generously shared insights into how he drew on a wide range of world history to build the stories of the *Star Wars* galaxy. We were equally fortunate in the historians who contributed to this volume. They combined their own scholarship with an abiding respect for *Star Wars* to produce fabulous chapters that exceeded our expectations, time and again. We also thank our husbands, Bill Offutt and Mike Myatt, whose endless patience and knowledge of history, American and ancient, helped us improve this collection. When research questions took us further afield, many others stepped in with timely guidance. We particularly benefited from the expertise and generosity of Anne Rubenstein, James Fallone, Pamela Fuentes, and David Leeson, who answered all of our questions.

This book would not have been possible without the help of our cunning and resourceful editors at Wiley: Eric Nelson, Connie

Santisteban, Lisa Burstiner, and Becky Yeager. They helped with thousands of important tasks that turned this volume from a good idea into a beautiful reality and kept us both on track during the long process. We are also profoundly grateful to J. W. Rinzler of Lucasfilm, whose encyclopedic knowledge of the *Star Wars* galaxy and elegant way with words saved us, time and again.

Finally, we thank our fellow fans who've been with us every step of the way, from the very first time a Star Destroyer cast its shadow across the screen. In movie theaters and in bookstores, at conventions and online, we've come together through the joy we've found in following the stories of Jedi and Sith, smugglers and royalty. *Star Wars* has inspired generations of fans who've enriched our lives with their creativity and enthusiasm. This collection is our way of giving back to the fans who have been an integral part of our lives for decades. May the Force be with you . . . always!

NOTES

1. Why Rebels Triumph

1. Sanchez, quoted in Andrew J. Bacevich, "The Petraeus Doctrine," *Atlantic Monthly*, October 2008, 17–20.

2. Photo by 1352 Photo Group AAVS, Number 1274, Detachment 5, Unclassified, dated 1965, in the author's possession.

3. The fictional wars of *Star Wars* and the real wars of the American Revolution and Vietnam are not perfect analogs, of course. In the *Star Wars* universe, both sides were fighting for keeps, whereas in the United States in the 1780s and in Vietnam in the 1970s, one side could choose to withdraw across the ocean and go away. Thus, after Yorktown in 1781, the British decided that the cost of defeating the American revolutionaries was simply too high; ditto the United States in the early 1970s, whose leaders decided that the war in Vietnam was no longer winnable at a reasonable cost.

4. Harold Holzer, *Lincoln at Cooper Union: The Speech That Made Abraham Lincoln President* (New York: Simon & Schuster, 2004). Instrumental in his selection as a presidential candidate, Lincoln's brilliant speech, which further decoupled slavery from federal authority and sanction, antagonized supporters of slavery, sowing yet another seed for Southern secession and Civil War after Lincoln won the election later that year.

5. Militarily, the Tet Offensive was a clear defeat for the North Vietnamese and especially for the Viet Cong. The general uprising they sought to provoke did not materialize, and VC cadres were mauled by superior American firepower. Strategically, however, the extent and violence of the Tet Offensive shocked Americans at home, who had been told by the military that the war had already nearly been won. The U.S. media also tended to exaggerate—if not sensationalize—the effectiveness of the offensive. See Don Oberdorfer, *Tet!: The Turning Point in the Vietnam War* (Baltimore: Johns Hopkins University Press, [1971], 2001); and Peter Braestrup, *Big Story: How the American Press and Television Reported and Interpreted the Crisis of Tet 1968 in Vietnam and Washington*, 2 vols. (Boulder, CO: Westview Press, 1977).

6. See Samuel B. Griffith II, *Mao Tse-Tung on Guerrilla Warfare* (Garden City, NY: Anchor Press, 1978); and Vo Nguyen Giap, *People's War, People's Army* (Washington, DC: U.S. Government Printing Office, 1962).

7. Forrest McDonald, *Novus Ordo Seclorum: The Intellectual Origins of the Constitution* (Lawrence: University Press of Kansas, 1985).

8. As one American military adviser noted, "Charlie [the Viet Cong] doesn't need advisers when he conducts a sapper attack. He doesn't need Tac[tical] air [support], or gunships or artillery. He's hungry and he's got a cause and he's motivated. Therein lies the difference. On our side [the South Vietnamese army] nobody is hungry and few are motivated." Quoted in Guenter Lewy, *America in Vietnam* (Oxford: Oxford University Press, 1978), 172.

9. French general Jacques Hogard, who fought in Indochina and Algeria in the 1950s, spoke of five stages of people's (or revolutionary) warfare: (1) Reconnaissance of the population by propagandists and agitators; (2) the creation of nodes and networks of sympathizers, while simultaneously intimidating opponents and neutrals; (3) the deployment of armed cells to commit acts of terror to weaken the government's legitimacy; (4) guerrilla warfare to gain control over portions of the countryside, to include setting up a parallel rebel government; and (5) a conventional offensive to overthrow the government. Hogard's stages 1 to 3 are commonly collapsed into "Phase One" of People's War, with stages 4 and 5 becoming Phases Two and Three, respectively. See Peter Paret, *French Revolutionary Warfare from Indochina to Algeria* (New York: Praeger, 1964).

10. Literature on guerrilla warfare is vast. One might start with Lawrence of Arabia's classic entry on "guerrilla warfare," written for the fourteenth edition of the *Encyclopedia Britannica* (1929), reprinted in Clifton Fadiman, ed., *The Treasury of the Encyclopaedia Britannica* (New York: Viking, 1992). For an extended treatment, see Robert B. Asprey, *War in the Shadows: The Guerrilla in History*, 2 vols. (Garden City, NY: Doubleday, 1975).

11. Lucas's original script for *Star Wars* includes an extended scene with Luke's best friend and fellow pilot on Tatooine, Biggs Darklighter. Prior to Luke's decision to follow Ben and join the Rebellion, Biggs entrusts Luke with his own

secret: that he's leaving the Imperial Academy to join the Rebels because he wants "to be on the right side—the side I believe in." In the extended canon of *Star Wars*, Biggs's principled decision to join the Rebel Alliance surely influences Luke at this pivotal moment in his life. Carol Titelman, ed., *The Art of Star Wars, including the Complete Script of the Film by George Lucas* (New York: Ballantine Books, 1979), 28–29.

12. Richard M. Ketchum, *Saratoga: Turning Point of America's Revolutionary War* (New York: Henry Holt, 1997). In destroying the Empire's "ultimate weapon" and defeating its ultimate enforcer (Vader), the Rebels show they are a force to be reckoned with—and they show the Empire's supporters there is no place safe for them.

13. John M. Gates, "People's War in Vietnam," *Journal of Military History* 54 (July 1990): 325–344.

14. Certainly, the most powerful cinematic depiction of People's War remains *The Battle of Algiers*, directed by Gillo Pontecorvo, Rialto Pictures, Italy/Algeria, 1966.

15. Cited in Marshall McLuhan and Quentin Fiore, *War and Peace in the Global Village* (New York: Bantam Books, 1968), 97.

16. See, for example, Robert Cowley, ed., *What If? The World's Foremost Military Historians Imagine What Might Have Been* (New York: Berkley Books, 2000).

17. Brian McAllister Linn, *The Philippine War, 1899–1902* (Lawrence: University Press of Kansas, 2002); Robert Grainger Ker Thompson, *Defeating Communist Insurgency: The Lessons of Malaya and Vietnam* (New York: Praeger, 1966); Anthony Short, *The Communist Insurrection in Malaya, 1948–60* (London: Frederick Muller, 1975). The insurgents in Malaya and the Philippines were effectively isolated from external support, whereas the American rebels of the 1770s had extensive help from France, and the North Vietnamese had considerable support from China and the Soviet Union.

18. For the events that ended with the fall of South Vietnam in 1975, one might say that both the United States and South Vietnam lost faith with each other. Put differently: perhaps they never fully understood each other, a cultural and communication gap that proved unbridgeable precisely because it was so poorly perceived. See, for example, Stephen T. Hosmer et al., *The Fall of South Vietnam: Statements by Vietnamese Military and Civilian Leaders* (New York: Crane, Russak and Co., 1980), esp. 82–83.

19. Bernard B. Fall, *Hell in a Very Small Place: The Siege of Dien Bien Phu* (Philadelphia: J. B. Lippincott, 1967); and Johnson, quoted by George C. Herring, "'Cold Blood': LBJ's

Conduct of Limited War in Vietnam," in Dennis E. Showalter and John Albert, eds., *An American Dilemma: Vietnam, 1964–1973* (Chicago: Imprint, 1993), 63–85. Such overconfidence was seen in the earliest days of American involvement in Indochina. In 1953, for example, when the United States was aiding France in its long and debilitating war, a U.S. Marine colonel boasted that "two good American divisions with the normal aggressive American spirit could clean up the situation in the Tonkin Gulf in ten months." Cited in George C. Herring, "The Legacy of the First Indochina War," in John Schlight, ed., *The Second Indochina War Symposium: Papers and Commentary* (Washington, DC: Center of Military History, 1986), 9–34.

20. Obviously, the Ewoks in their primitive innocence are nowhere near as nasty as the real-life Viet Cong, who as insurgents were quite skilled at using torture and terror to advance their cause. It is hard to imagine Ewoks terrorizing villages to extort loyalty, for example, tactics that the VC employed on a regular basis in the vicious war that was Vietnam.

21. I am indebted to Peter Carr for this analysis.

22. "Southeast Asia" includes the bombing of Laos and Cambodia, as well as Vietnam. The "Little Boy" uranium bomb used at Hiroshima exploded with a force of roughly 16 kilotons, or 16,000 tons of TNT. So many bombs were dropped in so many rural areas that the death toll of Vietnamese, Cambodian, and Laotian civilians remains impossible to measure accurately; reliable sources suggest casualties from aerial bombing alone in the hundreds of thousands. For example, citing U.S. military estimates, PBS records that Operation Rolling Thunder, a "graduated" bombing campaign from 1965 to 1968, killed 182,000 North Vietnamese civilians. See "Battlefield: Vietnam" Timeline, entry for November 1, 1968, http://www.pbs.org/battlefieldvietnam/timeline/index2.html. Together with the dead and the wounded, of course, were all of the civilians who lost their homes and livelihoods in the bombing.

23. See Stanley Karnow, "Vietnam War Commander Westmoreland Dies at 91," *NPR Morning Edition*, July 19, 2005, http://www.npr.org/templates/story/story.php?storyId=4760273.

24. Many would disagree with this conclusion, of course. For a range of opinions on the Vietnam War and its meaning, see Gil Dorland, *Legacy of Discord: Voices of the Vietnam Era* (Washington, DC: Brassey's, 2001); and Norman A. Graebner, "The Scholar's View of Vietnam, 1964–1992," in Dennis E. Showalter and John Albert, eds., *An American Dilemma: Vietnam, 1964–1973* (Chicago: Imprint, 1993), 13–52.

25. In some ways, the Death Star is reminiscent of the V1 and V2 "vengeance weapons" of Adolf Hitler in World War II. In spreading terror through destruction, they were meant to be decisive, war-winning weapons. In its sheer destructiveness and massive expense, the Death Star also echoes the Manhattan Project of World War II that led to the atomic bombs of 1945 and later to the hydrogen (or thermonuclear) bombs that haunted the world during the Cold War. For more on the Death Star, see chapter 8, "Fear Is the Path to the Dark Side."

26. On COIN strategy, see David Galula, *Counterinsurgency Warfare: Theory and Practice* (Westport, CT: Praeger Security International, 1964, 2006); and John Nagl, *Learning to Eat Soup with a Knife: Counterinsurgency Lessons from Malaya and Vietnam* (Chicago: University of Chicago Press, 2005).

27. A good summary of Nixon's "liberal" social agenda is provided by Kurt Andersen, "The Madman Theory," *New York Times*, August 5, 2011, http://www.nytimes.com/2011/08/06/opinion/the-madman-theory.html.

28. See the U.S. Army official website at www.army.mil and the article "School of Advanced Military Studies Reflects and Looks Forward after 25 Years," May 26, 2009, http://www.army.mil/article/21643/school-of-advanced-military-studies-reflects-and-looks-forward-after-25-years.

29. See Fred Kaplan, "*Force Majeure*: What Lies behind the Military's Victory in Iraq," *Slate*, April 10, 2003, www.slate.com/id/2081388/.

30. Michiko Kakutani, "The Training of Navy Seals Commandos," May 8, 2011, http://www.nytimes.com/2011/05/09/books/seal-team-six-and-the-heart-and-the-fist-reviews.html.

31. Nick Turse, "2014 or Bust: The Pentagon's Building Boom in Afghanistan Indicates a Long War Ahead," www.tomdispatch.com, November 5, 2009, http://www.tomdispatch.com/blog/175157. The United States also built a colossal embassy in Baghdad and sprawling military bases in Iraq. In a linguistic form of jiu-jitsu, the United States described these bases as "enduring" facilities, rather than as "permanent."

32. Sebastian Junger, *War* (New York: Twelve Books, 2010), 99–100.

33. Ibid., 83.

34. This is reminiscent of the "gook syndrome" of the Vietnam War, as discussed by Cecil Currey in *Self-Destruction: The Disintegration and Decay of the United States Army during the Vietnam Era* (New York: W. W. Norton, 1981), 84–91.

35. Nick Turse, "A Secret War in 120 Countries: The Pentagon's New Power Elite," www.Tomdispatch.com, August 3, 2011, http://www.tomdispatch.com/post/175426/.

36. Ketchum, *Saratoga: Turning Point of America's Revolutionary War*; and William Astore, "Freedom Fighters for a Fading Empire: What It Means When We Say We Have the World's Finest Fighting Force," www.tomdispatch.com, January 6, 2011, http://www.tomdispatch.com/blog/175337.

2. "Part of the Rebel Alliance and a Traitor"

1. Maurice Agulhon, "Marianne, réflexions sur une histoire," *Annales historiques de la Révolution française* 289 (1992): 313–318.

2. Kelly de Vries, *Joan of Arc: A Military Leader* (Stroud: Sutton, 1999), 38–53.

3. Larissa Juliet Taylor, *The Virgin Warrior: The Life and Death of Joan of Arc* (New Haven: Yale University Press, 2009), 94–118. See also Marina Warner's *Joan of Arc: The Image of Female Heroism* (Berkeley: University of California Press, 1999).

4. Joie Karnes, "Constance Markievicz: To-Day Life *Is* Politics," Ph.D. dissertation, Drew University, 2006, 5–7, 29–37.

5. Quoted in Heidi Konkel, "Female Spies and Soldiers of the Civil War: Being a Woman Had Its Advantages," M.A. thesis, California State University Dominguez Hills, 2005, 30.

6. H. Donald Winkler, *Hidden Heroines of the Civil War* (Naperville, IL: Sourcebooks, 2010), 3–27.

7. Lisa Margaret Lines, *Milicianas: Women in Combat in the Spanish Civil War* (Lanham, MD: Lexington Books, 2011), 80–81. See also Mary Nash, *Defying Male Civilization: Women in the Spanish Civil War* (Denver: Arden Press, 1995).

8. Hanna Diamond, *Women in the Second World War in France 1939–48: Choices and Constraints* (New York: Longman, 1999), 104.

9. Bonnie Smith, *Changing Lives. Women in European History since 1700* (Lexington, MA: D.C. Heath, 1989), 487–488.

10. Diamond, *Women and the Second World War in France*, 102–108.

11. Smith, *Changing Lives*, 488.

12. Ibid., 489. See also Diamond, *Women and the Second World War in France*, 119.

13. Margaret Collins Weitz, *Sisters in the Resistance:*

How Women Fought to Free France, 1940–1945 (New York: Wiley, 1995), 147–151.

14. Sarah Helm, *A Life in Secrets: Vera Atkins and the Missing Agents of WWII* (New York: Nan A. Talese, 2005), 9–27.

15. Nancy Wake, *The Autobiography of the Woman the Gestapo Called the White Mouse* (Melbourne: Macmillan, 1985), 43–75.

16. Russell Braddon, *Nancy Wake: The Story of a Very Brave Woman* (London: Cassell, 1956), 192–193.

17. Rosemary Lancaster, *Je Suis Australienne: Remarkable Women in France, 1880–1945* (Crawley: University of Western Australia Press, 2008), 171–180.

18. Elizabeth R. Kindleberger, "Charlotte Corday in Text and Image: A Case Study in the French Revolution and Women's History," *French Historical Studies* 18, no. 4 (Fall 1994): 974–980.

19. Weitz, 258–261. See also Lucie Aubrac's own account, *Outwitting the Gestapo* (Lincoln: University of Nebraska Press, 1994).

20. Anna Macias, "Women and the Mexican Revolution, 1910–1920," *Americas* 37, no. 1 (July 1980): 58–62.

21. Patricia Flynn, "Women Challenge the Myth," in *Revolution in Central America*, edited by John Altoff and the Stanford Central America Action Network (Boulder, CO: Westview, 1983), 416–422; Margaret Randall, *Sandino's Daughters Revisited: Feminism in Nicaragua* (Piscataway: Rutgers University Press, 2004), 230–244.

3. Elegant Weapons for Civilized Ages

1. Laurent Bouzereau, *Star Wars: The Annotated Screenplay* (New York: Ballantine Books, 1997), 34.

2. Joseph Campbell, *The Hero with a Thousand Faces* (New York: Princeton University Press, [1949] 1968), 3.

3. Though that won't stop me from still trying after thirty-three years.

4. Daniel Wallace, *The Jedi Path: A Manual for Students of the Force* (Bellevue, WA: Becker & Meyer, 2010), 8.

5. Celibacy is enforced during most of the Jedi Order's long history, though the Order occasionally makes exemptions to this rule, as in the case of Ki-Adi-Mundi, whose home world of Cerea is so depopulated by war that he is allowed to have a family without renouncing his membership in the Jedi Order. Similar exceptions to celibacy rules were made in the Shaolin Temple in 621 CE, when the monks were allowed to marry as a reward for their courage in battle. Also,

the reformed Jedi Order under Luke Skywalker does not require celibacy.

6. Meir Shahar, *The Shaolin Monastery: History, Religion, and the Chinese Martial Arts* (Honolulu: University of Hawaii Press, 2008), 9.

7. Ashley Croft, *The Shaolin Temple: A History and Evolution of Chinese Martial Arts, Zen Buddhism and the Shaolin Warrior Monks* (London, UK: Martial Arts Publishing, 2010), 15.

8. Robin Reilly, *Karate Training* (Rutland, VT: Charles Tuttle, 1985), 30.

9. Croft, *The Shaolin Temple*, 19.

10. Bouzereau, *Star Wars: The Annotated Screenplay*, 180.

11. Shahar, *The Shaolin Monastery*, 102.

12. Croft, *The Shaolin Temple*, 17.

13. Shahar, *The Shaolin Monastery*, 122.

14. Wallace, *The Jedi Path*, 70

15. Croft, *The Shaolin Temple*, 31.

16. Ibid., 30.

17. David Chow and Richard Spangler, *Kung Fu: History, Philosophy and Technique* (Burbank, CA: Unique Publications, 1982), 11.

18. Croft, *The Shaolin Temple*, 22.

19. Ibid., 26.

20. Bouzereau, *Star Wars: The Annotated Screenplay*, 35.

21. Thanks to Rebecca Kemnitz MacMullan for her clear and insightful lessons on the nature of *qi*.

22. Waysun Liao, *T'ai Chi Classics* (Boston: Shambala Publications, 1990), 17.

23. Wallace, *The Jedi Path*, 26.

24. "The Jedi Temple," in *The Complete Star Wars Encyclopedia*, 152.

25. Croft, *The Shaolin Temple*, 33.

26. Japan has a history of warrior monks called *sohei* or *yamabushi*. For more on them, see Mikael Adolphson, *The Teeth and the Claws of the Buddha: Monastic Warriors and Sohei in Japanese History* (Honolulu: University of Hawaii Press, 2007).

27. Thomas Cleary, *Code of the Samurai: A Modern Translation of the* Bushido Shoshinsu (Rutland, VT: Tuttle Publishing, 1999), x.

28. Victor Harris, "Translator's Introduction," *A Book of Five Rings* (Woodstock, NY: Overlook Press, 1974), 2.

29. Even Darth Vader's helmet looks a great deal like the lacquered helmets of the samurai.

30. An important point of divergence between these

two communities is that Jedi, by definition, do not fight other Jedi in combat, because all Jedi serve the light side of the Force. Jedi who oppose others are called either Fallen or Dark Jedi, or, if they cross over to the dark side, the Sith. Each individual samurai, on the other hand, served his particular lord unto death and very frequently crossed blades with other samurai.

31. Cleary, *Code of the Samurai*, 6.

32. Miyamoto Musashi, *A Book of Five Rings*, Victor Harris, trans. (Woodstock, NY: Overlook Press, 1974).

33. Takuan Soho, *The Unfettered Mind*, William Scott Wilson, trans. (Tokyo: Kodansha International, 2002), 15.

34. Bouzereau, *Star Wars: The Annotated Screenplay*, 34.

35. Stephen Sansweet, Pablo Hidalgo, et al., "The Jedi Code," in *The Complete Star Wars Encyclopedia*, vol. 2 (New York: Ballantine, 2008), 146.

36. Cleary, *Code of the Samurai*.

37. Although the samurai were formally abolished in the nineteenth century, their spirit lives on in many of the Japanese martial arts. The samurai's devotion to his master continues in the close and formal relationship between a master or senior student (*sempai*) and the student or junior (*kohai*).

38. Rielly, *Karate Training*, 61.

39. Tsunetomo Yamamoto, *Hagakure: The Book of the Samurai*, William Scott Wilson, trans. (Tokyo: Kodansha International, 1979), 18.

40. Wallace, *The Jedi Path*, 99.

41. Soho, *The Unfettered Mind*, 55.

42. Bouzereau, *Star Wars: The Annotated Screenplay*, 59.

43. Soho, *The Unfettered Mind*, 55.

44. All dates in the *Star Wars* universe are measured in years before the Battle of Yavin (BBY) or after it (ABY).

45. Bouzereau, *Star Wars: The Annotated Screenplay*, 115.

46. Eugen Herrigel, *Zen in the Art of Archery*, R. F. C. Hull, trans. (New York: Vintage Books, 1971), 35.

47. Michael Haag, *The Templars: The History and the Myth* (New York: Harper Collins, 2009), 145.

48. Barbara Frale, *The Templars: The Secret History Revealed* (Dunboyne, Ireland: Maverick House, 2009), 62.

49. Haag, *The Templars*, 96.

50. The Order of Knights of the Hospital of St. John, or the Hospitallers, was founded in 1099 and took up arms in 1118 under their master Raymond de Le Puy.

51. Robert Payne, *The Dream and the Tomb: A History of the Crusades* (New York: Stein and Day, 1984), 125.

52. Haag, *The Templars*, 101.

53. Ibid.

54. Ibid., 121.

55. Interestingly, some of the Jedi who fight in the Mandalorian Wars are called the Revanchists or the Jedi Crusaders.

56. Frale, *The Templars*, 58.

57. Ibid., 65.

58. We see an excellent example of this tension in Jedi Battlemaster Skarch Vaunk's caution regarding Form VII Lightsaber Combat: *Juyo* or "the Ferocity Form." *Juyo* is highly effective in the hands of a Master such as Mace Windu, for it harnesses the power of the Jedi's passion. Yet it is also a controversial form that is taught only to select Jedi because it risks drawing the Jedi to the dark side. See Wallace, *The Jedi Path*, 135–136.

59. Haag, *The Templars*, 103.

60. As the wise Chancellor Palpatine would say, this hair-splitting logic might be easier to swallow if you take a broader view.

61. Frale, *The Templars*, 67.

62. Ibid.

63. Haag, *The Templars*, 217.

64. Another fascinating historical parallel involves the clone troopers of *Star Wars* and the Mamelukes: slaves primarily from Turkey, Russia, and Greece who served as the elite core of the Egyptian army. The Mamelukes, similar to the clones, were outsiders who were bred to fight for a society that denied them freedom and whose rewards they could not enjoy.

65. Malcolm Barber, *The Trial of the Templars* (Cambridge, UK: Cambridge University Press, 2006), 202.

66. "Jedi Order," in *The Complete Star Wars Encyclopedia*, vol. 2, 150.

67. Frale, *The Templars*, 186.

68. Abbé Augustin Barruel, *Memoirs* (1797), as quoted in Haag, *The Templars*, 266.

69. I would like to thank my good friend Kevin Decker for his invaluable and knowledgeable critiques that greatly improved the quality of this chapter.

4. "A House Divided"

1. Benjamin Irvin, "Tar, Feather, and the Enemies of American Liberties, 1768–1776," *New England Quarterly* 76, no. 2 (June 2003): 237.

2. Orlando Figes, *A People's Tragedy: The Russian Revolution, 1891–1924* (New York: Penguin, 1996), 773–793.

3. From the opening crawl of *A New Hope*.

4. From the opening crawl of *The Phantom Menace*.

5. Eric R. Wolf, *Europe and the People without History* (Berkeley: University of California Press, 1982) masterfully describes the rise of global empires that came to control and monopolize the surplus production of local societies, often through extracting taxes. Wolf's work is a useful lens with which to view the *Star Wars* story.

6. W. E. B. Du Bois, *Black Reconstruction in America* (New York: Harcourt, Brace, and Co.,1935), 61, for a quotation from Frederick Douglass in 1865 on how the war started with both sides fighting for slavery—the Confederates for its survival out of the United States, the North fighting for its survival in the United States.

7. Robin Blackburn, *The Making of New World Slavery: From the Baroque to the Modern 1492–1800* (London, New York: Verso, 1997).

8. James M. McPherson, *Battle Cry of Freedom: The Civil War Era* (New York: Oxford University Press, 1988), 100.

9. Du Bois, *Black Reconstruction in America*, 100.

10. Ibid., 115.

11. J. Tracy Power, "'Brother against Brother': Alexander and James Campbell's Civil War," *South Carolina History* 95, no. 2 (April 1994): 130–132.

12. For an overview of the divisions and conflicts in "Bleeding Kansas" and in the border states of Missouri and Kentucky, see McPherson, *Battle Cry*, 145–169, 290–297. For Kansas, see Nicole Etcheson, *Bleeding Kansas: Contested Liberty in the Civil War Era* (Lawrence: University Press of Kansas, 2004).

13. See McPherson, *Battle Cry*, 297; see also Lowell Harrison, *The Civil War in Kentucky* (Lexington: University of Kentucky Press, 1975).

14. Carol Berkin, *Civil War Wives: The Lives and Times of Angelina Grimke Weld, Varina Howell Davis, and Julia Dent Grant* (New York: Knopf, 2009), 227–260. See also the official White House biography online at http://www.whitehouse.gov/about/first-ladies/juliagrant.

15. McPherson, *Battle Cry*, 854.

16. James McPherson, *Crossroads of Freedom: Antietam* (New York: Oxford University Press, 2002).

17. McPherson, *Battle Cry*, 818, 856.

18. Eric Foner, *Reconstruction: America's Unfinished Revolution 1863–1877* (New York: Harper & Row, 1988), 18.

19. Lincoln's Second Inaugural Address, March 4, 1865, in William E. Gienapp, *This Fiery Trial: The Speeches and Writings of Abraham Lincoln* (New York: Oxford University Press, 2002), 221.

5. I, Sidious

1. The career of Augustus is covered in a volume in *The Routledge History of the Ancient World*, Martin Goodman, *The Roman World, 44 BC—AD 180* (London: Routledge, 1997). The equivalent volume for the end of the Republic, Edward Bispham, *The Roman Republic 264–44 BC* (Abingdon: Routledge, forthcoming), will be published in May 2012. Sir Ronald Syme's account in *The Roman Revolution* (Oxford: Oxford University Press, 1939) remains worth reading.

2. The position of *dictator* in the early Republic gave the holder sole executive power, which was usually split between two consuls, but did so for a strictly limited period, usually for six months. The dictatorship of Lucius Cornelius Sulla (82–81 BC) had not been limited, but Sulla had resigned after a year.

3. Lucas's use of Rome is covered in Peter Bonadella, *The Eternal City: Roman Images in the Modern World* (Chapel Hill: University of North Carolina Press, 1987), 227–237, and in Martin M. Winkler, "*Star Wars* and the Roman Empire," in *Classical Myth and Culture in the Cinema*, edited by Martin M. Winkler (Oxford: Oxford University Press, 2001), 272–290.

4. For a good introduction to Roman religion, see James Rives, "Religion in the Roman World," in *Experiencing Rome: Culture, Identity and Power in the Roman Empire*, edited by Janet Huskinson (London: Routledge, 2000), 245–275.

5. He did also have the title *imperator*, from which the modern word *emperor* derives, but this was a title indicating that the holder had been celebrated as a successful military commander.

6. There was also the Social War of 91–88 BC, fought by allies of Rome in Italy who wanted access to Roman citizenship, a servile war or slave revolt (that of Spartacus in 73–71 BC), and numerous wars of overseas conquest.

7. According to Lucasfilm reference materials, Palpatine is born in 82 BBY (Before the Battle of Yavin), so this would make him forty-nine to fifty when he is made chancellor and sixty-two to sixty-three when he assumes the imperial throne in *Revenge of the Sith*.

8. Anne Lancashire, "*The Phantom Menace*: Repetition, Variation, Integration," *Film Criticism* 24, no. 3 (2000): 27–28.

9. For Napoleon, see Frank McLynn, *Napoleon: A Biography* (London: Jonathan Cape, 1997).

6. Teen Queen

1. Great Britain abolished the law of primogeniture only when it came to the royal succession in 2011. Now, if a daughter is the firstborn, she will inherit before a younger brother. See Christa Case Bryant, "Kate Middleton: New Succession Rules Could Make Her Mother of Britain's Next Queen," *Christian Science Monitor*, October 28, 2011.

2. Daniel Wallace with Kevin J. Anderson, *Star Wars: The New Essential Chronology* (New York: Del Rey, 2005), 9.

3. Joyce Tyldesley, *Cleopatra: Last Daughter of Egypt* (New York: Basic Books, 2008), 28–40.

4. Duane W. Roller, *Cleopatra: A Biography* (Oxford: Oxford University Press, 2010), 58–64.

5. Tyldesley, *Cleopatra*, 142–191.

6. Roller, *Cleopatra*, 153–154.

7. Ibid., 80–82.

8. Natalie Mears, *Queenship and Political Discourse in the Elizabethan Realms* (Cambridge, UK: Cambridge University Press, 2005), 223–224.

9. See the entries for Amidala, Padmé, and Naberrie, Padmé, in *The Complete Star Wars Encyclopedia* (New York: Del Rey, 2009), vol. 1, 27–28, and vol. 2, 352.

10. Éva Deák, "'Princeps non Principissa': Catherine of Brandenburg, Elected Prince of Transylvania (1629–1630)," in *The Rule of Women in Early Modern Europe*, edited by Anna J. Cruz and Mihoko Suzuki (Champaign: University of Illinois Press, 2009), 80–88.

11. Jonathan Sumption, *The Hundred Years' War: Trial by Battle* (Philadelphia: University of Pennsylvania Press, 1999), 102–107.

12. P. G. M. Dickson, *Finance and Government under Maria Theresia, 1740–1780*, vol. 2 (Oxford: Clarendon Press, 1987), 3.

13. Derek Beales, *Joseph II: In the Shadow of Maria Theresa, 1741–1780*, vol. 1 (Cambridge, UK: Cambridge University Press, 2008), 24–26.

14. Margaret R. Hunt, *Women in Eighteenth-Century Europe* (Harlow, UK: Pearson, 2010), 327–328.

15. Isabel de Madariaga, *Catherine the Great: A Short History* (New Haven, CT: Yale University Press, 1990), 4.

16. Hunt, 329–330.

17. Richard Hingley and Christina Unwin, *Boudica: Iron Age Warrior Queen* (London: Hambledon, 2005), 8.

18. Hingley and Unwin, 56–69. Also Natalie B. Kampen, "Boudicca," in *The Oxford Encyclopedia of Women in World History* (Oxford: Oxford University Press, 2008),

http://www.oxford-womenworldhistory.com/entry?entry=t248.e124.

19. David J. Hay, *The Military Leadership of Matilda of Canossa, 1046–1115* (Manchester, UK: Manchester University Press, 2008), 70–90.

20. Bernard Hamilton, "Women in the Crusader States: The Queens of Jerusalem (1100–1190)," in *Medieval Women*, edited by Derek Baker (Oxford: Blackwell, 1978), 149–156.

21. Maria Perry, *The Word of a Prince: A Life of Elizabeth I* (London: Boydell, 1990), 286.

22. Robert Lacey, *Monarch: The Life and Reign of Elizabeth II* (New York: Simon & Schuster, 2003), 141–142.

23. David P. Jordan, *The King's Trial: Louis XVI vs. the French Revolution* (Berkeley: University of California Press, 1981), 26.

24. Martyn Atkins, "Jacqueline, suo jure countess of Hainault, suo jure countess of Holland, and suo jure countess of Zeeland (1401–1436)," in *Oxford Dictionary of National Biography* (Oxford: Oxford University Press, 2004), http:/oxforddnb.com/view/article/58930. Also Véronique Flammang, "Partis en Hainaut? La place de la noblesse hainuyère dans la lutte entre Jacqueline de Bavière et Jean IV de Brabant (1424–1428)," *Bijdragen en mededelingen betreffende de geschiedenis der Nederlanden*, 123, no. 4 (2008): 546–549.

25. Joseph F. Patrouch, *Queen's Apprentice: Archduchess Elizabeth, Empress Maria, the Habsburgs and the Holy Roman Empire, 1554–1569* (Leiden: Brill, 2010), 29.

26. Barbara Watson Andaya, "Women and the Performance of Power in Early Modern Southeast Asia," in *Servants of the Dynasty: Palace Women in World History*, edited by Anne Walthall (Berkeley: University of California Press, 2008), 40.

27. Neil Thomas Proto, *The Rights of My People: Liliuokalani's Enduring Battle with the United States, 1893–1917* (New York: Algora, 2009), 93–107.

7. "There's Always a Bigger Fish"

1. Stephen J. Sansweet and Peter Vilmur, *The Star Wars Vault: Thirty Years of Treasures from the Lucasfilm Archives* (New York: Harper/Lucasfilm, 2007), 22.

2. Civic virtue includes the responsibility not only to hold office, but also to deliberate on important affairs, pay fair taxes, and maintain respect for fellow citizens, even in times of intense disagreement. So you can see how contemporary America is *not* a republic!

3. Bruni, as interpreted by J. G. A. Pocock, *The Machiavellian Moment: Florentine Political Theory and the Atlantic*

Republican Tradition (Princeton, NJ: Princeton University Press, 1975), 88.

4. A parallel development occurs in ancient China, as the virtue- and duty-based philosophy of Confucius (551–479 BC) becomes the standard by which the vast Chinese bureaucratic structure of the Mandarins would judge themselves; see John Keay, *China: A History* (New York: Basic Books, 2009), chap. 2.

5. Aristotle, *Politics*, 1295a 20–23, in *The Complete Works of Aristotle*, vol. 2, edited by Jonathan Barnes (Princeton, NJ: Princeton University Press, 1984), 2056.

6. McCormick, "From Constitutional Technique to Caesarist Ploy," in Baehr and Richter, *Dictatorship in History and Theory: Bonapartism, Caesarism, and Totalitarianism* (Washington, DC, and New York: German Historical Institute and Cambridge University Press, 2004), 198.

7. Herodotus, "Tyranny in Corinth," in Donald Kagan, ed., *Problems in Ancient History, Volume One: The Ancient Near East and Greece* (New York: Macmillan, 1966), 205.

8. Aristotle, *Politics* 1310b, 15–16, 2070.

9. Aristotle, "Constitution of Athens," in *The Complete Works of Aristotle*, vol. 2, edited by Jonathan Barnes (Princeton, NJ: Princeton University Press, 1984), 2056.

10. Ibid., 2349.

11. Chester Starr, *A History of the Ancient World*, 2nd ed. (New York: Oxford University Press, 1974), 254.

12. Aristotle, "Constitution of Athens," 2352.

13. Daniel Wallace with Kevin J. Anderson, *Star Wars: The New Essential Chronology* (New York: Ballantine Books, 2005), 35.

14. Reynolds, Mack, James Luceno, and Ryder Windham, *Star Wars: The Complete Visual Dictionary* (New York: Dorling Kindersley, 2006), 78.

15. William V. Harris, "Power," in Alessandro Barchiesi and Walter Scheidel, eds., *The Oxford Handbook of Roman Studies* (New York: Oxford, 2010), 564.

16. Starr, *A History of the Ancient World*, 468.

17. Sheldon Wolin, *Politics and Vision: Continuity and Innovation in Western Political Thought*, expanded ed. (Princeton, NJ: Princeton University Press, 2004), 76.

18. Quoted in Hannah Arendt, *Between Past and Future* (New York: Penguin, 1977), 123.

19. Arno J. Mayer, *The Furies: Violence and Terror in the French and Russian Revolutions* (Princeton, NJ: Princeton University Press, 2000), 100.

20. Daniel Wallace and Jason Fry, *Star Wars: The Essential Atlas* (New York: Ballantine Books, 2009), 158.

21. Harris, "Power," 570.

22. "The Account of Dio Cassius," in Donald Kagan, ed., *Problems in Ancient History, Volume Two: The Roman World* (New York: Macmillan, 1966), 269.

23. Robin Lane Fox, *The Classical World: An Epic History from Homer to Hadrian* (New York: Basic Books, 2006), 358–359.

24. Starr, *A History of the Ancient World*, 552.

25. Jean Bethke Elshtain, "St. Augustine," in David Boucher and Paul Kelly, eds., *Political Thinkers*, 2nd ed. (New York: Oxford University Press, 2009), 126.

26. Scott L. Waugh, "The Court, Politics, and Rhetoric in England," in David R. Knechtges and Eugene Vance, eds., *Rhetoric and the Discourses of Power in Court Culture: China, Europe, and Japan* (Seattle: University of Washington Press, 2005), 38.

27. Joseph B. Pike, ed. and trans., *Frivolities of Courtiers and Footprints of Philosophers: Being a Translation of the First, Second, and Third Books and Selections from the Seventh and Eighth Books of the Policratus of John Salisbury* (Minneapolis: The University of Minnesota Press, 1938), 11.

28. Niccolò Machiavelli, *The Prince*, in Peter Constantine, ed. and trans., *The Essential Writings of Machiavelli* (New York: Modern Library, 2007), 65, 67.

29. Quentin Skinner, *The Foundations of Modern Political Thought*, vol. 1 (New York: Cambridge University Press, 1978), 73.

30. Ibid., 113.

31. Paul Strathern, *The Artist, the Philosopher, and the Warrior* (New York: Bantam Books, 2009), 5961.

32. Skinner, *Foundations of Modern Political Thought*, vol. 1, 134–135.

33. Maurizio Viroli, *Niccolò's Smile: A Biography of Machiavelli*, translated by Antony Shugaar (New York: Farrar, Straus & Giroux, 2000), 155–156.

34. It's unlikely that Machiavelli would have approved of the forced conscription of human stormtroopers, but the Imperial Academy for the training of officers—where Han trained and Luke aspired to go as well—was a stroke of genius; Wallace, *Star Wars: The Essential Chronology*, 87, 92.

35. Keay, *China: A History*, 94

36. Reynolds, Luceno, and Windham, *Star Wars: The Complete Visual Dictionary*, 12.

37. Machiavelli, *The Prince*, in *The Essential Machiavelli*, 69.

38. Ibid., 65.

39. There's a myth that Mussolini, the Fascist leader of Italy from 1922 to 1943, made the trains run on time. The

cliché is often used (sometimes ironically) to demonstrate that even dictatorial regimes have some practical good to them. Overall, the Italian railway system was no more efficient under Mussolini than under his liberal predecessors; see R. J. B. Bosworth, *Mussolini's Italy* (New York: Penguin, 2007), 439.

40. Eric Nelson, "The Problem of the Prince," in James Hankins, ed., *The Cambridge Companion to Renaissance Philosophy* (New York: Cambridge University Press, 2007).

41. Skinner, *Foundations of Modern Political Thought*, vol. 1, 78.

42. Wolin, *Politics and Vision*, 189.

8. "Fear Is the Path to the Dark Side"

1. Speech at Brown University, June 4, 1983, http://tedkennedy.org/ownwords/event/cold_war. Kennedy first called SDI "Star Wars" just after Reagan's speech. He is quoted by Lou Cannon in the *Washington Post*, March 24, 1983, A1, as saying, "Sen. Edward M. Kennedy (D-Mass.) characterized the speech as 'misleading Red-scare tactics and reckless *Star Wars* schemes.'" This extract is obviously taken from a later speech, where he reused the image.

2. Remarks at the Annual Convention of the National Association of Evangelicals, Orlando, Florida, March 8, 1983, http://www.hbci.com/~tgort/empire.htm. Will Kaufman, *American Culture in the 1970s* (Edinburgh: Edinburgh University Press, 2009), 93, talks of "Reagan's transformation of the ironic rhetoric and vision of *Star Wars* into a serious mode of political discourse." He also observes, "There was something very serious in his appropriation of the cartoon or comic-book phrase, 'the Evil Empire,' for a statement on the direction of United States foreign policy, as though the departments of Defense and State could be guided by the ethics of a Saturday afternoon sci-fi adventure."

3. Juan Williams of the *Washington Post* wrote an article on March 29, 1983, A10, titled "Writers of Speeches for President Claim Force Is with Him," mocking the "bellicose tone" of his recent speeches.

4. Although it contains a number of mistakes, David Meyer discusses this in "Star Wars, *Star Wars* and American Political Culture," *Journal of Popular Culture* 26, no. 2 (Fall 1992): 99–115. Lincoln Geraghty has commented, "Right wing Cold War politics were indelibly etched onto the characters and back story that informed the *Star Wars* universe: heroic rebels versus the evil empire became America against the Soviet Union. Intriguingly, for those opposed to the SDI, the rebellion in *Star Wars* could be seen as a metaphor for the left's struggle against Reaganism and the politics of big business." See Lincoln Geraghty, ed., *American Science Fiction Film and Television* (Oxford: Berg, 2009), 59.

5. Laurent Jullier in his book *Star Wars: Anatomie d'une saga* (Paris: Armand Colin, 2005), 17, wrote of how the prequel trilogy shows "our world" and "our anxieties."

6. Press release by the White House, August 6, 1945, http://www.trumanlibrary.org/whistlestop/study_collections/bomb/large/documents/pdfs/59.pdf#zoom=100.

7. Brian Cameron, "'What Is Thy Bidding, My Master?': *Star Wars* and the Hegelian Struggle for Recognition," in Kevin Decker and Jason Eberl, eds., *Star Wars and Philosophy* (Chicago: Open Press, 2005), 164, notes that "like all weapons of mass destruction, the Death Star's military function cannot be easily separated from its political and policing functions—its purpose as a method of domestic control. Its objective power lies not in its actual use, but in the threat of its use, and herein lays the secret of the political function of justifying the exercise of power."

8. Mary Henderson, in *Star Wars: The Magic of Myth* (New York: Bantam, 1997), 149, for example, comments, "The ultimate weapon of the Empire was also similar to that which played such a prominent role in the Cold War. In real life this was the atom bomb, and in *Star Wars* it was the Death Star. The goals of these weapons were identical: to render the enemy incapable of making war."

9. David Allen Rosenberg, "The Origins of Overkill: Nuclear Weapons and American Strategy, 1945–1960," *International Security* 7, no. 4 (Spring 1983): 11–12. For more on Truman, see Richard F. Haynes, *The Awesome Power: Harry S Truman as Commander in Chief* (Baton Rouge: Louisiana State University Press, 1973). For more on the decision to use the bomb at Hiroshima and Nagasaki, see J. Samuel Walker, *Prompt and Utter Destruction: Truman and the Use of Atomic Bombs against Japan* (Chapel Hill: University of North Carolina Press, 2004); Gar Alperovitz, *The Decision to Use the Atomic Bomb* (New York: Knopf, 1995); Barton J. Bernstein, "The Atomic Bombings Reconsidered," *Foreign Affairs* (January–February 1995): 135–152; and Martin Sherwin, *A World Destroyed: Hiroshima and the Origins of the Arm Race* (New York: Vintage Books, 1987).

10. The President's News Conference, November 30, 1950, http://trumanlibrary.org/publicpapers/viewpapers.php?pid=985.

11. See, for example, Rosenberg, "The Origins of Overkill: Nuclear Weapons and American Strategy, 1945–1960,"

or Beatrice Heuser, "Victory in a Nuclear War? A Comparison of NATO and WTO War Aims and Strategies," in *Contemporary European History* 7, no. 3 (November 1998): 311–327.

12. Rosenberg, "The Origins of Overkill: Nuclear Weapons and American Strategy, 1945–1960," 27–32. See also Douglas Kinnard, *President Eisenhower and Strategy Management: A Study in Defense Politics* (Lexington: University Press of Kentucky, 1977).

13. The entire text of NSC-162/2 is available online at http://www.fas.org/irp/offdocs/nsc-hst/nsc-162-2.pdf.

14. For a general overview of U.S. nuclear strategy, see *Fred Kaplan, The Wizards of Armageddon* (Stanford, CA: Stanford University Press, 1983). Also important is Lawrence Freedman, *The Evolution of Nuclear Strategy*, 3rd ed. (New York: Palgrave, 2003). For more on Kahn, see *Sharon Ghamari-Tabrizi, The Worlds of Herman Kahn: The Intuitive Science of Thermonuclear War* (Cambridge, MA: Harvard University Press, 2005). The literature on Kissinger is immense (and much of it written by the man himself). Most of it obviously concerns his time as national security adviser and secretary of state. A few books that consider earlier periods are Jeremi Suri, *Henry Kissinger and the American Century* (Cambridge, MA: Harvard University Press, 2009), and Stephen Graubard, *Kissinger: Portrait of a Mind* (New York: Norton, 1974).

15. Speech on January 12, 1954 (Department of State Bulletin, vol. 30, 107–110), http://wadsworth.com/history_d/special_features/ilrn_legacy/waah2c01c/content/amh2/readings/dulles.html. For background information, see Samuel F. Wells Jr., "The Origins of Massive Retaliation," *Political Science Quarterly* 96, no. 1 (Spring 1981): 31–52; Richard Immermann, *John Foster Dulles and the Diplomacy of the Cold War* (Princeton, NJ: Princeton University Press, 1992); or Frederick Marks, *Power and Peace: The Diplomacy of John Foster Dulles* (Westport, CT: Praeger, 1993).

16. Speech given in San Francisco, September 18, 1967, http://www.atomicarchive.com/Docs/Deterrence/Deterrence.shtml. For more on this, see Henry Sokolski, *Getting MAD: Nuclear Mutual Assured Destruction, Its Origins and Practice* (Washington, DC: Strategic Studies Institute, 2004), http://www.strategicstudiesinstitute.army.mil/pdffiles/PUB585.pdf.

17. Walter Pincus, "Neutron Killer Warhead Buried in ERDA Budget," *Washington Post*, June 6, 1977, A1. See also his subsequent articles in the *Post*, such as "Senate Pressed for Killer Warhead" on June 21, 1977, A2, or "Pentagon Wanted Secrecy on Neutron Bomb Production," June 25, 1977, A1.

18. For more on this, see Clive Rose, *Campaigns against Western Defense: NATO's Adversaries and Critics*, 2nd ed. (Basingstoke, UK: Macmillan, 1986), "Brezhnev Offer on the Neutron Bomb Accompanied by Threat," *The Times* (London), December 24, 1977. The Soviet propaganda on the subject and much of the Western press reporting on the neutron bomb were exaggerated. *Scientific American* came to the conclusion that "the enhanced-radiation warhead promises to be neither the collateral-damage-free weapon that its supporters see nor the 'ultimate capitalist weapon' (destroying only people not property) that many people in peace groups fear." Fred Kaplan, "Enhanced Radiation Weapons," in *Arms Control and the Arms Race: Readings from* Scientific American (New York: Freeman, 1985). The original article was published in the *Scientific American* for May 1978.

19. For more on the controversy, see Vincent Auger, *The Dynamics of Foreign Policy Analysis: The Carter Administration and the Neutron Bomb* (London: Rowman & Littlefield, 1996), and Robert Strong and Marshal Zeringue, "The Carter Administration and the Neutron Bomb," *Southeastern Political Review* 16, no. 1 (March 1988): 147–174.

20. Tony Blair, speech on Iraq, House of Commons, March 18, 2003, House of Commons Debates, vol. 401, col. 762, http://www.publications.parliament.uk/pa/cm200203/cmhansrd/vo030318/debtext/30318-06.htm.

21. As Meyer points out, on page 113: "In stark contrast with the technological escalations that drive the arms race, Luke's battles are fought with progressively less sophisticated weapons."

22. There are a number of websites that support the idea that Artoo is the real hero of *Star Wars*. See, for example, http://kevinforsyth.net/weblog/?p=103, or http://boards.theforce.net/the_star_wars_saga/b10456/19722655/r19724406/. There is even a Facebook page titled "R2D2 Is the REAL hero of Star Wars."

23. For more on this, see Elizabeth Cook, "'Be Mindful of the Living Force': Environmental Ethics in *Star Wars*," in Decker and Eberle, eds., *Star Wars and Philosophy*.

24. "The Evaluation of the Atomic Bomb as a Military Weapon," June 30, 1947. President's Secretary's File, Truman Papers, 36, http://www.trumanlibrary.org/whistlestop/study_collections/bomb/large/documents/pdfs/81.pdf#zoom=100.

25. The Italian general Giulio Douhet was one of the first to recognize the importance of air power for warfare in

his book *Command of the Air* (Rome: Stabilimento poligrafico per l'amministrazione della Guerra, 1921, republished in English in the United States by the Government Printing Office, 1983). He warned that "to get an idea of the nature of future wars, one need only imagine what power of destruction that nation would possess whose bacteriologists should discover the means of spreading epidemics in the enemy's country and at the same time immunize its own people. Air power makes it possible not only to make high-explosive bombing raids over any sector of the enemy's territory, but also to ravage his whole country by chemical and biological warfare." For the impact on Britain, see Uri Bialer, *The Shadow of the Bomber: The Fear of Air Attack on British Politics, 1932–1939* (London: Royal Historical Society, 1980). See also Tami Davis Biddle, *Rhetoric and Reality in Air Warfare: The Evolution of British and American Ideas about Strategic Bombing, 1914–1945* (Princeton, NJ: Princeton University Press, 2002); Lee Kennett, *The First Air War, 1914–1918* (New York: Free Press, 1991); and Raymond H. Fredette, *The Sky on Fire: The First Battle of Britain, 1917–1918* (Washington, DC: Smithsonian Institution Press, 1991).

26. For more on this, see H. R. Southworth, *Guernica! Guernica! A Study of Journalism, Diplomacy, Propaganda and History* (Berkeley: University of California Press, 1977); Ian Patterson, *Guernica and Total War* (Cambridge, MA: Harvard University Press, 2007); Tom Buchanan, *Britain and the Spanish Civil War* (Cambridge, UK: Cambridge University Press, 1997).

27. Stanley Baldwin, November 10, 1932 (*Parliamentary Debates*, Series 5, vol. 270, col. 632), http://hansard.millbanksystems.com/commons/1932/nov/10/international-affairs.

28. See, for example, Alastair Horne, *To Lose a Battle. France 1940*, rev. ed. (London: Penguin, 1990), and Julian Jackson, *The Fall of France: The Nazi Invasion of 1940* (Oxford: Oxford University Press, 2003).

29. Speech of Joseph McCarthy, Wheeling, West Virginia, February 9, 1950, at http://historymatters.gmu.edu/d/6456.

30. For more on McCarthy, see David Oshinsky, *A Conspiracy So Immense: The World of Joe McCarthy* (New York: Free Press, 1983); Robert Griffith, *The Politics of Fear: Joseph R. McCarthy and the Senate* (Amherst: University of Massachusetts Press, 1970). There has been a recent attempt on the American right, led by Anne Coulter, to rehabilitate McCarthy, and a number of books with this aim have appeared. For HUAC, see John Joseph Gladchuk, *Hollywood and Anticommunism: HUAC and the Evolution of the Red Menace, 1935–1950* (London: Routledge, 2006).

31. Susan Sontag, "The Imagination of Disaster," in *Against Interpretation* (New York: Farrar, Straus & Giroux, 1966). See also Brian Murphy, "Monster Movies: They Came from beneath the Fifties," *Journal of Popular Film* 1, no. 1 (Winter 1972): 31–44; Lori Maguire, "The Destruction of New York City: A Recurrent Nightmare of American Cold War Cinema," *Cold War History* 9, no. 4 (November 2009): 513–524; Joyce Evans, *Celluloid Mushroom Clouds: Hollywood and the Atomic Bomb* (Boulder, CO: Westview Press, 1998); Toni Perrine, *Film and the Nuclear Age: Representing Cultural Anxiety* (New York: Garland, 1998); and Paul Boyer, *By the Bomb's Early Light: American Thought and Culture at the Dawn of the Atomic Age* (New York: Pantheon Books, 1985).

32. January 17, 1961. The text of it can be found at http://www.americanrhetoric.com/speeches/dwightdeisenhowerfarewell.html.

33. See http://www.merriam-webster.com/dictionary/military-industrial%20complex.

34. For a detailed presentation of popular reactions to *Sputnik*, see "The Impact of *Sputnik I*: Case Study of American Public Opinion at the Break of the Space Age," compiled by Martha Wheeler George (Washington, DC: NASA, 1963), http://history.spacebusiness.com/sputnik/files/sputnik65.pdf. See also Robert A. Divine, *The Sputnik Challenge* (New York: Oxford University Press, 1993), and Barbara Barksdale Clowse, *Brainpower for the Cold War: The Sputnik Crisis and National Defense Education Act of 1958* (Westport, CT: Greenwood Press, 1981).

35. R. W. Apple Jr., June 23, 1996, http://topics.nytimes.com/top/reference/timestopics/subjects/p/pentagon_papers/index.html?scp=1-spot&sq=pentagon%20papers&st=cse. In June 2011, the complete text of the Pentagon Papers became available online at http://www.archives.gov/research/pentagon-papers/.

36. Laurent Bouzereau, *Star Wars: The Annotated Screenplays* (New York: Ballantine Books, 1997). James Curtis in "From *American Graffiti* to *Star Wars*," *Journal of Popular Culture* 13, no. 4 (Spring 1980): 600, relates the film to Watergate. Stephen Paul Miller, in *The 1970s Now: Culture as Surveillance* (Durham, NC: Duke University Press, 1999), sees *Star Wars* as a reflection of the decade's preoccupation with surveillance, noting that like Watergate, "*Star Wars* involves a struggle for tapes." He also places it in relation to Vietnam: "After the Vietnam War, a credible war can only

occur in the outer space of a distant future or past. . . . However, there is an ideological need for such a fantastic war."

37. Will Brooker, *Star Wars* (London: British Film Institute, 2009), 81.

9. From Slavery to Freedom in a Galaxy Far, Far Away

1. See, generally, John Hope Franklin and Evelyn Brooks Higginbotham, *From Slavery to Freedom: A History of African Americans*, 9th ed. (New York: McGraw Hill, 2011). I thank Avery Edison, Abigail Finkelman, and Mike Pusatere for their helpful comments on this essay. Their insights from the next generation were particularly useful. I finished this chapter at Nanzan University in Nagoya, Japan, while on a fellowship from the Japan Society for the Promotion of Science. I thank the JSPS for its support of my scholarship. I finished the final work on this essay while visiting at Duke Law School, where I was the John Hope Franklin Professor of American Legal History. I thank Duke Law School for itrs support as well. Portions of this essay dealing with international law are taken from Seymour Drescher and Paul Finkelman, "Slavery," in Bardo Fassbender and Anne Peters, eds. *The Oxford Handbook of the History of International Law* (Oxford: Oxford University Press, 2012), chap. 37.

2. Orlando Patterson, *Slavery and Social Death: A Comparative Study* (Cambridge, MA: Harvard University Press, 1982).

3. Max Farrand, ed., *The Records of the Federal Convention of 1787*, rev. ed. (New Haven, CT: Yale University Press, 1966), vol. 2, 371. On the issue of slavery in the Convention, see Paul Finkelman, *Slavery and the Founders: Race and Liberty in the Age of Jefferson*, 2nd ed. (Armonk, NY: M. E. Sharpe, 2001).

4. Patterson, *Slavery and Social Death: A Comparative Study*, vii.

5. See Sue Peabody *"There Are No Slaves in France": The Political Culture of Race and Slavery in the Ancien Régime* (New York: Oxford University Press, 1996).

6. *Somerset v. Stewart*, 98 Eng. Rep. 499 (1772).

7. Ibid., at 510.

8. Ibid., at 509.

9. Paul Finkelman, *An Imperfect Union: Slavery, Federalism and Comity* (Chapel Hill: University of North Carolina Press, 1981).

10. Quoted in Donald Robinson, *Slavery in the Structure of American Politics* (New York: Harcourt Brace Jovanovich, 1981), 80. See also Finkelman, *Slavery and the Founders*, for a discussion of slaveholding by Jefferson and other Founders.

11. Ratification of a constitutional amendment requires the support of three-fourths of the states. To this day, in 2012, it would be impossible to amend the Constitution if the fifteen slave states that existed in 1860 still had slavery and still opposed emancipation. The ratification of the Thirteenth Amendment ending slavery was possible only because the secession of eleven slave states allowed for constitutional change, which they were forced to accept as a cost of military defeat.

12. Suzanne Miers, *Slavery in the Twentieth Century* (New York: Altamira Press, 2003), 20–25.

13. Renee C. Redman, "The League of Nations and the Right to Be Free from Enslavement: The First Human Right to Be Recognized as Customary International Law," *Chicago-Kent Law Review* 70 (1994): 759–802.

14. Although *Star Wars* is clearly "futuristic," with its technology and space travel, the movie is set "A long time ago, in a galaxy far, far away."

15. Stephen J. Sansweet and Pablo Hidalgo, *The Complete Star Wars Encyclopedia*, 3 vols. (New York: Ballantine Books, 2008), vol 1, 122.

16. Ibid., 166–167.

17. Gardulla is described as having a large slave trading operation, *The Complete Star Wars Encyclopedia*, 322–323.

18. See, for example, the cases discussed in Bernie Jones, *Fathers of Conscience: Mixed-Race Inheritance in the Antebellum South* (Athens: University of Georgia Press, 2009).

19. See Judith Kelleher Schafer, *Brothels, Depravity, and Abandoned Women: Illegal Sex in Antebellum New Orleans* (Baton Rouge: Louisiana State University Press, 2009).

20. Ibid.

10. "Greed Can Be a Powerful Ally"

1. Augustine of Hippo, *City of God* (New York: Penguin, 1984), Book IV, chap. 4.

2. This idea is briefly touched on in an article for slate .com, posted on May 24, 1999, titled "The Economics of the Phantom Menace," http://www.slate.com/articles/business/moneybox/1999/05/the_economics_of_the_phantom_menace.html.

3. Lynn Pan, *Sons of the Yellow Emperor: A History of the Chinese Diaspora* (New York: Kodansha International, 1994), 6.

4. For a comprehensive overview of the South China Sea in this period, see John Wills, ed., *China and Maritime Europe 1500–1800* (Cambridge, UK: Cambridge University Press, 2010), and Anthony Reid, *Southeast Asia in the Age of*

Commerce, 1450–1680, Volume II: Expansion and Crisis (New Haven, CT: Yale University Press, 1995).

5. For Japanese pirates, or "sea lords," as he calls them, see Peter Shapinsky, "With the Sea as Their Domain: Pirates and Maritime Lordship in Medieval Japan," in Jerry Bentley, Kären Wigen, and Renate Bridenthal, eds., *Seascapes, Littoral Cultures and Trans-Oceanic Exchanges* (Honolulu: University of Hawaii Press, 2007), 221–238.

6. Probably the best description of piracy along the Chinese coast in the sixteenth century is in Robert Antony, *Like Froth Floating on the Sea: The World of Pirates and Seafarers in Late Imperial South China* (Berkeley: University of California Institute for East Asian Studies, 2003).

7. Kenneth Swope, *A Dragon's Head and a Serpent's Tail: Ming China and the First Great East Asian War, 1592–1598* (Norman: University of Oklahoma Press, 2009).

8. Derek Massarella, *A World Elsewhere: Europe's Encounter with Japan in the Sixteenth and Seventeenth Centuries* (New Haven, CT: Yale University Press, 1990).

9. Richard Cocks's fascinating diary and a selection of his letters were edited in two volumes by Edward Thompson, *Diary of Richard Cocks: Cape Merchant in the English Factory in Japan, 1615–1622, with Correspondence* (London: Hakluyt Society, 1883).

10. John Wills, "Maritime China from Wang Chih to Shih Lang: Themes in Peripheral History," in Jonathan Spence and John Wills, eds., *From Ming to Ching: Conquest, Region, and Continuity in Seventeenth Century China* (New Haven, CT: Yale University Press, 1981), 216–218.

11. Tonio Andrade, *Lost Colony: The Untold Story of China's First Great Victory over the West* (Princeton, NJ: Princeton University Press, 2011).

12. Om Prakash, *Precious Metals and Commerce: The Dutch East India Company in the Indian Ocean Trade* (London: Ashgate-Variorum, 1994).

13. Probably the best comprehensive account of the VOC in English is Feeme Gaastra, *The Dutch East India Company* (Zutpen: Walburg Pers, 2007); see also Els Jacobs, *In Pursuit of Pepper and Tea: The Story of the Dutch East India Company* (Zutphen: Walburg Pers, 1991). A good comparison of the various European trading companies can be found in Holden Furber, *Rival Empires of Trade in the Orient, 1600-1800* (Minneapolis: University of Minnesota Press, 1976).

14. Although it is in Dutch, a concise description of this process is to be found in Femme Gaastra, "De VOC in Azië tot 1680," in *Algemene Geschiedenis der Nederland 5* (Bussum: Unieboek, 1980).

15. Niels Steensgaard calls this moment a "metamorphosis." Niels Steensgaard, "The Dutch East India Company as an Institutional Innovation," in *Dutch Capitalism and World Capitalism*, edited by Maurice Aymard (Cambridge, UK: Cambridge University Press, 1982), 239.

16. For Dutch ship production, see Charles Boxer, *The Dutch Seaborne Empire, 1600–1800* (London: Penguin Books, 1990).

17. According to *The New Essential Chronology to Star Wars*, the Trade Federation was created in 350 BBY "to represent the needs of major shipping corporations." See Daniel Wallace and Kevin Anderson, *The New Essential Chronology to Star Wars* (New York: Del Ray, 2005), 31. See also Steve Miller and J. D. Wiker, *Secrets of Naboo* (Renton, WA: Wizards of the Coast, 2001).

18. Jan Pieterzoon Coen was responsible for locating the capital of the VOC in Asia at Batavia on the island of Java and was extremely influential in laying out a vision of comprehensive trade throughout Asia, using a network of several factories. He has also been criticized for his often violent and inhumane treatment of natives. See Steven R. Bown's accessible account of Coen's life in *Merchant Kings: When Companies Ruled the World, 1600–1900* New York: Thomas Dunne Books, 2009), 7–56.

19. Kristof Glamann, *Dutch Asiatic Trade, 1620–1740* (The Hague: Martinus Nijhoff, 1958), 6–7.

20. Eiichi Katō, "Unification and Adaptation, the Early Shogunate and Dutch Trade Policies," in Leonard Blussé and Femme Gaastra, eds., *Companies and Trade* (Leiden: Leiden University Press, 1981), 220–221.

21. Niels Steensgard, in Blussé and Gaastra, eds., *Companies and Trade*, 55–56.

22. For a list of Dutch blockades of Portuguese ports, see Ernst van Deen and Daniël Klijn, *A Guide to the Sources of the History of the Dutch-Portuguese Relations in Asia* (Leiden: Institute for the History of European Expansion, 2001).

23. For a good firsthand account of the combined fleet at Hirado, Japan, see Thompson, ed., *The Diary of Richard Cocks*.

24. Glamann, *Dutch-Asiatic Shipping*, 7.

25. A good source for the history of the EIC, based on extant primary sources, is Anthony Farrington, *Trading Places: The East India Company and Asia, 1600–1834* (London: British Library, 2002).

26. Sushil Chaudhary, *The Prelude to Empire: Plassey Revolution of 1757* (New Delhi: Manohar, 2000).

27. This trade network is described in Femme Gaastra,

De Geschiedenis van de VOC (Zutplen: Walburg Pers, 1991), 124–127.

28. Kees Zandfleet, *The Dutch Encounter with Asia* (Amsterdam: Rijksmuseum, 2002), 159.

29. See, for example, Victor Enthoven, Steve Murdoch, and Eila Williamson, eds., *The Navigator: The Log of John Anderson VOC Pilot-Major 1640–1643* (Leiden: Brill, 2010), 68–69.

30. Mary Lindemann, "'Dirty Politics or Harmonie?' Defining Corruption in Early Modern Amsterdam and Hamburg," *Journal of Social History* 45, no. 3 (Spring 2012): 587.

31. Donald Keene, *The Japanese Discovery of Europe, 1720–1830* (Stanford, CA: Stanford University Press, 1969), 5.

32. For a good, accessible overview of Dutch policy vis-à-vis the islanders of the Spice Islands, see Giles Milton, *Nathaniel's Nutmeg: Or the True and Incredible Adventures of the Spice Trader Who Changed the Course of History* (New York: Penguin Press, 2000), chap. 11.

33. For a helpful discussion of Western power in South and Southeast Asia, see P. J. Marshall, "Western Arms in Maritime Asia in the Early Phases of Expansion," *Modern Asian Studies* 14, no. 1 (1980): 13–28.

11. Coruscant, the Great Cities of Earth, and Beyond

1. Louis Wirth, "Urbanism as a Way of Life," in Richard Sennett, ed., *Classic Essays on the Culture of Cities* (New York: Appleton-Century-Crofts, 1969), 143–164.

2. Tacitus, *Annals*, Book XV, chap. 44.

3. Jane Jacobs, *The Death and Life of Great American Cities* (New York: Random House, 1961).

4. Richard Sennett, *Flesh and Stone: The Body and the City in Western Civilization* (New York, London: W. W. Norton & Co , 1994), 263.

5. Georg Simmel, "The Metropolis and Mental Life," http://www.altruists.org/static/files/The%20Metropolis%20and%20Mental%20Life%20%28Georg%20Simmel%29.htm.

6. Fernand Braudel, *Civilization and Capitalism, 15th–18th Century*, vol. 3: *The Perspective of the World*, translated by Sian Reynold (Berkeley: University of California Press, 1992), 32.

7. William Dunbar, "London, Thou Art of Townes a Per Se," in *The Poems of William Dunbar* (London: Blackwood, 1893), 276–278.

8. James Boswell, *Life of Johnson* (New York: Charles Scribner's Sons, 1917), 341.

9. Benjamin Disraeli, *Tancred* (London: Henry Colburn, 1847); Ralph Waldo Emerson, *Essays and English Traits*; *Harvard Classics Vol. 5* (New York: P. F. Collier & Son, 1909)

10. Richard Dennis, *Cities in Modernity: Representations and Productions of Metropolitan Space, 1840–1930* (Cambridge, UK: Cambridge University Press, 2008), 51

11. Sam Bass Warner Jr., "Slums and Skyscrapers: Urban Images, Symbols, and Ideology," in Lloyd Rodwin and Robert M. Hollister, eds., *Cities of the Mind: Images and Themes of the City in the Social Sciences* (New York and London: Springer, 1984), 181–195.

12. Jane Austen, *Mansfield Park*, (New York: W. W. Norton & Co, 1998).

13. Ezra Pound, "Patria Mia," *New Age* 11, no. 21, September 19, 1912, 492.

14. Thomas Wolfe, *The Web and the Rock (Voices of the South)* (Baton Rouge: Louisiana State University Press, 1999).

15. Christopher Gray, "Not Just a Perch for King Kong," *New York Times*, September 23, 2010, RE9.

16. Lewis Mumford, *The Culture of Cities* (London: Routledge, 1997), 258.

17. William Shakespeare, *Coriolanus*, act III, scene 1, line 200.

18. David Harvey, *Consciousness and the Urban Experience* (Baltimore: Johns Hopkins University Press, 1985), 47.

ILLUSTRATION CREDITS

176–177, [LC-DIG-ppmsca-19305]; 107, Library of Congress, Prints & Photographs Division, Frank Leslie's illustrated newspaper, vol. 33, no. 836 (1871 Oct. 7), p. 61; 109 (inset), Billy Hathorn, creativecommons.org/publicdomain/zero/1.0/deed.en; 115, Library of Congress, Prints & Photographs Division, Purchase, William A. Gladstone, 1995 (DLC/PP-1995:113.21), [LC-DIG-ppmsca-10900]; 117, Library of Congress, Prints & Photographs Division, Brady-Handy Photograph Collection, [LC-DIG-cwpbh-01159]; 118, Library of Congress, Prints & Photographs Division, *Grant and Lee, the Virginia Campaigns* by William Frassanito (New York: Scribner's, 1983), [LC-USZ61-903]; Library of Congress, Prints & Photographs Division, [LC-USZ62-15887]; 127, Augustus of Prima Porta, Vatican Museums, Chiaramonti Museum, Braccio Nuovo (New Wing), photo by Till Niermann, creativecommons.org/licenses/by-sa/3.0/deed.en; 128, *The Death of Caesar*, Jean-Léon Gérôme, Walters Art Museum; 129, Library of Congress, Prints & Photographs Division, BI, Shelf, sources checked: LC/MUMS, [LC-USZ62-84591]; 130 (inset), *Cicero (106–43 BC) in the Senate Accusing Catiline of Conspiracy on 21st October 63 BC*, 1889 (fresco), Maccari, Cesare (1840–1919) / Palazzo Madama, Rome, Italy / Ancient Art and Architecture Collection Ltd. / The Bridgeman Art Library; 137, *Antony and Cleopatra*, Sir Lawrence Alma-Tadema, Private Collection; 140, *Coronation of Emperor Napoleon I and Coronation of the Empress Josephine in the Notre-Dame de Paris, December 2, 1804*, Jacques-Louis David, Louvre Museum; 142, the Yorck Project; gnu.org/licenses/fdl.html; 143, the National Archives and Records Administration, Heinrich Hoffmann–National Socialist Pictures Press/Press Illustrations Hoffmann; 144 (top), courtesy of Jim Payne at throughtheireyes2.co.uk; 147, Library of Congress, Prints & Photographs Division, Germany Nuremburg 1934, Nazis . . . Meetings, parades, rallies, etc., BI (3), Shelf, Himmler, H-, 1900–1945, Hitler, A-, 1889–1945, Lutze, V-, 1890–1943, [LC-USZ62-76094]; 154 (inset), Library of Congress, Prints & Photographs Division, Plate no. 4.LC no. 5, [LC-USZ62-115872]; 160, H. F. Helmolt, *History of the World*, vol. VII (Dodd Mead, 1902), plate between pp. 524 and 525; 164, Library of Congress, Prints & Photographs Division, [LC-USZ62-116782]; 169, Library of Congress, Prints & Photographs Division, Rice, James Rogers, [LC-DIG-pga-02485]; 171 (inset), *Jacoba of Bavaria (1401–1436), Countess of Holland and Zeeland*, Zeelandic Museum; 173, Library of Congress, Prints & Photographs Division, [LC-USZ62-105895], © Edgeworth; 178, *Portrait of Machiavelli*, Santi di Tito, Palazzo Vecchio; 180, Ludovisi Collection, photo by Jastrow; 181, William C. Morey, *Outlines of Greek History* (Chicago: American Book Co., 1903), 125; 182, Library of Congress, Prints & Photographs Division, Athens, Egypt, Rhine, Switzerland, Tyrol, Salzburg, opposite p. 19, left side, [LC-USZ62-108943]; 189, Bust of Cicero, Musei Capitolini, Rome, photo by Glauco92, creativecommons.org/licenses/by-sa/3.0/deed.en; 193, statue of Niccolò Macchiavelli (Serie "the Great Florentines"), by Lorenzo Bartolini, Uffizi gallery, Florence, Italy, photo by Jebulon, creativecommons.org/publicdomain/zero/1.0/deed.en; 194, Library of Congress, Prints & Photographs Division, 40180 U.S. Copyright Office, reproduction of painting by Federico Faruffini (1833–1869), [LC-USZ62-100795]; 204 (top), United States Senate; 204 (bottom), the National Archives and Records Administration, ARC Identifier 198535, Collection RR-WHPO: White House Photographic Collection, 01/20/1981–01/20/1989; 206, Getty Images, Omikron Omikron; 208 (inset), Federal Government of the United States; 210, Library of Congress, Prints & Photographs Division, [LC-USZ62-70080], © Chase-Statler, Washington; 214, Service Depicted: Air Force; 219, National Archives and Records Administration; 226, the National Archives and Records Administration. National Archives Identifier: 541900, Local Identifier: 306-NT-901B(3), U.S. Information Agency; 230, *Slave Combing a Girl's Hair*, Herculaneum, Third Style (fresco), Roman, (1st century AD) / Museo Archeologico Nazionale, Naples, Italy / the Bridgeman Art Library; 232, Library of Congress, Prints & Photographs Division, Saint-Mémin and the Neoclassical profile portrait in America / Ellen G. Miles. Washington, D.C.: National Portrait Gallery, 1994, no. 657, [LC-USZ62-54941]; 234, Library of Congress Rare Book and Special Collections Division , LOT 4422-A-1, [LC-USZ62-34160]; 236, Library of Congress, Prints & Photographs Division, *The Graphic*, London, June 7, 1884, p. 548, [LC-DIG-ppmsca-15836]; 247, Library of Congress, Prints & Photographs Division, *Lincoln's Photographs: A Complete Album* by Lloyd Ostendorf (Dayton, OH: Rockywood Press, 1998), pp. 6–7, [LC-USZ62-36582]; 248, Attic red-figure cup depicting Cassandra chased by Ajax seeking refuge by a xoanon of Athena, c. 430 BC (pottery), Greek, (5th century BC) / Louvre, Paris, France / Giraudon / the Bridgeman Art Library; 252, Henry London's free papers, Port Royal, SC, 22 August 1862 (pen & ink on paper), American School, (19th century) / Private Collection / Courtesy of Swann Auction Galleries / the Bridgeman Art Library; 260, Library of Congress, Prints & Photographs Division, Japanese prints and drawings, [LC-DIG-jpd-00378]; 261, Library of Congress, Prints & Photographs Division, Japanese prints and drawings, [LC-DIG-jpd-00083]; 264 (inset), "In Busy Life: Traces of the VOC in the Old Church," Summer 2002, De Oude Kerk, Amsterdam; 266, *The Capture of Kochi and Victory of the Dutch V.O.C. over the Portuguese in 1656, on the Coast of Mallabar*, 1682, Coenraet Decker, Atlas van der Hagen, Koninklijke Bibliotheek; 268, John Ogilby, *Asia: Being an Accurate Description of Persia, and the Several Provinces Thereof* (1673); 276 (top), *Defeat of the Peishwas Army before Jhansi by General Rose on 1st April 1858*, from *The History of the Indian Mutiny* published in 1858 (engraving), English School (19th century) / Private Collection / Ken Welsh / the Bridgeman Art Library; 280, Library of Congress, Prints & Photographs Division, Chadbourne collection of Japanese prints, [LC-USZC4-9983]; 286 (bottom), Roman Kirillov, creative commons.org/licenses/by-sa/3.0/deed.en; 288, the Yorck Project: 10.000 Meisterwerke der Malerei; 292, Library of Congress, Prints & Photographs Division, Subways NY NYC 1901, NY NYC Union Sq., NY NYC Views 1901, Photog. I., NY NYC Transit systems 1901, Geogr., Shelf, [LC-USZ62-63514]; 294 (bottom), © Stephen Power; 300 (bottom); Library of Congress, Prints & Photographs Division, New York World-Telegram and the Sun Newspaper Photograph Collection, [LC-USZ62-120810]; 303, used with the acknowledgment of the Frank R. Paul Estate

Insert Illustration Credits

Insert 1: p. 1 (top), 2 (symbol), 2–3, 4 (inset), 5 (symbol), 6 (symbol), 6–7, 8 (symbol and inset), © Lucasfilm Ltd. & TM. All Rights Reserved; 1 (bottom), U.S. Government; 3 (inset), Library of Congress, Prints & Photographs Division, Detroit Publishing Company, [LC-D416-256]; 4–5, *Washington Crossing the Delaware River*, 25th December 1776, 1851 (oil on canvas) (copy of an original painted in 1848), Leutze, Emanuel Gottlieb (1816–1868) / Metropolitan Museum of Art, New York, USA / the Bridgeman Art Library; 7 (inset), Library of Congress, Prints & Photographs Division, Reproduction Number: LC-USZ62-39586, published in *The American Revolution in Drawings and Prints: A Checklist of 1765–1790 Graphics in the Library of Congress* / compiled by Donald H. Cresswell, with a foreword by Sinclair H. Hitchings (Washington: [For sale by the Supt. of Docs., U.S. Govt. Print. Off.], 1975), no. 324; 8 Library of Congress, Prints & Photographs Division, [LC-DIG-pga-01711]. *Insert 2:* 1 and symbol, 2 and symbol, 4 (symbol), 4–5, 6–7, 7 (symbol), 8 and symbol, © Lucasfilm Ltd. & TM. All Rights Reserved; 1 (inset), Library of Congress, Prints & Photographs Division, Reproduction Number: LC-USZ62-48839; 3, Library of Congress, Prints & Photographs Division, Reproduction Number: LC-D416-567, Detroit Publishing Co. no. 050334; 3 (inset), Library of Congress, Prints & Photographs Division, Cabinet of American illustration, *Haloed Joan of Arc on Horse with Lion Flag Leading Army* by Walter Appleton Clark; 4 (inset), *Cleopatra and Caesar*, Jean-Léon Gérôme, mezzomondo.com/arts/mm/orientalist/european/gerome/index _b.html; 6 (inset), Library of Congress, Prints & Photographs Division, Reproduction Number: LC-DIG-jpd-01519, *Shinkan no tsuki*, Yoshitoshi Taiso. *Insert 3:* 1 and symbol, 2 (symbol), 2–3, 4 (symbol), 4–5, 6–7, 7 (symbol), 8 (symbol and bottom), © Lucasfilm Ltd. & TM. All Rights Reserved; 1 (inset), photo by Andreas Wahra; 2 (inset), Library of Congress, Prints & Photographs Division, Reproduction Number: LC-USZC2-1958, *The Battle of Malvern Hill, Va. July 1st 1862*, Currier & Ives: A Catalogue Raisonné / compiled by Gale Research (Detroit, MI : Gale Research, 1983), no. 0458; 4 (inset), Library of Congress, Prints & Photographs Division, Reproduction Number: LC-USZ62-2582, *A Slave Auction at the South* / from an original sketch by Theodore R. Davis, *Harper's Weekly*, vol. 5, no. 237, 1861 July 13, p. 442; 7 (inset), *The Slave Market*, c.1867 (oil on canvas), Gerome, Jean Leon (1824–1904) / Sterling & Francine Clark Art Institute, Williamstown, USA / the Bridgeman Art Library; 8 (top), Library of Congress, Prints & Photographs Division, Reproduction Number: LC-USW33-059244, Office of War Information, Overseas Picture Division, Washington Division, 1944. *Insert 4:* 1 and symbol, 3 (inset and symbol), 4 (symbol), 4–5, 6–7, 7 (symbol), 8 and symbol, © Lucasfilm Ltd. & TM. All Rights Reserved; 1 (inset), Library of Congress, Prints & Photographs Division, Reproduction Number: LC-USZC2-2711, *John Hancock's Defiance: July 4th 1776*, Currier & Ives: A Catalogue Raisonné / compiled by Gale Research (Detroit, MI: Gale Research, 1983), no. 3528; 2–3, *The Return to Amsterdam of the Second Expedition to the East Indies on 19th July 1599* (oil on copper), Eertvelt, Andries van (1590–1652) / Johnny van Haeften Gallery, London, UK / the Bridgeman Art Library; 5 (inset), courtesy of Professor Frances Pritchett, Columbia University; 6 (inset), Library of Congress, Prints & Photographs Division, Reproduction Number: LC-D4-73392, Detroit Publishing Co. no. 073392; 8 (inset), Library of Congress, Prints & Photographs Division, Reproduction Number: LC-USZ62-99149, by G.A. Davis, the Arkell Weekly Company, Frank Leslie's illustrated weekly, 1894 Sept. 27, p. 206.

INDEX

Page numbers in *italics* refer to illustrations.